EMPERORS AND GLADIATORS

EMPERORS AND GLADIATORS

Thomas Wiedemann

London and New York

First published 1992
First published in paperback 1995
by Routledge
11 New Fetter Lane, London EC4P 4EE

Simultaneously published in the USA and Canada
by Routledge
29 West 35th Street, New York, NY 10001

Reprinted 1996, 2000, 2001

Routledge is an imprint of the Taylor & Francis Group

© 1992, 1995 Thomas Wiedemann

Typeset in 10 on 12 point Baskerville by
Florencetype Ltd, Stoodleigh, Devon
Printed in Great Britain by
Butler & Tanner Ltd, Frome

British Library Cataloguing in Publication Data
Wiedemann, Thomas
Emperors and Gladiators
I. Title
937

Library of Congress Cataloguing in Publication Data
Wiedemann, Thomas E.J.
Emperors and Gladiators / Thomas Wiedemann.
p. cm.
Includes bibliographical references and index.
1. Gladiators. 2. Games—Rome—Social aspects. 3. Sports and
state—Rome. I. Title.
GV35.W54 1992
796.8—dc20 92–10519
ISBN 0–415–12164–7

In memory of
Helen
30.4 – 5.5.1989

CONTENTS

FIGURES

(between pp. 101 and 102)

1 The Corn Exchange, Leeds (1861–3): one of many nineteenth-century buildings whose form was inspired by that of Roman amphitheatres, even though this one was intended for quite different functions. Photograph by D.B. Milburn.

2 The Colosseum on a coin of Alexander Severus (AD 223). Reproduced by courtesy of the Trustees of the British Museum.

3 Terracotta lamp with a representation of two gladiators, one raising his finger to admit defeat. Reproduced by courtesy of the Trustees of the British Museum.

4 Terracotta lamp in the shape of a gladiator's helmet. Reproduced by courtesy of the Trustees of the British Museum.

5 Scenes from the 'Villa di Dar Buc Amméra' mosaic (Zliten, Libya), representing a *venatio*, executions, and gladiators, with orchestral accompaniment. Courtesy of the German Archaeological Institute, Rome. DAI 61–1889/92.

6 Relief from Apri (Thrace), representing a *venatio* with bull- and bear-leaping, a *pyrricha* with a dancing bear, and an execution (bottom right). L. Robert, *Les Gladiateurs*, no. 27 (drawn by Sue Grice).

7 Execution scene: a woman tied on to a bull is mauled by a leopard. The crouching figure holding a shield is presumably the *confector* (executioner). Terracotta from Kalaa Scira, N. Africa. Louvre, inc. CA 2613. Cliché des Musées Nationaux, Paris.

ix

ABBREVIATIONS

AE	*Année Epigraphique* (Paris) – cited by year and number of inscription.
CIL	*Corpus Inscriptionum Latinarum*, many vols (Berlin, 1869 on).
CTh.	*Theodosian Code*: English translation by C. Pharr (NY, 1952)
D–S	C. Daremberg and E. Saglio (eds), *Dictionnaire des Antiquités*, 5 vols (Paris, 1877 on).
ILS	H. Dessau (ed.), *Inscriptiones Latinae Selectae*, 3 vols (Berlin, 1892–1914).
JRS	*The Journal of Roman Studies* (1910 on).
MGHAA	*Monumenta Germaniae Historica, Auctores Antiquissimi* (Berlin, 1878 on).
PG	P. Migne, *Patrologiae Cursus Completus. Series Graeca* (Paris, 1886 on).
PL	P. Migne, *Patrologiae Cursus Completus. Series Latina* (Paris, 1878 on).
RE	G. Wissowa (ed.), *Paulys Realencyclopädie der Classischen Altertumswissenschaft* (Stuttgart, 1894 on).
ZPE	*Zeitschrift für Papyrologie und Epigraphik* (Cologne).

DATES

EMPERORS AND GLADIATORS

68/9	Civil wars (Galba, Otho, Vitellius)
69–79	Vespasian ('Flavian' dynasty)
79–81	Titus
79	Eruption of Vesuvius
80	Inauguration of Flavian amphitheatre (Colosseum)
81–96	Domitian
98–117	Trajan
100	Younger Pliny consul (*Panegyric*)
109	*Ludi* to celebrate conquest of Dacia
117–38	Hadrian
138–61	Antoninus Pius
161–80	Marcus Aurelius
180–92	Commodus
193–211	Septimius Severus ('Severan' dynasty)
212	*Constitutio Antoniniana*
222–35	Alexander Severus
286–93	Carausius emperor in Britain
306–36	Constantine
354	Calendar of Furius Dionysius Philocalus
394	Theodosius defeats Eugenius (the last pagan emperor)
429–534	Vandal kingdom in N. Africa
438	Theodosian Code
493–526	Theoderic king in Italy
538	Justinian's *Digest*

xiii

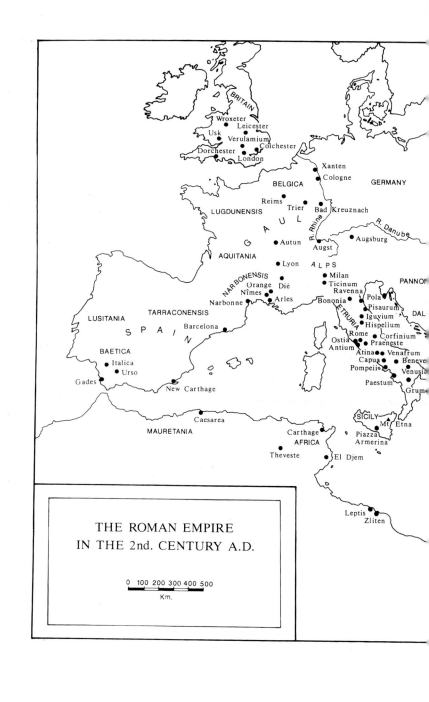

THE ROMAN EMPIRE
IN THE 2nd. CENTURY A.D.

0 100 200 300 400 500
Km.

DACIA

Durostorum

THRACE

Heraclea Amastris

Constantinople

Amphipolis BITHYNIA

CEDONIA Ancyra

Pergamum

GREECE ASIA

Smyrna

Patras Ephesus

Nysa Laodicea

Corinth Athens Perge

LYCIA Antioch

Rhodes SYRIA

Berytus

JUDAEA

Jerusalem

Alexandria

EGYPT

PARTHIAN EMPIRE

INTRODUCTION

Scholars have tended to avoid betraying too much interest in gladiators and amphitheatres. They have perhaps been put off by the popularity of the games, the fact that they fascinated the Romans, and – worse – fascinate ordinary people today. Much of the literary and epigraphical evidence relating to gladiators was assembled a century ago by Friedländer in his *Sittengeschichte Roms* and by Lafaye and others in articles in Daremberg and Saglio's *Dictionnaire des Antiquités*. More recent popular accounts by Grant, Auguet, and Weber (in English, French, and German respectively) are hampered not so much by their dependence on these earlier collections of material, as by their lack of sympathy for this important aspect of Roman culture; in the first edition of his book on *Gladiators*, Grant grotesquely listed *munera* alongside the Nazis (and ahead of Genghis Khan) as 'the two most quantitatively destructive institutions in history' (p. 8). In Chester Starr's words, 'there appears to be an orthodoxy here which is not to be challenged . . . Without admiring bloodshed, nonetheless, the recruitment, training and organization of the gladiatorial profession deserves investigation as a reflection of the skill and efficiency of Roman administrative structure' (*Past and Future in Ancient History* (1987), p. 63). Recent decades have indeed seen more objective investigations of the topic, in particular by George Ville, M. Hönle (especially on the art historical evidence) and J.-C. Golvin (on architectural aspects). It has not been my intention to compile a comprehensive collection of the surviving evidence about *munera*, and readers will have to go to these books for such evidence. Nor have I wished to repeat competent descriptions of different types of gladiators and their styles of fighting (I hope that the *Glossary* may suffice for technical terms). I wish rather to try to explore the significance of gladiatorial combat in the context of Roman ideas about society, morality and mortality. Four passages on pp. 78–82 are based on translations in *Early Christian Writings*, tr. M. Staniforth (Penguin Classics, 1968), copyright © Maxwell Staniforth, 1968, and one on p. 148 f. is from Augustine's *Confessions*, tr. R.S. Pine-Coffin (Penguin Classics, 1961), copyright © R.S. Pine-Coffin, 1961, reproduced by permission of Penguin Books Ltd.

I should like to thank the students who took part in a course on gladiators which I gave at Bristol in 1987/8 and 1988/9: Rosemary Bowling, Peter Claxton, Tessa Coombs, Alexander Crum-Ewing, Karen Downie, Jonathan Drake, Geraldine Geddy, Barbara Guynn, Jonathan Martin, Annabel Middlemas, Chippy Moss, Justin Murphy, Marcus Pailing, Astrid Petersen, Laura Stanley, Gail Thomas, Hilary Vickers and Fiona Yates. I should like to thank those who commented on the issues raised in discussions about gladiators following papers I was invited to give at Gregynnog, the Oxford Triennial Conference in 1988, Bonn and elsewhere. Many other scholars and museums have given me assistance; I am particularly grateful to Roger Ling (on Roman wall-painting), to Debora Schmid (for sending me material on the *Gladiatorenmosaik* from Augst), and to Catharine Edwards and Jürgen Malitz, for drawing my attention to interpretations and materials that I would not otherwise have been predisposed to use.

This paperback edition differs from the hardback edition only in respect of some minor changes. I am grateful to a number of friends, colleagues and reviewers for their comments on the hardback edition, and particularly to Pat Witts for much helpful information about representations of gladiators on mosaics.

Thomas Wiedemann

1

GLADIATORS AND ROMAN IDENTITY

MUNIFICENCE, GAMES AND GLORY

Gladiatorial contests, *munera gladiatoria*, hold a central place in modern popular perceptions of Roman behaviour. They were without a doubt also of major significance to the way the Romans themselves ordered their lives. Although the popular image of the Roman mob spending most of the year looking on from its comfortable seats in the Colosseum while men killed each other and killed or were killed by wild beasts in the arena is a considerable distortion, the investment of time, wealth, and emotion into the games was nevertheless enormous. Attending the games was one of the practices that went with being a Roman. They were held in the most visible single building in a Roman city – whether a purpose-built amphitheatre as was usual in the west, or a reconstituted theatre as in the Greek east. Notwithstanding the unease and embarrassment that many apologists for Rome have felt at what went on in these buildings, they cannot be dissociated from Roman civilization.

Roman tradition held that the activities that took place in the amphitheatre were not originally Roman at all. Where they came from, in terms of both cultural and geographical origins, is considerably less certain than many scholars, ancient as well as modern, have assumed. Roman writers believed that the traditional spectacles of the Roman community were not *munera* but the *ludi*, ceremonial processions followed by chariot-races which took place in the Circus Maximus or in the so-called Circus Flaminius, an open space (not a building) in the Campus Martius. These *ludi* were thought to have developed hand-in-hand with Rome's own development as a Mediterranean city-state under the 'Etruscan' kings in the sixth century BC. Other

1

activities, especially theatrical ones, came to be associated with these 'games' in the course of the centuries. The circus-games were state occasions, presided over by magistrates, and financed (at least in part) by the state treasury. On the other hand gladiatorial shows and the wild-beast 'hunts' (*venationes*) which came to be associated with them did not appear at Rome until very much later.

There were respects in which the two types of spectacle played a similar social and ritual role, and many studies of Roman social life rightly discuss them together; but there are also significant distinctions to be made between them. The Romans themselves, before the third century AD, used different words for the two types of ceremonies: chariot races in the Circus and theatrical shows were called *ludi* ('games' or 'exercises': the same Latin word was used for 'school', including – confusingly – gladiatorial schools), while the activities associated with the amphitheatre were *munera*.[1] The two words reflect their different origins. Gladiatorial contests did not originate as state occasions, but as obligatory offerings (*munera*) owed to important men at their deaths. It would be misleading to call them 'private' occasions, since the men so honoured had generally been public figures, and the object of the exercise was to broadcast their prestige, and that of their families, to the Roman public in general. When the Caesars permanently took on the role of being Rome's rulers, and monopolised the giving of *munera* in the capital, the distinction between public and private as applied to the imperial family lost much of its relevance. Nevertheless it is not without significance that, in the context of wild-beast hunts and gladiatorial games, emperors were generally acclaimed and referred to as 'Caesar', rather than by any of their constitutional titles such as 'Augustus', 'Imperator' or 'Princeps'.[2]

The traditional public ceremonies of Rome did not, then, include gladiatorial games. Nevertheless it is worth examining the role of such *ludi*, since they give us a context for public spectacles at Rome. When Cicero drew up a blueprint for a revised Roman constitution, probably during Pompey's sole consulship in 52 BC, he defined the *ludi publici* as follows:

> Public games are to be divided into those which take place in the *cavea* (theatre) and those which take place in the Circus. In the Circus, footraces, boxing, wrestling, and

chariot racing; in the theatre, singing, lyre-playing and flute-playing.[3]

The public nature of the *ludi* can be seen from the description given by Dionysius of Halicarnassus in the time of Augustus. Originally, Dionysius tells us, the people took their places by *curiae*, tribal or electoral units. The Circus, and at least some theatres, were *templa*, sacred places belonging to the gods. And the Circus Maximus was said to have been laid out by Tarquinius Priscus at the same time as he laid out the Roman Forum. Although the individual magistrate who presided over each occasion was given credit for putting on a particularly splendid programme – credit which would be realised in the form of votes at his next election – *ludi* were an offering to the gods by the whole community, and not by the presiding magistrate alone. They were suitable occasions for parading the power of the Roman community. Once Rome had come to dominate the entire Mediterranean, one way of symbolising that power was to display various exotic beasts imported from the territories Rome had conquered, and then slaughter them in the presence of the Roman people assembled in the Circus or theatre as a visual symbol of Roman control: perhaps the most famous such display was presented by Pompey during his second consulship in 55 BC, when over a thousand lions and leopards were killed, and the Roman people was shown a northern European lynx and an Indian rhinoceros for the first time.[4]

Roman spectacles were a public display of power, and that power was primarily military. The central role which the exercise of power in warfare played within the system of political competition and in the self-esteem of the Roman elite (and in Roman life generally) during the republic is well-known. Military success was rewarded in all ranks of the Roman army; for those who commanded successful armies, the highest sign of public recognition was the award of a triumph. Triumphal processions, with the associated games thanking or repaying the gods for their support ('votive games'), were another of the occasions on which the power of the Roman state was publicly associated with the glory of an individual political leader. They have to be distinguished from the regular *ludi*. Although triumphal games had to be authorised by the Roman Senate, they were financed by the general who had won the victory, normally

3

out of the spoils, and reflected on him: as Livy says of Romulus, the first Roman to hold a triumph, it had the effect of making him personally more respected, *augustiorem*.[5] Unlike *ludi*, the triumphal display centred on the person of the returning general to such an extent that it temporarily gave him a monarchical position, visibly represented by his dress – something that conflicted with the ideals of a republican city-state, and made his peers, and even his followers, uneasy: hence the need to break the tension by letting the soldiers make obscene jokes about the *triumphator*, and even placing a slave behind him on his chariot to remind him that he was only another mortal. At the same time the power that the triumphal procession advertised was the power of the Roman people, as put into effect by a Roman army. The extent of that power was visually symbolised by placards containing written statements and representations of the army's successes under the general's command ('I came, I saw, I conquered'), as well as by the procession of captured prisoners. A fragment from Sallust's *Histories* describing how Sulla's supporter Metellus Pius returned to his provincial base from a successful campaign illustrates both how these displays symbolised Rome's claim to universal power, and the unease and resentment that a general's peers might feel against such private claims:

> When Metellus returned in great glory from his year in Further Spain, men and women came to meet him from everywhere, and people watched him in every street and from the rooftops. His quaestor Gaius Urbinus and others knew what he wanted; when they invited him to dinner, they took greater pains than Romans and indeed human beings generally do to adorn the house with tapestries and insignia, and set up stages for actors to perform. The ground was covered with crocuses and other flowers, as the finest temples are. When he had sat down, they sprang a surprise on him by letting down a representation of Venus to the sound of artificial thunder, to place a crown on his head. As he went in to dine, they honoured him with incense like a god. As he reclined, he wore the embroidered toga and cloak (sc. of a *triumphator*), and the banquet included the choicest foods, not just from all the provinces but even from across the seas, with many varieties of fowl and flesh from Mauretania that had not been known

4

before. These things lost him some of his reputation, especially among the older and more conservative men, who
thought such things haughty and dangerous and unworthy
of Roman power (*superba illa, gravia, indigna Romano
imperio*).[6]

These features of traditional Roman displays, the *ludi* and the
triumph, deserve our attention because in the course of time
they became associated with something that had developed
under different circumstances as a different form of display, the
gladiatorial *munus*, originally connected not with public power,
but with individual mortality.

The historical tradition pinpointed the first occasion of a
munus at Rome: it was at the funeral of Junius Brutus Pera in
264 BC, on the eve of the first Punic war. His sons Marcus and
Decimus had three pairs of gladiators fight to the death on the
Forum Boarium (between the Palatine and the Tiber).[7] The
very fact that references to this, and many subsequent, gladiatorial displays survive in the historical record shows their ambiguous position between Roman private and public life. Like
other funerals of members of the Roman elite, Junius Pera's
funeral was a private occasion which his sons chose to turn into a
public one in order to enhance their father's status, and of
course their own. The importance of funerals as occasions which
the deceased's personal or political heirs tried to exploit for their
own purposes is well attested: Mark Antony's speech over the
body of Julius Caesar is perhaps the most notorious. The Greek
historian Polybius, in his account of the workings of the Roman
political system in the first half of the second century BC, had
already remarked upon the public and political nature of these
private events, with the procession of actors bearing the wax
masks (*imagines*) of earlier members of the deceased's kin-
group. The competitive nature of republican politics meant that
ever more *imagines* were displayed on these occasions. At the
funeral of M. Claudius Marcellus after his death at the Battle of
Petelia in 208 BC, in his fifth consulship, the funeral masks of
600 Claudii were paraded; at the funeral of the dictator Sulla in
78 BC, there were said to have been 6,000.[8]

It was in the context of such *munera*, obligations carried out in
honour of the dead, that gladiatorial contests at Rome are first
recorded. They were, literally, a spectacular way of attracting

the attention of the Roman public to the importance of the deceased man and his family. The relative completeness of Livy's account of the period 218–167 BC allows us to trace how, over this period, the competitiveness of Roman public life meant that on each occasion the spectacle presented – like the number of ancestral masks – had to improve on what had gone before; for Romans felt the need to compete, not just with their contemporaries, but also with those who had achieved great honour before them. In 216 BC, at the funeral of Marcus Aemilius Lepidus, there were twenty-two pairs of gladiators; in 200 BC, at that of Marcus Valerius Laevinus, twenty-five; in 183 BC, at that of Publius Licinius, sixty pairs. Of several shows presented in 174 BC, that given by Titus Flamininus at his father's funeral was the most spectacular. Seventy-four men were said to have fought over a period of three days.[9]

Hitherto the *editores*, the men who presented these displays, had been *privati*, men who were not holding (and sometimes had not yet held) any public magistracy, and who hoped that by drawing attention to the virtues of their deceased parents they would improve their own standing in the eyes of the electorate. Unlike the funerals themselves, the *munera* had the very great advantage that they did not have to be put on immediately after the death of the deceased: his son could make a vow promising to put on gladiatorial contests, but leave the fulfilment of that vow to some occasion which suited his own political calendar, such as the campaign for election to a higher magistracy (when the competition would be fiercest). Towards the end of the republic, politicians seeking election to a praetorship or consulship were under great pressure to find appropriate relatives to honour in this way. Where there was no famous father, even a deceased woman, who had played no formal political role, would do: in 45 BC, Julius Caesar honoured his daughter Julia (who had died eight years before) with a *Munus*. There is no clear evidence for gladiators at the funeral of his aunt in 65 BC, when Caesar was aedile; but after his election to that office, he promised the electorate that he was going to put on a spectacle greater than any before, so much so that his rivals in the Senate introduced restrictions on the allowable expenses; as a result, he was prevented from presenting the 320 pairs of gladiators he had advertised.[10]

There is no conclusive evidence that in the late republic

munera were ever given by magistrates in their public capacity, though they might be given by men who happened to be holding a magistracy at the time. Although the distinction between public and private affairs was a very important one to the Romans, the fact that gladiatorial displays were public events put on by public figures in their private capacity sometimes confused both later Roman writers and modern scholars, particularly after Augustus made the blurring of that distinction between private and public an essential feature of his new imperial system. In late antiquity, it was argued that in the year 105 BC, or even regularly from 105 BC on, the consuls had provided gladiatorial games on behalf of the state. This story has been accepted by many scholars, and seems to be based on Valerius Maximus' reference to the consul of that year, P. Rutilius Rufus, using gladiatorial trainers to give hastily raised recruits basic weapons training after the Roman defeat at Arausio. But Valerius' account in no way implies that Rufus put on *munera* either in a private or still less in an official capacity, and the idea of publicly provided gladiatorial shows in the late republic has to be dismissed.[11]

Although by the end of the first century BC the Roman electorate had come to expect that aediles and praetors, who might at a later stage wish to be appointed to the higher magistracy of the consulship, would be giving *munera*, these were still formally not being provided for the Roman people by its magistrates. Funerals continued to be the occasion on which games were presented by private individuals with social, but not necessarily political ambitions. In one of Horace's *Satires*, a social climber called Staberius is said to have imposed on his heir the obligation to engrave on his tomb the amount of money he had left in his will; should the heirs fail to do so, they would be obliged to give the people a show consisting of 100 pairs of gladiators and a feast. The *munus* is an alternative way of expressing publicly the wealth and social importance of the deceased.[12] This was more than just a literary joke. Tiberius had to send military units to quell a riot at Pollentia in Liguria when the population, with the support or connivance of their magistrates, refused to allow the funeral of a principal centurion (*primus pilus*) to take place until his heirs had promised to provide a *munus*.[13]

Apart from funerals, we find gladiatorial games being promised in connection with death in other ways. During Caligula's reign, a wealthy individual is said to have vowed to put on a show of 100 gladiators in thanksgiving for the emperor's alleged escape from a conspiracy which may or may not have been hatched against him by his former associate Lepidus. Another man is said to have taken a vow to appear as a gladiator himself if the emperor should recover from a serious illness.[14]

By concentrating political power in his own hands, Augustus turned claims to prestige by anyone in public life who was not a member of the imperial family into potential challenges to his own position. It was in the emperor's interest to control any such claims by senators at Rome to independent sources of popularity. As early as the 20s BC, Augustus restricted the praetors to two gladiatorial shows during their year of office, with a maximum of 120 participants.[15] Further restrictions on the opportunities for gaining popularity, including *ludi* and electoral contests as well as *munera*, were imposed by Tiberius. From Domitian's time on, no gladiatorial games could any longer be presented at Rome except by the emperor or by a relative or magistrate on his behalf. Hand-in-hand with this control of *munera* by the emperors went the establishment of the system of imperial gladiatorial training institutions (*ludi*) in the city, probably also originating under Augustus.[16]

Like the monopolisation of other visible public and private institutions at Rome, Augustus' control of gladiatorial *munera* had the effect of blurring the distinction between his own public and private roles. That confusion between public and private has made it difficult for some scholars to realise that, while the *munera* given by the Caesars were public, they must be distinguished from state occasions like religious or triumphal *ludi*. Gladiatorial contests remained the personal gifts of those who gave them, and not obligations formally required of magistrates. The original distinction, as well as its later blurring, can most clearly be seen in the provisions for their financing. *Ludi* were regularly financed by grants from the *Aerarium*, the state treasury of the Roman people. Dionysius of Halicarnassus says that up to the second Punic war the sum allocated by the *aerarium* was 200,000 Asses (= 80,000 HS: *Antiquities*, 7, 71.2). The Calendar of Antium states that in AD 51, the *Ludi Romani* were granted 760,000 HS, the *Ludi plebeii* 600,000 HS, and the *Ludi Apollinares* 380,000 HS.[17] Individual magistrates would top up these grants from the treasury in accordance with their means;

8

but it was only after the third century, when emperors were rarely present at Rome, that Roman magistrates (praetors and quaestors) were required to finance the traditional Roman games out of their own resources.[18]

Surviving laws regulating the functioning of Roman colonies in the provinces also testify to the importance of ensuring that *ludi* were regularly and properly celebrated. The charters of Spanish municipalities established by Caesar specify the sums of money to be paid out by the city treasury; they are of course very much smaller than those that applied for Rome. At Urso, each of the two chief magistrates (*duumviri*) are to be granted 2,000 HS to cover the four-day games honouring Juppiter, Juno and Minerva; they were obliged to match this sum with at least as much from their own purses. In requiring individual magistrates to match the money provided by their city with funds from their private resources, Julius Caesar was in effect institutionalising what was by now common practice at Rome. For the less honorific aedilician games, the city and the magistrates had to provide 1,500 HS each. But no sums of money are allocated to gladiatorial *munera*: not because they did not take place, but because, as at Rome, they were provided by individuals in their private capacity, not by the community.[19]

In the provinces and Italy outside Rome, the distinction between spectacles provided by magistrates on behalf of the community, and those provided for the community by its richest members as semi-voluntary obligations, became increasingly blurred. Pollentia expected a *munus* when a leading citizen died. The greater the honours a local magistrate attained, the greater the expectation that he would provide a *munus*: when Aulus Clodius Flaccus was *quinquennalis* (the equivalent to holding the censorship at Rome) of Pompeii, he provided bulls, wild boars and bears together with thirty pairs of athletes and five pairs of gladiators 'by himself' (*solus*); the expenses of a second *venatio* plus thirty-five pairs of gladiators were shared with his fellow-*quinquennalis* (*cum collega*).[20] An inscription from Nimes honours a freedman's son for 'the munificence of the spectacles which he either gave of his own accord or did not begrudge when they were demanded'.[21]

Not all municipal and provincial office-holders had the resources to provide the expensive spectacles that were expected by the people. In AD 27, Tiberius banned anyone without an equestrian property-rating (400,000 HS) from providing *munera* in Italian municipalities; that is itself the figure Petronius mentions as the cost of a three-day *munus* in a Campanian municipality, no doubt a characteristic satirical exaggeration. Later emperors had to legislate to set an upper limit for what might be expected, to the relief of provincial magnates (see Chapter 4). On occasion, cities had to make grants to their magistrates to enable them to provide what were in theory free gifts to the people. At Allifae, L.Fadius Pierus 'gave a full *venatio* and twenty-one pairs of gladiators during his duumvirate, having received 13,000 HS from the municipality'.²² In the course of time, the incentives for members of the municipal elites to invest their resources in such public shows became considerably weaker, as the attractions of public office-holding and even of prestige in the wider sense within the local community gradually waned. The effect was that the responsibility for providing games, like other liturgies, had to be made semi-official. From being voluntary gifts to the community, gladiatorial shows had turned into obligatory offices required of the wealthiest citizens, or wealthy outside patrons. At Praeneste, the holder of this position was called a *curator*: Gnaeus Voesius Aper 'was curator of the public gladiatorial show thrice'. The same title is found at Grumentum and Ticinum (Pavia) in southern and northern Italy, and at Dié (Dea Vocontiorum) in southern Gaul. At Beneventum, he was called a *munerarius*.²³

One of the reasons why municipal inscriptions mention gladiatorial *munera* as evidence of a local dignitary's liberality was precisely because they were exceptional, and not formally required of municipal office-holders. Some inscriptions proudly record the first *editor* to put on a show in a particular municipality, erected 'because he was the first of all *editores* to have provided five wild beasts at his own expense', or 'the first to be an *editor*' at Paestum. At Ostia an *editor* boasted that he 'was the first of all since Rome was founded to make women fight'.²⁴ Because such expenditure was irregular, it may have totalled less cumulatively than that devoted to regular municipal *ludi*. It will not necessarily have been insignificant, although the sums involved on individual occasions might be quite small. The Urso charter lays down a minimum of 8,000 sesterces; at Iguvium, an inscription mentions the magistrate Gnaeus Satrius Rufus, who donated 7,750 HS towards Augustus' victory games, the *ludi victoriae Caesaris Augusti.*[25] On the other hand the city of Pisaurum was left a legacy of 600,000 HS intended to provide a gladiatorial show once every five years; if we assume that the capital was invested with a return of 4 per cent, 120,000 HS would have been available at the end of every five-year period.[26]

What direct evidence there is for the sums of money spent on gladiatorial *munera* at Rome is literary and necessarily very incomplete, and stresses only the most remarkable occasions. With a few exceptions, it concentrates on particularly lavish (or otherwise extraordinary) emperors, in particular triumphal games associated with imperial victories. References to *munera* in the republican period suggest that costs might be as great as those of the public *ludi*, though of course without any state support. In Polybius' time, a fine display of gladiators is said to have cost 30 talents.[27] Cicero's speeches and letters contain several references to private individuals giving extraordinary *munera* at great personal expense in order to improve their chances of election to office. In the 50s BC Milo 'provided most magnificent *ludi* – I have to admit that no one had provided anything more costly', in his attempt to win the consulship for 52 BC, using up three separate inheritances.[28] Cumulative totals for the *munera* provided by an emperor during the whole of his reign might impress the public. In his *Res gestae*, Augustus advertised that 'On three occasions I gave a gladiatorial show on my own behalf, and fifteen times on behalf of my sons or grandsons. About ten thousand men fought in these shows.' Augustus' statement illustrates another aspect in which emperors used a public spectacle to fulfil a private, or at least family, interest, by displaying the current emperor's preferred successor to the Roman people, and to bind the community's loyalty to him by associating him with the 'favour' of granting games in excess of anything that was required. Trajan's victory games were presided over by Hadrian. Hadrian was Trajan's closest male relative, and Trajan granted him four million sesterces for the games, thus effectively marking him out as a potential successor. They lasted for 120 days, and 11,000 beasts were said to have been slaughtered.[29]

The frequency with which emperors presented special games (and the fact that it is not always easy to establish whether literary sources refer to the execution of prisoners and slaughter of beasts in the context of regular gladiatorial displays or of exceptional triumphal *ludi*) makes it more difficult than some scholars have thought to quantify the number of days a year during which Romans might expect to watch gladiators. What is clear is that they were far fewer than the days dedicated to *ludi* in the form of chariot-races or theatrical shows. When Juvenal and other moralists said that ordinary Romans were kept happy by 'bread and circuses', they meant exactly that: subsidised food and chariot-races, not gladiatorial shows. The most ancient of these festivals, the *Ludi Romani* in September, was originally just a chariot-race; from 364 BC, the day of the race was preceded by three days of theatrical shows. By the time of Augustus, the seven annual state *ludi* together took up 65 days (13 for chariot races, 48 for *ludi scaenici*). The number of festivals increased considerably during the first century of the principate; the late antique *Historia Augusta* ascribed to Marcus Aurelius (AD 161–80) a decision to cut down the number of festival days in order to increase those on which courts could sit to 230 (leaving 135 days of *ludi* in an ordinary year).[30] Our only certain information about gladiatorial shows is contained in the so-called Calendar of Furius Dionysius Philocalus, which tells us that in AD 354, 176 days were set aside for spectacles of various kinds: 64 for chariot races, 102 for theatrical shows, and only 10 days in December for gladiatorial contests and *venationes*. The *Historia Augusta* ascribes to the author's ideal emperor, Alexander Severus (AD 222–35), the intention to spread the gladiatorial games out to one a month throughout the year; that is a programmatic statement confirming that the dozen or so days of gladiatorial *munera* were bunched together at the end of the year. Although extraordinary *munera*, and some regular spectacles in Italian and provincial municipalities, might be held in the summer or other times of the year, the association of the regular gladiatorial games at Rome with the year end is noteworthy. *Munera* were a way of coming to terms both with the deaths of particular individuals, and also with the annual cycle of death and rebirth in nature.[31]

But the relatively limited total of days per year devoted to *munera* is not necessarily the best indicator of the extent to which emperors were prepared to dedicate resources to them. As with other spectacles, the cost of providing wild beasts from every territory which Rome's power could reach was enormous. So was the effort put into transporting to Rome the prisoners of war and criminals who were forced to fight as gladiators. A particularly fine list of both is provided in the imaginative accounts of Probus' and Aurelian's triumphs in the *Historia Augusta*:

> One hundred Libyan leopards were produced, and one hundred Syrian ones; one hundred lionesses, together with three hundred bears; it was thought that the spectacle of all these animals was impressive rather then enjoyable. Three hundred pairs of gladiators were also produced, with several Blemmyans who had been paraded in the triumphal procession fighting, as well as some Germans and Sarmatians, and also some Isaurian brigands . . .
>
> Four tigers, spotted giraffes, elks and other such, eight hundred pairs of gladiators in addition to the prisoners taken from barbarian races: Blemmyes, Exomites, Yemenites, Indians, Bactrians, Iberians, Saracens, Persians (each with their accoutrements), Goths, Alans, Roxalani, Sarmatians, Franks, Suabians, Vandals, Germans, all captives with their hands bound. The procession was led by the Palmyrenes who had survived.[32]

One has to be even more circumspect than normal in evaluating any references to spectacles in the *Historia Augusta*; whether we accept the view that the author wished to defend pagan customs, or alternatively believe with Syme that he was a 'rogue grammarian' writing for a pupil with a teenager's enthusiasm for *munera*, the author was not an objective reporter. Although certainly fictitious, the account shows how such spectacles were occasions for demonstrating the power which the *triumphator* had exercised on behalf of Rome over exotic and distant peoples, just as in the days of Metellus Pius.

The display of outlandish and expensive animals was one way in which the *editores* of gladiatorial *munera* could prove how much wealth they were putting at the disposal of their people. Another was the use of precious metals: in the funeral games for his father which Caesar put on as aedile, all the equipment used in the arena was made of silver. It was the first occasion on which even the criminals condemned to fight wild beasts bore equipment made of silver, a practice which (Pliny comments with disapproval) was later emulated in the municipalities of Italy. In Nero's day, the amber which a Roman equestrian brought back from an expedition to northern Europe was used to decorate the knots in the nets that protected the parapet surrounding the arena from wild beasts (this at a gladiatorial *munus* presented by one Julianus). As so often in Pliny, what superficially looks like objective description masks moralising judgements. But the amphitheatre both gave emperors (and other *editores*) an opportunity to display their munificence, and gave the audience an opportunity to evaluate that munificence in terms of praise or blame. A good example is the story of the 120 foot long beam of larch wood which Tiberius had transported from the Alps as part of a platform for a *naumachia* (naval display); it was later used by Nero for his amphitheatre. Nero used it to win glory by disproving Vitruvius' view that the use of a beam of that length was not possible. Tacitus' scathing comment that there were some historians who filled their annals with this sort of anecdote reveals the ambiguity of such claims to glory.[33] There are references to gladiators' armour being gilded, or decorated with gold thread and precious gems.[34] Apart from precious metals, armour might be decorated with peacock or ostrich feathers.[35] Surviving examples of gladiators' helmets and greaves illustrate the extent of decoration which could have been of no practical use, though such decoration was not allowed to impede the wearer's capacity to fight: thus the helmet of the *secutor* tended to be plain, in order not to give any potential hold for the net wielded by his opponent, the *retiarius* (see Glossary).

There were further ways of spectacularly investing money in such shows. There appear to be several references to the use of artificial lighting to illuminate the Colosseum during the regular games which preceded the Saturnalia in December during Domitian's reign,[36] and, like other metropolitan Roman practices, it was copied elsewhere in Italy. At Lanuvium a man 'gladiatores dedit lumina ludos', and an inscription from the amphitheatre of Pompeii (and therefore just pre-dating Domitian's reign) refers to lights being given for, or perhaps instead of, games.[37]

As we have seen, *munera* were attractive to public figures as a way of keeping the memory of the deceased in the forefront of the public consciousness because they could be held a considerable time after a funeral, and even repeated at annual or five-yearly intervals. Romans adopted other strategies at different times for ensuring that the status of the deceased and their political heirs would not be forgotten: they included the enormous mausolea of late republican families such as that of the Metelli on the Via Appia, or most spectacularly that which Augustus had built for himself on the Campus Martius, or in late antiquity the intricate and expensive sarcophagi in which senators and bishops were laid to rest in church buildings. Unlike tombs, funeral displays are by their very nature temporary affairs, and the fame they bring the provider is liable to be forgotten. Those who invested so much in *munera* thought that their liberality deserved to be remembered. One way of making their gifts more permanent was through visual representations in public places. Pliny the Elder tells us that 'the practice of painting gladiators has been very popular for centuries'; the fashion was started in the late second century BC by one Gaius Terentius Lucanus. He had put on a *munus*, in honour of the grandfather who had adopted him, in the Roman Forum over three days with thirty pairs of gladiators, and then had a painting of it made to be placed in the grove of Diana; if this was the Diana of the Aventine, then the temple was closely associated with the Roman *plebs*.[38] A number of examples of murals representing gladiators survive, especially from the north-western provinces of the empire; a notable one was recovered from the villa of La Liégeaud at La Croisille-sur-Briance, and another was discovered some years ago at Colchester (figure 10).[39]

The representations of public spectacles on the tombs of their *editores* and on mosaics laid on the floors of Roman houses in various parts of the empire were similar attempts to keep fresh claims to exceptional munificence. From the Severan period on, there are mosaics by the score representing wild beast shows, particularly from north Africa. Yet it is noteworthy that mosaics depicting gladiators are, in comparison, very few. Some are also unusually early: the coloured mosaic from the 'Villa di Dar Buc Amméra' at Zliten in Libya has been dated to the Flavian period (ca. AD 80–100; figure 5). It was laid as a frieze, probably surrounding a dining area, and depicts (in a clockwise sequence) four musicians (one playing a trumpet, *tuba*, one a water-organ and two, seated, playing the horn, *cornu*); six pairs of gladiators, together with a couple of umpires; four *bestiarii*; and three particularly gruesome figures

of prisoners being attacked by wild beasts. It is possible that
the mosaic records games associated with the execution of
Garamantine marauders who took advantage of the confusion
of Rome's civil wars in AD 69.[40] Another representation which
includes executions, on a mosaic from the so-called 'Domus
Sollertiana' at El Djem in Tunisia, also seems to be exceptional.
It has been dated to ca. AD 180, and shows a number of
bearded prisoners, naked apart from loincloths, being pro-
pelled towards wild leopards by attendants with whips. The
prisoners' beards suggest that they are meant to represent
captured barbarians, so this mosaic too may commemorate a
particular incident.[41]

Such representations of *munera* from Africa appear to pre-
date the fashion for hunting mosaics, confirmation of the impression that private individuals increasingly found the expense
of gladiatorial contests too much, and devoted themselves to
presenting wild beast shows instead; where later mosaics include
the odd human figure among several panels depicting wild
beasts, he is more likely to represent a famous *bestiarius* (see
Glossary) than a gladiator (e.g. Bardo mosaic inv. 2816). The
circus and the *venatio* continued to be popular themes for
mosaicists, so much so that there were parodies with scenes of
children or *erotes* as the participants.[42] Some of these mosaics will
have been selected out of sheer pleasure in the scenes portrayed
or more particularly because they would attract attention (cf. the
emphasis on violent images in modern television news reportage); but the element of glory-seeking by creating a permanent
reminder of private munificence is sometimes obvious. The
third-century mosaic found at Smirat in Tunisia honouring an
editor called Magerius is the most striking example. Around the
outside, four leopards are shown being put to death; they are
named (Victor, Crispinus, Luxurius and Romanus), as are their
killers (Mamertinus, Spittara, Bullarius, Hilarinus); the group of
bestiarii to which they belong, the 'Telegenii', is known from
other north African inscriptions. Two further figures represent
Diana and, probably, Apollo. What is without parallel is the
scene in the centre of the mosaic. A man in a tunic bears a richly
decorated tray on which are four bags of money, and to the left
and right there are inscriptions recording what happened. On
the left, 'Proclaimed by the *Curio* (president): My lords, in order
that the Telegenii should have what they deserve from your

favour for (fighting) the leopard, give them five hundred denarii'; the words on the right represent the acclamations of the crowd, welcoming Magerius' gift to the Telegenii: 'They shouted: may future generations know of your *munus* because you are an example for them, may past generations hear about it; where has such a thing been heard of? When has such a thing been heard of? You have provided a *munus* as an example to the quaestors; you have provided a *munus* from your own resources. . . . By your *munus* they were dismissed with money-bags.' Nothing can be clearer than the wish to make permanent both a particular moment of munificence, and the glory bestowed on the *editor* by the crowd in return. Although the *munus* is a *venatio*, not a gladiatorial spectacle, it illustrates how *editores* wanted their gift to the community to be remembered.

Another early representation was on a tomb found outside Pompeii on the road to Herculaneum, and ascribed by the early nineteenth-century excavators to the *duumvir* Umbricius Scaurus; the stucco relief itself has not survived, but was drawn at the time by the French draughtsman F. Mazois. It was in three sections; one contained a hunting scene, the other two six and two pairs of gladiators respectively, including the types known as *equites*, Thracians, heavily armed *hoplomachoi*, and *retiarii* (see Glossary). There has been considerable controversy both about the proper attribution of this relief, and about the nature of the games depicted; they are unlikely to have been funeral games, but rather the events presented on the last day ('summo die') of the *munus* Scaurus provided for his home town. Another monumental representation of a *munus* found at Pompeii is discussed below (p. 93 f.); others have been found in cemeteries at Amiternum (Chieti) and Venafrum. Some of these representations come from the tombs of successful gladiators, but others were intended to remind the local population of the generosity of the *editor*. Indeed, tombs were sometimes set up to defeated gladiators by the *editor*, as much in his own memory as in that of the gladiators. An archpriest of Bithynia erected a tomb listing, in writing, the results of a three-day *munus* at Claudiopolis. On Umbricius Scaurus' tomb, the name of the *lanista* M. Festus Ampliatus is prominently displayed, as is the fact that the gladiators were provided by the imperially owned training school at Capua, the *ludus Julianus* – facts which doubtless raised the cost and status of the *munus*. A *duumvir* from Cirta in Numidia thought of a cheap way of immortalising his *munus*: he raised a statue to himself out of the revenue from entrance fees.[43] One of the most effective ways of advertising their munificence to the widest possible audience through visual representations was available to emperors alone: the coinage. The representations of the Colosseum on coins of Titus and Philip the Arab (celebrating the milleniary festival of AD 247) are well-known. On Titus' issue of brass *sestertii*, we are not only shown the outside, but also details of the inside: stairways, an entrance, and several dozen dots representing the heads of members of the audience. A series of gold and bronze coins of AD 223 commemorates Alexander Severus' re-opening of the Colosseum after a fire in AD 217 (figure 2). On a bronze medallion of Gordian III dating to AD 243 we can see both the crowd of spectators inside the building, and a bull attacking a rhinoceros in the arena.[44] But that virtually exhausts the number of known coin issues with representations of the arena; and none of them depicts a gladiator. What few coins there are advertising imperial munificence in providing games bear images of the animals presented: there is a particularly fine series from the reign of Antoninus Pius. The contrast with the regular and frequent commemoration of the emperor's liberality in providing the people (and, of course, the army) with distributions of money, and especially of his concern for the corn-supply (Annona), is striking.[45] The evidence suggests that what emperors thought ought to be commemorated was not a particular *munus*, even on exceptional occasions such as triumphs, but rather their provision of a great public building. Several buildings of this kind are commemorated on coins, such as the harbour at Ostia begun by Claudius, or Trajan's column. It is as one of these magnificent constructions that the Colosseum appears on coins, when Titus inaugurated it and when Alexander Severus repaired it. The exceptional nature of this gift to the Roman people can also be seen in another attempt to give its inauguration permanence, the celebration of Titus' games in a unique collection of epigrams, the *Book of Spectacles* ascribed to Martial.

The most spectacular permanent way to make one's investment long term is by buildings, of which tombs were one category. Vitruvius' handbook on architecture includes a section on the construction of permanent theatres for *ludi scaenici* (5, 3–5). But in his time, many spectacles were still presented in

temporary wooden buildings hastily (and sometimes danger-
ously) put up for the occasion: 'This shortcoming occurs both in
permanent buildings and in the gladiatorial displays which
magistrates present in the forum and in stage plays, where no
period of delay is permitted, but arrangements have to be completed in a limited time.'[46] These wooden structures resulted in
some notorious catastrophes, of which the most famous was one
at Fidenae in AD 27, described by Tacitus. Although permanent
amphitheatres began to be constructed in various Italian cities
during the second half of the first century BC, many Italian
amphitheatres continued to be temporary, or at least wooden:
during Antoninus Pius' reign, a man left the city of Salutium
money for a gladiatorial show with a wooden arena, 'munus
gladiatorium et saepta lignea'.[47] Even the Circus Maximus at
Rome continued to have wooden seating, with ensuing disasters:
the worst occurred under the same Antoninus Pius, when
wooden seats collapsed, with the loss of 1,112 lives.[48]

The Circus Maximus pre-dated the republic; and throughout
the republican period the Circus Flaminius appears to have been
a normal setting for *ludi*, without any permanent buildings. The
construction of a permanent site at Rome for both theatrical *ludi*
and gladiatorial and wild-beast shows would have seemed a
necessity, as well as a major source of enduring prestige for
whoever built it. The transitoriness of the structures erected for
such spectacles so long as the republic continued to function
parallels the circulation of magisterial power among short-term
office-holders. Permanent buildings would indicate permanent
political control. Major public building, including temples, roads
and aqueducts, was in the hands of the censors, the pair of five-
yearly officials. In 154 BC, the censors Valerius Messala and
Cassius Longinus wished to build a theatre, but were forbidden
by the Senate; it would have made their censorship too permanent.[49] A century later, in 58 BC, Aemilius Scaurus as aedile
constructed seating for 80,000 spectators at the *ludi*, and in 55
BC Pompey built a permanent theatre, formally as the steps
leading up to a temple of Venus (and therefore a religious site
which no envious rivals would be allowed to pull down).[50]
Augustus not only had Pompey's theatre repaired, but also
constructed a permanent stone theatre honouring his deceased
nephew Marcellus (13/11 BC), and authorised his loyal supporter
Cornelius Balbus to build a theatre out of the spoils of an

African triumph (13 BC). The late first century BC and the early first century AD was also the time when it began to be fashionable to build such theatres outside Rome.[51]

But these buildings were specifically designed for the state *ludi* and not for gladiatorial or animal *munera*. Buildings for gladiatorial shows seem already to have existed at Pompeii and perhaps elsewhere in Campania since at least the beginning of the first century BC. The elliptical shape of such amphitheatres represented the optimum compromise between giving the entire audience a frontal view of the arena (for which a circular building would of course have been best), and allowing the performers, men or beasts, a longer area to advance and retreat in. Doubtless there were also ideological reasons behind the adoption of this format. A circular building implies the equality of all spectators (at least, all those seated in each row); an ellipse makes most of the spectators face two specific points on the circumference, thus enabling attention to be drawn to the box of the presiding magistrate. But there were also historical reasons why that particular shape developed. At Rome, since *munera* were not provided by the state, those who gave them had to erect temporary structures for each show; like the seating in the Circus, these would originally appear to have consisted of two long banks of seats facing each other, with straight or (later) semicircular short sides. This shape is suggested by the lay-out of the four underground passages underneath the Roman Forum which are associated with Julius Caesar's provision of wild beast shows, and the early first-century AD amphitheatre built at Cherchell (Caesarea) in Mauretania by the Roman client-king C. Julius Juba II (reigned ca. 24 BC–AD 23).[52]

One of the earliest references to seating arrangements at Rome tells how Gaius Gracchus had such temporary seats torn down in 122 BC so that ordinary Romans, and not just those invited by the elite, could have a good view of the show. Like the shows themselves, these temporary wooden structures became more complicated as time went on: Pliny has a curious account of a pair of wooden theatres which Scribonius Curio is said to have had constructed in 53 BC. They could be turned round on themselves to form the full circle required for a *venatio* or gladiatorial spectacle. Caesar may have had a more permanent wooden amphitheatre built in 46 BC. But the first stone amphitheatre at Rome appears at the same time as Augustus imposed his control over public shows; it was built by another of his trusted commanders, C. Statilius Taurus in 29 BC. By Augustus' time, the use of the word *amphitheatrum* had become standard for such permanent elliptical buildings.[53]

The destruction of Statilius Taurus' amphitheatre by fire during Nero's reign gave Vespasian the opportunity to present the people of Rome with the Roman world's most spectacular building, the Colosseum. Vespasian was able to have the Colosseum built on a prime inner-city site only because the land was already in the possession of the Caesars, having been sequestrated by Nero after the great fire for his hated new palace, the 'Golden House'. Much of the rubble which went to build the Colosseum too was already available and on the site, from the spoils of the Golden House (the symbolism of Vespasian's act in converting the site of a tyrant's palace into a place for granting the Roman people gladiatorial shows will be discussed more fully in Chapter 5). The Colosseum's overall dimensions are 188 by 156 metres, and the arena measures 86 by 54; it has four levels of arcades, originally rising to about 50 metres, and required 100,000 cubic metres of Travertine stone as well as 300 tons of iron to hold it together. Modern estimates show that it could hold an audience of 40–45,000 seated, plus 5,000 standing, though ancient sources exaggeratedly suggest 80–90,000.[54] Earlier amphitheatres, such as that at Pompeii, had been comparatively shallow buildings, constructed as much by digging into the soil as by building upwards; and the ratio of height above ground to cross-section at Pompeii is about 1:12, while the ratio for the Colosseum is 1:3.26 (in other words, the Colosseum is much higher in comparison with its breadth). Once the Colosseum had been built, it became the prototype for all later amphitheatres. It is possible that Nero's amphitheatre had already had similar proportions: it is interesting that the painting at Pompeii depicting the riots of AD 59 shows the amphitheatre there as a much higher building than it really is, and the assumption must be that, when that picture was painted, it was felt that any amphitheatre ought to look like the Colosseum. The exceptional nature of Vespasian's gift to the Roman people was illustrated by its appearance on the coins struck at the time of its formal inauguration by his son Titus. There can have been few more successful attempts at giving munificence a permanent form.[55] The Colosseum continued to inspire large buildings in recent centuries, whether they fulfilled similar theatrical functions (like the Albert Hall in London) or quite different ones, such the Corn Exchange at Leeds, designed by Bradwick in 1861–3 with an elliptical shape like a Roman amphitheatre, and now a shopping arcade (figure 1). Associated with the Colosseum were permanent 'schools' (Lat. *ludi*) in which gladiators were trained at the expense of the imperial household. A fourth-century chronicle ascribes these *ludi* to Domitian, but a recently discovered inscription suggests that at least one imperial school was already functioning under Tiberius, and it is tempting to associate the creation of imperial training schools with Augustus, as another aspect of his extension of control over *munera* at Rome.[56] A procurator in charge of the imperial gladiators is attested for Claudius' reign; and inscriptions show that from Domitian's time on this procurator was of equestrian rank. Domitian may have been responsible for re-organising them after the completion of the Flavian amphitheatre. The four schools were known as the *ludus magnus* ('great' school), the *Gallicus*, *Dacicus* (perhaps established by Trajan), and *Matutinus*; the last of these, the 'Morning School', trained the *bestiarii* whose wild-beast shows took place in the mornings. One half of the remains of a building which appears to have been the *ludus magnus* was excavated in the 1960s on the north side in the Via S. Giovanni in Laterano to the north-east of the Colosseum. The centre of the rectangular building consisted of an elliptical training ground, with underground passages leading directly to the Colosseum.[57]

If the Colosseum could not be emulated any more than Rome itself could, that did not stop municipalities throughout the western Mediterranean from devoting their financial resources to the erection of similar massive stone structures. Greek cities had a financial advantage here, in that they already had public theatres suitable for such spectacles, and only minor architectural alterations for safety reasons were required; and in the Celtic north-west of the empire, both the availability of funds and local experience with massive earthworks meant that earthen rather than masonry structures were preferred. Reliable lists are now available of sites known to have possessed such buildings; Golvin lists 186 certain, and another 86 probable, purpose-built amphitheatres.[58] That of Carthage, the second city of the Latin world, may stand as an example of the effort which local elites put into such buildings: the estimated external dimensions of the building in its final phase (2nd/3rd century) were 156 by 128 metres, with an arena measuring 64.7 by 36.7 metres, and it could have held about 35,000 spectators.[59] The impression which its remains made on medieval visitors may be compared to that made by Rome's Colosseum, though they are not so familiar to European readers. They were described in AD 1082 by El Bekri, and then again in 1154 in the following terms by Edrisi in his geographical narrative:

There is a theatre which has no parallel in the entire world. The form of the building is circular and it consists of fifty surviving vaults. Above each vault there are five rows of arches, one rising above the other, all of the same form and size, made out of blocks of stone of the type called *Kaddzan*, of incomparable beauty. Above each row of arches, there is a circuit of panels, on which there are various reliefs and strange figures of persons, animals and ships, made with incredible skill. In antiquity, so far as we can tell, this building was used for games and public spectacles.

If members of the elite, from emperors to provincial worthies, were prepared to invest such enormous resources in gladiatorial displays as a means of winning favour with the people, then that implied that such shows were indeed popular with at least considerable sections of the population throughout the Roman empire. The evidence for that is overwhelming. Historical sources note that emperors who were unwilling to give games, like Tiberius, were unpopular as a direct result, while those who did, like Tiberius' successor Caligula, won great popularity, if only temporarily.[60] These spectacles were not just a public occasion: they also played a major role in the way people arranged their private experience. One thinks of the interesting graffiti recovered from Pompeii, and of the representations of contests between gladiators or of *venationes* on mosaics, on pottery tableware, on oil lamps and on glassware, from all parts of the empire (figures 3 and 4, the latter an oil lamp in the shape of a gladiator's helmet). In the words of the north African Christian critic of Roman habits Tertullian, these games were 'a most revered spectacle, and a very popular one'.[61] It is taken for granted by the educated elite in their literary creations that their audience will have attended such shows and will understand some of the technical vocabulary, and will admire and approve

23

of the skills and courage shown by gladiators. Games were a stock subject of conversation among the elite.[62] Children might play at being gladiators.[63] Advertisements in public places gave all classes details of forthcoming games, and there may have been souvenir programmes with information about those who fought in particular contests.[64]

While the number of wall-paintings and mosaics with representations of gladiators is by no means as large as those with chariot-races or animal fights, the fact that they are found in private houses suggests that in many parts of the Roman empire, these combats had an important place in the way in which wealthy people ordered their domestic lives. Unfortunately no comprehensive list of such mosaics appears to have been compiled to date. Some of these mosaics were placed in dining rooms, reminding us of the statement by the Augustan writer Nicolaus of Damascus (reported by Athenaeus) that some Romans liked to watch gladiators fighting while they feasted.[65] Roman dining rooms were of course to some extent public space; a mosaic placed there was intended to show off to guests the host's interest in *munera*, and perhaps to immortalise a particular *munus* he had provided for his municipality. Other mosaics may have been placed in the reception rooms in which important Romans received their clients at the morning *salutatio*; this is likely to have been the context of the Augst mosaic, whose panels are intended to be seen by persons standing around the walls of a room with an open, colonnaded entrance, rather than reclining in the middle as they would in a dining room.[66] A recently discovered wall-painting from a villa at Maasbracht near Maastricht appears to show scenes both of a *venatio* and of the distribution of largesse to clients, with a clerk taking records.

As we have seen, some mosaics record the names of individual gladiators, and it seems likely that these were not fictitious, but real persons, an attempt to give permanence to a particular *munus* paid for by the owner of the house. Some of the most striking of these representations have been found in North Africa; the Flavian one from Zliten has already been mentioned, with its representations not just of gladiators in combat and fights between wild animals (a bull and bear), but also of the execution of criminals by being left to the attentions of wild beasts (see p. 15 f. and figure 5). Not all mosaics including representations of gladiatorial duels as well as *venationes* are early: the famous Borghese mosaic is thought to date to ca. AD 300. It was discovered in the atrium of a villa near Tusculum in 1834, and was transported to the Villa Borghese at Rome, where it is on display, considerably restored. It is 27.90 metres in length, with representations of both wild-beast fighters and gladiators.[67] Another famous representation of a *retiarius* called Kalendio overcoming a *secutor* called Astianax, originally from Rome, is in Madrid;[68] there are many others. Comparatively few mosaics of gladiators have yet been recorded from the eastern half of the empire.[69]

Apparent differences in the frequency with which gladiators were represented on mosaics may merely reflect the rate of archaeological recovery. But the fashion seems to have been particularly popular in Gallia Belgica (covering the modern Benelux countries, the Rhineland, and much of Switzerland and north-eastern France), where it may be associated with the predilection for visual representations of scenes from daily life, e.g. the transportation, kitchen and feasting scenes on the tomb of the Secundinii at Igel near Trier. Representations of gladiators appear on mosaics from both urban and rural sites in this province, especially in the late second and early third centuries AD. They include Bad Kreuznach, Augsburg (in Rhaetia), Augst in Switzerland, Reims and Flacé-lès-Mâcon.[70] A large (and heavily restored) mosaic from what may have been a third- or fourth-century imperial villa at Nennig near Trier was found in 1852. But otherwise the many fine mosaics from the late third century onwards eschew gladiators and concentrate on scenes of chariot racing and *venationes*, including the hunting and capture of wild beasts which was a prerequisite of their display in the circus: examples of such scenes occur throughout the empire, with famous examples of a chariot race in Barcelona and of *venationes* in the baths of Caracalla at Rome and at Piazza Armerina in Sicily. A mosaic found at Cologne in 1885 and claimed as a fourth-century representation of a gladiatorial contest was far too heavily restored to have any evidential value, and may in fact have represented something quite different, for instance an imperial *adventus*.[71] While no such mosaics have hitherto been found in Britain, a wall-painting from the Roman colony of Colchester shows a defeated gladiator in a pose found in many other places, his shield on the ground and the finger of his left hand raised in an appeal for clemency (figure 10). There is much other if less spectacular artistic evidence from Roman Britain for interest in gladiators, including several terra sigillata beakers found at Colchester (see figure 12 for one with a *retiarius* fighting a *secutor*). No fewer than eighteen fragments of glass cups with representations of gladiators have been found from different sites in Britain, including two produced from the same mould (from Hartlip, Kent, and Southwark); others were found at London, Colchester, Wroxeter, Dorchester, Kingsholm (Glos.), Usk, and Leicester, almost all of them early legionary encampments. This suggests that interest in *munera* was more marked among soldiers and colonists than amongst wealthy members of local elites keen to emphasise their incorporation into Roman culture and political structures.[72]

VIRTUE AND VICE

Women as well as men found gladiatorial contests, and gladiators, attractive. Some much-quoted epigraphic evidence suggests that this attraction might be sexual: at Pompeii, the *retiarius* Crescens was known as 'the netter of girls by night' and 'the girls' darling'. Thracians were a favourite symbol of manliness because much of their body was left visible to the audience.[73] This obviously constituted a potential danger to the Roman male's control over his womenfolk. Augustus restricted women, other than the six Vestal Virgins, to watching gladiators from the rearmost rows of seats.[74] It proved impossible to put a stop to stories about sexual associations between gladiators and women of the elite, even including empresses. The wife of Marcus Aurelius, Faustina, was suspected of having had affairs with gladiators; only this could explain why her son Commodus was so interested in the sport.[75] This anxiety on the part of Roman males is prominent in fiction: it occurs in Petronius' *Satyricon*, and Juvenal's sixth satire makes much of the ultimate disgrace, a woman of senatorial status finding gladiators so interesting that she actually trains as one.[76] Roman anxieties about the sexual attractions of gladiators are given expression by the fact that they are classified together with prostitutes in Roman legislation, and that grammatical texts associate the Latin word for the gladiator's trainer (*lanista*) with that for a pimp (*leno*). Like pimps and prostitutes, public performers such as actors and gladiators sold their bodies for the delectation of others, if only visually.[77]

But ambivalence about gladiators went further than an anxiety about maintaining control over the sexual pleasures and preferences of women. There were anxieties about maintaining control over the gladiators themselves. Roman tradition could not forget that Spartacus' slave rebellion managed to sustain itself against major Roman forces for three years largely because it was led by trained gladiators.[78] Some years later, during Catiline's conspiracy, the Senate decreed that gladiators should be removed from Rome to Campania, where there were proper facilities for their policing; in the same year, 63 BC, Gaius Marcellus was expelled from Capua for trying to solicit the support of gladiators for an uprising. When Caesar invaded Italy in 49 BC, his opponents were particularly concerned about the five thousand gladiators owned by him whom he kept at or near Capua. To prevent them from causing any trouble (in favour of Caesar or in order to escape), these gladiators were distributed among the city's population with two to each household, although the consul L. Cornelius Lentulus considered promising them their freedom (from Caesar, their owner) if they fought on the Pompeian side. Gladiators continued to be involved in violent uprisings in the early empire. In AD 21, Sacrovir's Gallic rebellion was supported by gladiators who had been brought to Autun for training; there may have been special conditions in Gaul, but in Italy too force had to be used to prevent an incipient outbreak at Praeneste in AD 64, which brought back memories of Spartacus, so Tacitus tells us.[79]

This fear of gladiators offered Roman politicians the temptation of denigrating their opponents by accusing them of using gladiators as private security forces. In 57 BC, Cicero's enemy the tribune Clodius is said to have used gladiators belonging to his brother to prevent the passing of the law recalling Cicero from exile.[80] Decimus Brutus was invited to join the conspiracy to kill Caesar in 44 BC because he had a troupe of gladiators available in Rome which could be used to protect the conspirators. These stories were created by hostile sources, but it is not unlikely that, during the violent political conflicts of the last generation of the republic, public figures should wish to be accompanied and protected by slaves who had had some training in fighting. During the civil wars of AD 69, imperial gladiators are again mentioned as being used in the fighting; and again, such stories are likely to be based on fact as well as embellished by hostile reporting.[81]

27

There were thus real reasons why Romans had ambivalent attitudes towards gladiators. Notwithstanding the widespread popularity of *munera*, to call someone either a *lanista* or a gladiator is a standard term of abuse in classical invective, literary attacks denigrating an opponent.

> From the moment when Rufinus put on the adult toga, he abused adult freedom by attending gladiatorial exercises. He knew all the gladiators by name and knew all the details of their previous contests and their wounds. He even went through a training course under the supervision of a professional gladiator, although he came from a good family.[82]

The theme that young men are more interested than they should be in gladiators was a literary commonplace. The ultimate disgrace was for a free citizen to fight as a gladiator. 'The only thing that wealthy cavaliers (*trossuli*) think about is whether they should go and fight in the arena as swordsmen or *retiarii*. What would Cato the Elder have thought! . . .' One curious way of consoling a parent for the premature death of a son was to suggest that, had he grown older, he might have ended up squandering his fortune and sinking to the level of fighting as a gladiator.[83] Critics of Roman morality – whether classical pagan satirists or historians, or Christians like Tertullian and St Jerome – made a point of expressing their outrage at the ambivalence or even hypocrisy of attitudes towards professional gladiators: they were the lowest of the low, *perditi homines*, and yet senators favoured them, collected their armour, sometimes secretly practised as gladiators, and even on occasion sank to the level of performing in public themselves. In Tertullian's words, *Quanta perversitas*.[84]

Both gladiators and their trainers are déclassé, and suffer *infamia*, the loss of their identity as respectable citizens. The contrast between the fame of individual gladiators and the *infamia* with which gladiators as a group were stigmatised is striking. *Infamia* as a concept in Roman law was not so much an impediment imposed by the law, as a recognition by judicial officials (and increasingly by legislators and jurists) of the fact that certain individuals were not thought trustworthy by society at large, for example because they had committed a crime or had failed to manage their property to the point of declaring bankruptcy. Such persons were denied the right to witness wills or other legal transactions, and they could not appear before a court on anyone's behalf other than their own. Originally *infamia* was a state suffered by individuals for their personal misdeeds, formally recorded by the black marks the censors would place against their names in the register of citizens. But, from the late second century BC, it seems that anyone who had at any time fought as a gladiator was tainted with *infamia*, whatever their personal standing. The provisions of the Gracchan *Lex Acilia de repetundis* (122 BC) for the selection of juries to try cases of extortion by provincial governors survive; they may well repeat earlier regulations. The names put forward for the panel of jurors have to be those of *equites*; specifically excluded are any who have held minor magistracies, senators, and 'anyone who has or shall have fought having hired himself out for pay' (*queive mercede conductus depugnavit depugnaverit*), as well as those who have suffered a legal conviction and those who do not have a house within a mile of the city of Rome.[85]

That provision, imposing legal disabilities on gladiators as a class, was applied to other groups such as actors and prostitutes in subsequent Roman legislation. The municipal regulations of Julius Caesar (*Lex Iulia Municipalis*) exclude from membership of local councils 'anyone who is or has been a gladiatorial trainer or an actor'.[86] The law regulating the colony of Heraclea (*Tabula Heracleensis*) bans those who were or had ever been *lanistae* (trainers), gladiators, actors and convicted criminals from election to municipal councils. *Lanistae* and gladiators are classified along with actors and pimps in the very detailed regulations about who could and who could not appear on the stage and in the arena in a decree of AD 19 of which a copy was found at Larinum in central Italy.[87] The Julian/Papian laws on manumission provided that freedmen with two legitimate children born in freedom were to be exempted from fulfilling any more economic obligations towards their ex-owners: that privilege was explicitly denied to actors, and to those who had hired themselves out to fight in the arena (the texts do not specifically mention gladiators rather than *bestiarii*, but it is likely that any such specific references would have been edited out when the *Digest* was compiled in AD 538, when gladiatorial – but not wild-beast – games had long ceased).[88] Marcus Aurelius proclaimed that gladiators were not even worthy to be included amongst those who were to pay taxes: 'their money is contaminated by the stain of human blood', [pecunia] cruoris humani aspergine contaminata.[89] Private individuals shared the presumption enshrined in public law that the gladiator was not to be trusted. An inscription of republican date records the provision of a burial ground for the people of Sassina by one Horatius Balbus. He assimilates gladiators, even if they are free, to prostitutes and to those suicides who have hanged themselves, i.e. whose death is dishonourable. All these categories are banned from burial: 'extra auctorateis et quei sibei [la]queo manu attulissent et quei quaestum spurcum professi essent'.[90] The idea that a man who chose to fight in the arena was like one who had committed suicide is found in a literary attack on the institution by Cyprian, bishop of Carthage in the mid-third century: 'What madness, voluntarily to submit to attacks by wild beasts: both murderer and suicide!'[91]

The perception of gladiators as sinister might be represented in other ways as well. Some were said to be unusual in learning to fight left-handed in order to frighten their opponents; examples are attested by historical and rhetorical writers, on an inscription, and on visual representations on mosaics, reliefs and pottery.[92]

Both modern scholars and the Romans themselves tried to explain the paradox that the gladiators who provided one of their most important social activities were held in utter contempt. One widely held explanation, first formulated by W. Henzen in 1845, was in terms of the historical origins of gladiatorial contests: they were not Roman at all, but borrowed from the Etruscans. This theory was based on a statement by the Augustan writer Nicolaos of Damascus, quoted by Athenaeus, explicitly asserting that the Romans took the custom over from the Etruscans.[93] Support was found in the fact that the etymological dictionary compiled by Isidore of Seville in the early seventh century AD ascribed an Etruscan origin to the Latin word for a trainer of gladiators, lanista, and that Tertullian, in two of his attacks on the games, describes a figure dressed up as the god Dis Pater escorting the corpses of slaughtered gladiators from the arena in terms reminiscent of the hammer-wielding Etruscan god Charon, corresponding to Mercury in his role as guide of the souls of the deceased to the underworld.[94] Relevant archaeological evidence was harder to come by. Paintings of a figure called 'Phersu' are found in three different tombs at Tarquinia dating to the second half of the sixth century BC. 'Phersu' wears a conical cap and holds on a leash a large hound attacking another man whose head is covered in a hood.[95] These scenes have variously been interpreted as executions, funeral sacrifices, or a sporting event of some kind. But however similar the activities in which 'Phersu' participated may have been to the animal-fights and public executions that came many centuries later to be associated with Roman gladiatorial games, the masked man attacked by Phersu's hound was not a gladiator. A number of Etruscan tomb paintings from the sixth and fifth centuries BC contain representations of funeral games, but none of them includes pictures of gladiators. On the other hand a considerable number of south Italian vases of the second half of the fourth century BC bear representations of men engaged in single combat; and a Lucanian tomb at Paestum includes such combats among the scenes of funeral games in honour of the deceased. As Georges Ville persuasively argued, it was in Campania, not Etruria, that the Romans encountered gladiators fighting at funeral games. If we seek cross-cultural parallels, there are many examples of young men, especially in pastoral mountain societies, engaging in more or less ritualised combat in order to define a ranking order; sometimes they consist of unarmed wrestling matches – as among Swiss herdsmen – but fights with weapons, often resulting in bloodshed, are not unheard of. It is interesting that Procopius, centuries later, mentions fighting games amongst Samnite shepherd lads.[96]

If the belief that gladiators were Etruscan has persisted in spite of the absence of supporting evidence, it is because it provided modern scholars whose humanitarian presuppositions were affronted by gladiatorial contests with a morally satisfactory explanation. The Romans' reputation for civilised behaviour could be saved if these games were shown to have originated elsewhere. An Etruscan origin appealed to those who shared the widespread nineteenth-century belief that there was a link between morality and race: the (morally superior) Indo-European Romans had been tainted by contact with the (morally decadent) Etruscans. The argument was strengthened by reports in classical authors of both the Etruscans' immorality – for example, the unusually visible role which women were said to play in their social life – and their oriental origin. The story that the Etruscans reached Italy after having been forced to leave Lydia because of a famine is first found in Herodotus.[97] Whatever was unacceptable in Roman life could thus be traced back to, and blamed on, 'oriental' Etruscan decadence: like other aspects of racial theory, this was taken to absurd lengths by some Nazi thinkers, who argued that the 'priestcraft' which the Etruscans brought to Italy from the Orient explained why Romans had become decadent enough to accept Catholic Christianity, whose values were so opposed to the racial group loyalties which the Nazis ascribed to 'pure' Indo-Europeans.[98]

The considerable research devoted to the Etruscans during this century has made them rather less alien and 'mysterious'. It has reinforced the doubts, already voiced in antiquity, about the contribution of any significant immigration from the eastern Mediterranean (as opposed to cultural borrowing) to central Italy's development from the Villanovan bronze age to the Etruscan iron age.[99] If some Romans thought that certain aspects of their gladiatorial culture originated with the Etruscans, this was a moral statement rather than a historical one, and has to be seen in terms of the symbolic significance of 'Etruria' as a moral category in Roman thought. In archaic Rome, Etruria represented the nearest non-Latin speaking, 'foreign', community, across the river Tiber. Etruscan habits hence came to symbolise 'foreignness' in moral terms (exemplified by the lax control over women). Their 'foreignness' was reinforced by their mythical (and not, therefore, historical) Lydian origins. The category 'Etruscan' had an explanatory force with regard to customs and institutions about which the Romans had ambivalent feelings, in particular those associated with state power. An interesting list is given by Strabo: 'It is said that the triumphal garb and that of the consuls and basically that of any magistrate was brought there from Tarquinia, as were the *fasces*, trumpets, sacrifical rituals, divination and music, as they are used publicly by the Romans.'[100] It may as a matter of fact be historically true that some of these symbols were brought to Rome by a dynasty of 'Etruscan' kings. There is a strong tendency during periods of rapid social change associated with the formation of state power for political symbols to be borrowed from neighbouring cultures: this reinforces the status of the elite, whose contacts with 'foreign' cultures give them easier access to such symbolic objects (and the knowledge associated with them) than their humbler subjects. But not every institution which the Romans categorised as 'Etruscan' because of its moral ambiguity was historically borrowed from Etruria: the Roman theatre is a notable example.[101]

The ascription of an Etruscan origin to gladiatorial games similarly has to be explained as a result of Roman ambivalence about the games, and not vice-versa. Nevertheless the evidence suggests that, like other expensive activities symbolising the high status of the Roman elite, they were indeed consciously borrowed from a neighbouring culture, namely that of Campania. Such a borrowing was morally no less problematic than an 'Etruscan' origin. In an account of how the Romans and their Campanian allies celebrated a victory over the Samnites in 308 BC, Livy is anxious to differentiate between the two: while the Romans use the magnificent gold-inlaid shields captured from the enemy 'to adorn the forum' in honour of the gods, the Capuans use their spoils to arm the gladiators who perform at the private banquets of the Campanian elite.[102] The passage has rightly been used to support the view that the category of gladiators called 'Samnite' was actually connected with Samnium: it also exemplifies the moral uncertainties associated with any 'foreign' borrowing.

Speculations about the functional origins of *munera* have as little value as those about their geographical origins. Whatever the functions of reciprocal killing may have been in their original Campanian (or Etruscan) context, they will not necessarily have applied to the republican Roman society which thought them worth borrowing; and Augustus and his successors, and the Italian and provincial elites of the imperial period, will have had other reasons again for seeing *munera* as meaningful. The latter period is the focus of this book, but arguments about the original role and context of gladiatorial combats deserve a brief discussion.

The theory that they originated in human sacrifices looks to the accusations by Tertullian and other Christian writers that the gladiator was being sacrificed to the ghosts (*manes*) of the deceased;[103] and Roman *munera* were clearly originally associated with funerals. Unfortunately the Graeco-Roman elite was brought up on reading Homer, and they would have got the impression from the description of Achilles' slaughtering Trojan prisoners at Patroclus' funeral that such human sacrifice was typical of the heroic age. Herodotus ascribes human sacrifices at funerals to the Etruscans; when Octavian sacked Perugia in a civil war in 40 BC, he slaughtered captives on the pretext that such killings had once been an Etruscan tradition.[104] Tombpaintings from Caere have been interpreted in these terms, although other interpretations are possible. Whatever the Etruscans were reported by hostile sources as having done, there is no evidence that gladiators were sacrificed in this way, whether or not they were associated with Etruscan funerals; and there is no evidence at all that the Romans at any period thought that any such human sacrifices were appropriate in connection with funerals.

Another theory which has seemed superficially attractive is to see gladiators as analogous to 'scapegoats', beings whom a community loads with the guilt for the problem or problems it faces, and expels from its ranks so as to direct the wrath of the offended deity away from the community as a whole. The evidence for scapegoat-type killings in the Roman empire is slim, and in any case not relevant to gladiators: there is a story about a Christian called Dasius who was martyred at Durostorum on the Danube in the reign of Maximian and Diocletian for refusing to play the suicidal role of Cronos in a midwinter festival. What lies behind this story is unclear, but it does not constitute evidence that the execution of a 'scapegoat' was an acknowledged feature of Roman religious ritual, still less that gladiators were in any sense seen as scapegoats.[105]

What we can say with certainty is that there was a link between gladiatorial combat and death. From the time when gladiators first fought at Rome at the funeral of Junius Brutus Pera in 264 BC until the time of Augustus, they appeared only on occasions which (whatever the real reasons why their *editores* put them on) were overtly supposed to commemorate an individual who had recently died. To interpret that link in terms of human sacrifice, as Tertullian did, is to emphasise killing, rather than dying, as the central point of the spectacle: notwithstanding the widespread misconception that the phrase 'we who are going to die salute you' applied to gladiators, that phrase was spoken by condemned criminals, not gladiators.[106] Gladiators faced death every time they entered the arena, but they were not certain that they were going to die on any particular occasion: on the contrary, there were vested interests in favour of their surviving (see Chapter 3, pp. 120 ff.). Instead of seeing a gladiatorial combat as a public display of killing, it might be useful to see it as a demonstration of the power to overcome death. The victorious gladiator overcame death by showing that he was a better fighter than his opponent. But the loser, too, might win back his life by satisfying the audience that he had fought courageously and skilfully. If he did not prove this, he would be killed by the opponent with whom he had shared his gladiatorial training. He would die no lingering death, like a criminal, but would be dispatched quickly and with a minimum of pain: even though the gladiator was *infamis*, he would die by the sword, the death of a citizen on the field of battle. He was expected to take the *coup de grace* without protest, and the ritualised way in which it was carried out (p. 95 f. below) will have helped many defeated gladiators to fulfil this expectation. In that sense, even the gladiator who died in the arena had overcome death. The knowledge that he had proved his ability at fighting may have been small consolation to him (though latter-day cynicism is not to the point); his death was certainly a consolation to those who watched it. They had assembled in order to be reminded of the death of a great Roman. Each pair of gladiators brought the Roman audience face-to-face with death; through their skill in fighting, they might escape that death, just as the deceased in whose honour the *munus* was being given would overcome death because, while alive, he had demonstrated the qualities which for Romans constituted *virtus*.[107]

The connection between virtue and fighting in the Roman system of values is generally recognised. During the third and second centuries BC, it was primarily as military commanders that members of the Roman elite could prove to themselves and to their peers that they were good men, that they possessed *virtus*. Military *virtus* was not restricted to commanders, but could be demonstrated by, and rewarded in, ordinary soldiers, as is shown both by literary anecdotes and by the system of Roman military decorations.[108] *Virtus* was a complex concept which could include a variety of components relating to private and peaceful activities as well as behaviour in public life and warfare. The range of qualities which *virtus* covered is listed in a passage from a funeral speech which Q. Metellus gave in 221 BC in honour of his father, L. Caecilius Metellus.

35

He had to his credit ten of the greatest and best achievements which sages spend their lives trying to attain. Namely, he wished to be a warrior of the first rank; an outstanding public speaker; a most courageous general; one who won great military victories under his own auspices; to hold the highest offices; to have great wisdom; to be considered the foremost senator; to acquire a great deal of money in an honest fashion; to leave behind many children; and to be held in great fame in the community.[109]

Primarium bellatorem, to excel as a warrior, is not only distinguished from, but precedes, being a brave general, winning military victories under his own auspices, and being elected to magistracies. Courage and skill in hand-to-hand combat was something required from every Roman legionary. In Greek (and presumably archaic Italian) hoplite warfare, each soldier was one of thousands constituting a closely packed phalanx whose military effectiveness depended on everyone moving together in unison; any desire to show off individual courage at the expense of maintaining the battle line was frowned upon. The battle line of the republican Roman legion was much more open, and the individual soldier had more scope to use offensive weapons, as the Greeks found to their horror when they had to face Roman legionaries in the early second century BC. Roman success in battle was the result of the individual soldier's ability to survive hand-to-hand combat, rather than maximising the impact of the weight of the phalanx on the enemy line. As an example of such a display of individual *virtus*, we may cite the story of a 15-year-old Aemilius Lepidus, who 'advanced into battle, killed an enemy, and saved a fellow-citizen', for which he was rewarded with a statue on the Capitol.[110]

Single combat was therefore the context in which a Roman had to prove that he possessed one of the most important constituents of 'virtue'. Just what constituted virtue was no less problematic for the Romans than for others, and there will always have been uncertainty as to the relationship between courage in hand-to-hand combat and other virtues. The last century of the republic was particularly a period when different aspects of virtue came into conflict, and different political groupings laid claim to supreme or exclusive *virtus* on the grounds of possessing particular partial *virtutes*: the writings of Sallust express such conflicts between (for instance) the claims of inherited as opposed to personally acquired *virtus*, or between moral virtues and *virtus* in the sense of a purely technical ability to succeed. The description of the death in battle of Catiline and his associates bears witness to the bravery in hand-to-hand fighting expected of a virtuous Roman, no matter how decadent his personal and political life: 'mindful of his ancestry and of the high office he had held, he plunged into the thickest concentration of enemy soldiers, and there was cut down as he fought'.[111]

It was this same quality, the courage to confront an opponent coupled with the technical expertise to kill or maim him, which gladiatorial contests instantiated. Gladiatorial contests, because they were between men whose only claim to *virtus* was by fighting, isolated such virtue from all others. If the gladiators were women (figure 16), it even separated fighting ability from masculinity. For the onlookers, the match was analogous to an experiment in which fighting ability has been separated from other factors. That did not of course make the relationship between that fighting ability and other aspects of virtue less complex. The conflict between the *virtus* of the battlefield and other virtues may have been particularly problematic for Romans in the aftermath of the civil wars of the first century BC. Livy tries to re-integrate these virtues in a well-known and detailed description of gladiatorial games held by Scipio in honour of his father and uncle (who had both died in the fighting against the Carthaginians) at New Carthage in 206 BC:

> The gladiatorial games did not consist of the kind of persons from among whom the *lanistae* customarily make their purchases, i.e. slaves bought from slave-dealers or free men who offer their blood for sale; the skills of those who fought were offered voluntarily and gratis. Some of them were sent by their chieftains in order to demonstrate the *virtus* that was inborn in their tribe . . .

(Livy goes on to say that others fought out of respect for Scipio, and others again to settle disputes between them, and describes one such dispute and its resolution by battle).[112] We have already seen that Livy is uneasy about assigning gladiatorial contests the same moral stature as other, more 'Roman',

37

demonstrations of *virtus*. He has tried hard to distinguish
Scipio's games from the *munera* of Augustan Rome, in which the
audience could concentrate on the gladiators' fighting skills
precisely because they were otherwise worthless.
   The figure of the gladiator would not have been surrounded
with such ambiguity if he had simply been a social outcast. What
made him peculiar was that the particular *virtus* he exercised
gave him a claim to be a Roman. Inscriptions and graffiti show
the popular respect awarded to individual gladiators who were
known to the general public by name. The fighting skills of
particular gladiators were discussed in polite conversation.[113]
Their *virtus* was recognised by writers who had no hesitation in
using the word 'gladiator' as a term of abuse. Cicero expresses
reservations about gladiatorial games, and interestingly enough
they are the very opposite to those expressed by Livy – it was
because free men took part in them that they were cruel (no
treatment could be cruel against a criminal): 'A gladiatorial show
is apt to seem cruel and brutal to some eyes, and I incline to
think that it is, as now conducted. But in the days when it was
criminals who crossed swords in the death struggle, there could
be no better schooling against pain and death.'[114] A fine
example of such praise of the bravery of gladiators occurs in
Pliny's panegyric of the emperor Trajan. Pliny attacks certain
spectacles which Trajan's disgraced predecessor Domitian had
favoured, such as pantomime shows, but not *munera*: free citizens are made braver by seeing their inferiors set them a brave
example – 'A public entertainment, nothing lax or dissolute to
weaken and destroy the manly spirit of his subjects, but one to
inspire them to face honourable wounds and look scornfully
upon death, by demonstrating a love of glory and a desire for
victory even in the persons of criminals and slaves.'[115] As late as
the fourth century AD, the pagan orator Libanius – otherwise no
friend of spectacular shows, since they represented a threat to
his own rhetorical displays – can find praise for the bravery of
the gladiators who graced his uncle's games, 'whom you might
swear to have been the pupils of the three hundred at the Battle
of Thermopylae'.[116]
   The defeated gladiator had a weaker claim to manliness. It
is interesting that several reliefs show defeated gladiators awaiting the judgement of the crowd standing with their knees
close together in the stance which, since the fifth century BC, had

been used by sculptors to indicate femininity by emphasising the hips (figure 11). Praxiteles' Aphrodite of Cnidos was the proto-type; subsequently the stance was typically applied to her-maphrodites and to 'effeminate' male deities such as Apollo and Dionysus.[117] Too much should not be made of this, but even if the explanation for this type of representation is purely artistic, and there was no actual tradition of any real gladiators ever positioning themselves in this way to admit that they had no claim to manliness, it shows that sculptors and mosaicists, and the people they worked for, perceived defeated gladiators as effeminate.

In late antiquity it became particularly important for those pagans who wished to preserve the games in the face of Christian hostility, as one feature of the inherited culture, to emphasise the bravery publicly demonstrated by gladiators. It was argued that there was a very close link between gladiatorial combats and military training. There was a basis to this argu-ment, in that we are told that Roman commanders occasionally used gladiatorial trainers (*lanistae*) to train military recruits, especially in crises when mass levies had to be prepared for battle rapidly. The first known such example was in 105 BC, when the consuls P. Rutilius Rufus and C. Manilius needed to train a new army rapidly to face the threat of the northern invaders (cf. p. 7 above). The writer of the *Historia Augusta* generalised this into an argument of principle in favour of gladiators: 'Other accounts – which I think more likely – state that when the Romans went to war they had to look at fighting and wounds and weapons and unprotected men attacking one another, so that they would not be afraid of armed enemies in war or be frightened by wounds and blood.' Long after gladia-tors had disappeared from Italy, a Roman orator could still tell the Ostrogothic king Theoderic how the Romans of old had looked to gladiators for their military training.[118]

This makes the theory that gladiatorial games were promoted by the Roman emperors as a kind of substitute for warfare questionable. (It is in any case a variant of the dubious 'hy-draulic' theory of violence – that human beings are naturally prone to a certain amount of violence, and that if this can no longer be given expression either in violence against external enemies, or in civil strife, it has in some way to be allowed for by letting people watch it, e.g. on television.) What made the public display of fighting skills so critical for Romans was not the shift from a belligerent republic to a peaceful monarchy, but rather the crisis of Roman values brought about by the creation of a new Italian society in the late republic, a society which contained many different ethnic and cultural components and whose only shared experience was that of being part of the Roman military machine. The conditions of the late republic threatened the certainties of the inherited political culture. We have seen how Sallust's surviving monographs, the *Catiline* and *Jugurthan War*, illustrate doubts about the nature of *virtus*. It was no longer possible for the score or so of Latin families who had ruled the republic for generations to legitimate their claim to power because *virtus* was inherited from their ancestors. From the time of the Gracchi on, disagreement about what was legitimate in public life led to open violence: some argued that legitimacy was bestowed by *mos maiorum*, others that it lay in the will of the people (or its leaders). Even when there was no civil war, discord was endemic in the late republic. Common ground could not be based on the inherited culture, not only because it was challenged by aristocrats of Roman origin such as Catiline, but because many of the Italians who had become part of Roman political society in consequence of the Social War of 91–89 BC came from communities which did not share any common culture, either with Rome or with their fellow Italians.

Under these circumstances only new, artificially constructed, cultural symbols could replace violence as a means to a new consensus. Later, the emperors were to provide the political stability that enabled jurists to develop Roman law as a system of certain rules which would both allow Romans to know what behaviour was expected of them, and give them a symbol with which to identify their Roman citizenship. Before Augustus succeeded in monopolising political power, there was no source of authority within Rome that could impose consensus or the symbols that went with it. It helped if the symbols came from outside, so that they were not identified with any particular component of the Italian community. Far-sighted political leaders such as Cicero sought to provide the Italians with a basis for practical morality founded on Greek philosophy. Other Greek cultural borrowings (literary and artistic) can also be seen as attempts by those who won their way to the top at Rome, by whatever means, to legitimate their superior status by appealing to a point of reference which was outside Italy. This phase of the long and varied process known as the 'Hellenisation' of Italy can better be seen as the creation of a common culture, which was no longer Roman or Latin in any restrictive geographical or ethnic sense.[119]

The spread of gladiatorial games throughout Italy was part of that process of integration. The fact that gladiators were perceived as originally not Roman at all actually helped. It was at Capua, not Rome, where the leading gladiatorial *ludi* could be found, and literary references to the different categories of gladiators suggest that some of them were originally associated with ethnic groups: Samnites, Gauls and Thracians. During the first century BC, two of these groups (Samnites and at any rate those Gauls inhabiting Italy) were part of the process of Italian integration. By the time of Augustus, it had become inappropriate for them to be perceived as outsiders; and the *Samnis* turns into a *secutor*, while the *Gallus* becomes a *murmillo*.[120]

The evidence that it was Augustus who was responsible for giving gladiatorial games a major new role in the Roman ceremonial calendar is considerable (though there continued to be changes from time to time, e.g. in the officials responsible for staging shows). Just as he imposed his own solution on the question of Roman identity in other respects, so he took over both *ludi* and *munera* at Rome, monopolising the glory and legislating about who was to attend – i.e., who was a Roman. (The importance of the arena as the place where an emperor was particularly close to his people will be examined further in Chapter 5.)

It was in order to prove that they belonged to the Roman community that the cities first of Italy and later of the entire empire vied with one another in providing games and constructing amphitheatres. The interest shown in spectacles of all kinds by Caligula, Claudius and Nero will have helped to create an atmosphere in which being a Roman meant being prepared to take the games seriously. Thus Nero's visits to his new colony of Pozzuoli in AD 64–6 led directly to the rebuilding and enlargement of the amphitheatre there by L. Cassius Cerealis.[121] Popular involvement might lead to rioting, such as at Pompeii in AD 59. Bad behaviour on the part of the audience had to be punished: it was a failure to act in accordance with Roman morality.[122] During the civil wars of AD 68/9, rival emperors sought to turn their seizure of power into legitimate rule by providing expensive *munera* (perhaps most spectacularly on Vitellius' birthday, in each of the 265 *vici* (districts) of Rome).[123] The military leader who finally imposed his authority, Vespasian, legitimated it by constructing the Colosseum on the site of the tyrant Nero's palace, so that (in the words of the *Book of Spectacles*): 'Rome has been restored to herself, and under your presidency, Caesar, what used to be a source of pleasure for a master has become one for the whole people.'[124] The arena was a place of specifically Roman legitimacy, something which Vespasian was particularly anxious to claim since the principal source of his support, apart from his own army, had been a group of inter-related Hellenistic kings in the eastern half of the empire who were concerned that other candidates for the imperial office would disregard the obligations of the client–patron relationship with the Julio-Claudians that had brought them their kingdoms. Consequently he and his son Titus made a point of emphasising their Romanness in various ways, including holding gladiatorial shows in the Roman colony of Berytus and in other eastern cities.[125]

While the spread of gladiatorial spectacles outside Italy went hand-in-hand with Romanisation, there are some curious early references to such combats, most interestingly that put on at Antioch in Syria in 166 BC by the Seleucid king Antiochus IV; Antiochus had been a hostage in Rome during the rule of his elder brother Seleucus IV, and had seen there how effective *munera* were in asserting both the importance of the *editor*, and the power of the Roman people. It has been suggested that Antiochus was trying to upstage games put on by the Roman commander Aemilius Paullus at Amphipolis to celebrate his victory over Macedonia, though Livy's account suggests that it became a regular institution at Antioch.[126] Some other references to gladiatorial games outside Italy cannot necessarily be seen as attempts to emulate the Romans; at the funeral of the Lusitanian chieftain Viriathus in 140 BC gladiators were said to have appeared,[127] but we may be dealing here with a separate Celtiberian practice. In the Celtic world in general there is some evidence that some of the activities in the arena came to be assimilated to Celtic practices; a native Celtic method of execution had been to force convicted criminals to fight one another as so-called *trinquii*. Gladiatorial combats were certainly instituted in Gaul by Augustus, in the context of the ceremonial display of loyalty to himself (associated with Lug, the Celtic god of peace and civilised life, corresponding to the Roman Mercury) held annually at Lyon on 1 August; the inscription commemorating the erection of the first stone amphitheatre on the site under Tiberius survives. During Sacrovir's rebellion in AD 21, we are told of a *ludus* at Autun for training gladiators who were armed *more gentico* and called *cruppelani*, a term not otherwise attested. At Saintes, the *vergobret* dedicated an amphitheatre under Claudius. *Munera* had been introduced to southern Gaul by Roman settlers; the first certain reference to a gladiatorial spectacle is at Arles in 63 BC.[128] Some emperors seem to have attempted to limit or prevent such games in the provinces, perhaps out of fear that they might present a challenge to their own popularity as providers of games: Nero is said to have banned gladiatorial *munera, venationes*, and *ludi* of any kind in the provinces in AD 57, the year when he erected his wooden amphitheatre in Rome.[129]

It was shown half a century ago by Louis Robert that, in the eastern half of the empire too, gladiatorial games spread hand-in-hand with the identification by elites of their place within the Roman empire. Local populations will first have seen gladiators perform in shows put on by Hellenistic princes like Antiochus IV or, later, Herod Agrippa, or by the commanders of Roman armies such as Lucullus at Ephesus in 69 BC.[130] In Roman colonies such as Berytus and Corinth, *munera* could serve as a symbol that the population (whatever their ethnic origin) was genuinely Roman and superior to the Hellenistic communities in the rest of the province. The adoption of gladiators (μονομάχοι) by other cities was to a great extent a response to this challenge. Philostratus explicitly says that the Athenians introduced gladiatorial games out of rivalry with Corinth; Corinth was the seat of the provincial governor, but Athens the centre of philosophical culture.[131] For Greek-speakers, even if they were formally Roman citizens, the process of integration was a different phenomenon from the need of Romans in the provinces to maintain their superior identity as genuine Romans. Recent scholarship has shown just how few wealthy eastern landowners wished to become Roman senators during the first two centuries AD, and of course the east never identified with Latin literary culture, even if many decided to learn Latin in order to be able to practise the Roman law that applied to the east after Caracalla's grant of citizenship in AD 212. Although some Latin technical terms were simply transliterated into Greek (figure 17), the epigraphical evidence assembled by Robert shows that the gladiatorial spectacles held in Greek-speaking cities were conducted in a Greek ceremonial context. The motives of both cities and individuals will have been different from those of the Latin-speaking populations of the West: they will have been a result of the competition between cities and individuals to demonstrate their loyalty to the empire in general, and to win the favour of particular emperors. As early as the time of Augustus, amphitheatres had been built at Nysa in Caria and Alexandria in Egypt. An inscription from the Temple of Augustus at Ancyra in Galatia refers to thirty pairs of gladiators being displayed in the reign of Tiberius. Epigraphy confirms the existence of an amphitheatre at Laodicea on the Lycus by AD 79.[132] Generally, however, the Greek world did not need to construct buildings dedicated exclusively to *venationes* and gladiatorial combats, since it was already supplied with suitable public buildings in the form of theatres. Archaeological evidence illustrates how in the course of the centuries (and especially during the second half of the second century AD) more and more Hellenistic theatres were converted so that wild beasts could safely be displayed in them, and often so that what had once been the orchestra could be filled with water and used for *naumachiae* or other aquatic displays.[133]

Apart from direct acculturation through the planting of colonies, two of the most important factors in the process of Romanisation in the provinces were the imperial cult and the army. At Rome, and in Roman communities generally whether in Italy or the provinces, *munera* had begun as 'private' affairs. Augustus and his successors supported them once the distinction between 'private' and 'public' ceased to have any real application to the Caesars. Outside Italy, *munera* came to be given not just by private individuals within particular cities, but at the level of entire provinces, by the priest of the imperial cult for each province. As such, they came to be the responsibility of the provincial governor, who alone had the right to condemn criminals to execution. The association between gladiatorial games and the god-like honour awarded the emperor in the context of provincial cults has been well-studied for several provinces, east and west.[134] The western provincial capitals where the imperial cult was celebrated had amphitheatres whose size was substantially greater than those of ordinary colonies or municipalities: typically, external dimensions of ca. 140 by 120 metres, and an arena of 70 by 40 metres. The dimensions of the amphitheatre recently recovered on the Guildhall site at London, and in its final form associated with the period when London was the residence of emperors such as Carausius, Allectus, and Constantius, was 130 by 110 metres, with an arena estimated at 70 by 50 metres, similar to that of Trier and larger than Lyon, Carthage or El Djem.[135]

The role of the army is less easy to define. Because of the ancient references to *lanistae* as associated with military training, it has been assumed that the arenas invariably found in close proximity to legionary bases had some kind of training function. In the cities of Italy from the first century BC on, and later the western provinces, a *campus* was laid out for the military training of young men in the *juventus*-organisations; it was normally placed immediately outside the walls.[136] Although in some cities (including Pompeii, Corfinium and Narbo) these training grounds were sited in close proximity to the amphitheatre, and there is considerable evidence for the involvement of professional *lanistae* in the weapons-training which members of *juventus*-groups underwent (p. 110 n. 36 below), they were separate institutions and there is no evidence that arenas fulfilled any analogous function when they were constructed in proximity to a military fort. Rather, Roman legionaries in the provinces were a major source for the introduction of *munera* because they were Roman citizens, and wanted to display (to themselves and to others) their identification with Roman culture. If they were to be able to watch gladiators, then Roman soldiers had to provide their own: corporations of *lanistae* would not bring them to the less romanised parts of the empire, where there were few Roman *editores* who would pay for them. Hence the evidence for army units under the principate owning troupes of gladiators: an inscription from the lower Rhine mentions URSARIUS LEG[ionis] XXX U[lpiae] V[ictricis] S[everianae] A[lexandrinae], and one of the beakers found at Colchester with impressions of gladiators describes a *retiarius* as VALENTINVS LEGIONIS XXX. The Thirtieth Legion was based at Xanten on the Rhine; either

45

the cup, or the gladiator himself, must have been brought to Colchester.[137]

At the margins of the Roman empire, amphitheatres reassured Roman soldiers far from home that they were part of the Roman community. But the arena did not just serve to integrate into Roman society: it also symbolically divided off what was Roman from what was not. It was the limit of Roman civilisation in a number of senses. The arena was the place where civilisation confronted nature, in the shape of the beasts which represented a danger to humanity; and where social justice confronted wrongdoing, in the shape of the criminals who were executed there; and where the Roman empire confronted its enemies, in the persons of the captured prisoners of war who were killed or forced to kill one another in the arena. Amphitheatres could represent the dividing line between culture and the wild more directly. It is striking how many amphitheatres are sited at the edge of the city, either just inside (as in the case of Pompeii) or outside, as with many amphitheatres associated with military camps. Sometimes, as at Trier or Pula in Dalmatia, the amphitheatre was actually part of the circuit of walls surrounding the city. There could of course be practical reasons for this: when Aurelian's walls were thrown around Rome in the 270s, it was efficient to use pre-existing structures such as the amphitheatre linked to the Praetorian camp as part of the new defences. And not all amphitheatres were on 'marginal' sites: the Colosseum is an example, and its location can be explained with reference to a particular historical situation, the availability of land on the site of Nero's Golden House. But the frequency with which amphitheatres are associated with the edge of the city requires explanation, and Henze's theory that it was intended to minimise the noise pollution caused by the crowds attending spectacles is hardly convincing: by their nature spectacles are meant to attract the whole community. Nor is the idea that they were placed at the edge of cities for safety reasons, in case wild animals might escape.[138] The answer must lie in the symbolic nature of the activities which went on there. The arena was visibly the place where civilisation and barbarism met, and civilisation for the Romans meant the city.

The activities that went on in the arena were liminal in a number of further respects. The audience saw beasts and criminals passing from life to death; gladiators also passed from life to death, though in their case there was the possibility that their display of fighting skill might allow them to pass from the social death of *infamia* back to life as part of the Roman community again. They symbolised coming to terms with death in other ways, too: they were originally associated with funerals. When Augustus institutionalised them as annual ceremonies, they took place at the two times of the year that correspond to Christian Easter and Christmas. They were, in other words, symbols of spring regeneration and of the ending of one year and beginning of the next at the period of the winter solstice. The *munera* which formed part of the spring festival, the *Quinquatrus*, held from the 19–23 March, are attested by Dio and Ovid.[139]

The dates of the games provided by the magistrates in December are specified in the fourth-century list of festivals known as the 'Calendar of Philocalus': the games begin (*initium muneris*) on 2 December, and the 4th, 5th and 6th are listed as the days of the *munus arca*: the arca is the imperial exchequer. The 8th is stated to be the day of a *munus kandidati*, when the emperor's favoured candidate for the quaestorship added his own resources to make a particularly impressive showing. Then came the Saturnalia, with the main feast-day on the 17th; and afterwards five more days of *munera* (*munus arca* on the 19th, 21st and 23rd; *munus kandidati* on the 20th; and on the 24th, *munus consummatum*).[140] The cycle of (pagan) Roman festivals listed for the fourth century by Ausonius in *Eclogue* 23 ends with the gladiatorial games, which he says honoured Saturn/Cronos: 'We know that gladiators once fought out their funeral games in the forum; now the arena's sand claims those who at the end of December appease the sickle-bearing son of heaven with their last drops of blood.'[141] In the east, too, there is evidence that gladiatorial spectacles were associated not only with festivals honouring Rome and the emperor, but also the end of the Roman calendar year. During Hadrian's visit to Greece in AD 125, he instituted a new cycle of Nemean games at Argos to take place in December. Inscriptions reveal that such 'imperial Nemeans' took place in other cities too, and at least by the 30 December AD 214, might include gladiatorial combat.[142] A gladiatorial match was thought an appropriate accompaniment both to the funeral of an individual, and to the end of the year. The year's end is also a new beginning. Death and killing were essential associations of the arena: but so also was rebirth.

47

NOTES

1 J. Toutain, 'Ludi publici', in D–S III.1, 362–78.
2 In the *Book of Spectacles* (*Liber spectaculorum*) ascribed to Martial, the word 'Caesar' and its derivatives occur twenty-two times, but 'princeps' and 'Augustus' only once (leaving aside the historical Augustus in poem 28).
3 *De legibus* 2, 38.
4 Dionysius of Halicarnassus 7, 72 f.; 8, 68; Cicero, *De republica* 2, 20; Pliny NH 8, 20; 24; 28–9.
5 Livy 1, 8; H. Versnel, *Triumphus* (Leiden, 1970); cf. pp. 35 ff.
6 Sallust, *Histories* Fg. 2.70 Maurenbrecher = 2.59 McGushin = Macrobius, *Saturnalia* 3, 13.7.
7 Valerius Maximus 2, 4.7; Livy, *periocha* 16; cf. Servius, *ad Aen.* 3, 67.
8 Polybius 6, 53; Servius, *Ad Aeneid* 6, 862; and Appian, *Civilia* 105f.
9 Livy 23, 30.15; 31, 50.4; 39, 46.2; 41, 28.10 f.
10 Suetonius, *Julius* 26; Plutarch, *Caesar* 55; Dio 43.22; and Suetonius, *Julius* 10.2; the 320 referred to were presumably those originally intended for the display; cf. Plutarch, *Caesar* 5.
11 Ennodius, *Panegyricus dictus Theoderico* = MGHAA 7, 213, 25; Valerius Maximus 2, 3.2; G. Ville, *Mélanges de l'école Française à Rome* 72 (1960), 306; E. Baltrusch, 'Die Verstaatlichung der Gladiatorenspiele', *Hermes* 116 (1988), 324 ff.
12 Horace, *Satires* 2, 3.84 ff.
13 Suetonius, *Tiberius* 37.3.
14 Persius 6, 48; Suetonius, *Caligula* 27.2.
15 Dio 54, 2.4.
16 Imperial regulations: Dio 54, 2; 55, 32; 59, 14; 60, 5; Tacitus, *Annals* 11, 22; Suetonius, *Claudius* 24.2; Tacitus, *Annals* 13.5; Suetonius, *Domitian* 4.1.
17 *Fasti Antiatini* = CIL I(2), 248 f.
18 E.g., CTh. 6.4, which contains a number of fourth-century constitutions on the theatre and the circus.
19 ILS 6087. Cf. the provisions of the Flavian *Lex Irnitana*, AE 1986.333 §77.
20 ILS 5053 = CIL X.1074.
21 AE 1982.681; vel postulata non negavit.
22 ILS 5059 = CIL IX.2350: duumviratu suo acceptis a re p. xiii [m] n. venation. plenas et gladiatorum paria xxi dedit.
23 ILS 6252; ILS 6451, 6742, 6992; ILS 4186.
24 CIL IX.2237, quod primus omnium editorum sum‹ptu pr›oprio quinque fer‹as› dederit; AE 1975.252: primus ediderat; M. Cébeillac-Gervasoni and F. Zevi, 'Révisions et nouveautés pour trois inscriptions d'Ostie', *Mélanges de l'école Française à Rome* 88.2 (1976), 612: Qui primus omnium ab urbe condita ludus cum . . .] or et mulieres [a]d ferrum dedit . . . .
25 ILS 5531.
26 CIL XI.6377: ex DC usuris.

27 Polybius 32, 14.6: equivalent to 720,000 HS.
28 Cicero *ad Q.Fr.* 3, 6(8).6, *Pro Milone* 95; *Pro Murena* 19.38; *Pro Sestio* 54.116.
29 *Historia Augusta*, Hadrian 3.8; Dio 68, 15.1; AE 1933.30.
30 *Historia Augusta*, Marcus 10.10.
31 K. Latte, *Römische Religionsgeschichte* (Munich, 1960), 431 ff: 'Der römische Festkalender'. The significance of state *munera* coinciding with the end of the year is discussed on p. 47.
32 *Historia Augusta*, Probus 19, 7; Aurelian 33, 4 f., 34.1.
33 Pliny NH 33, 53; NH 37, 45; NH 16, 200; Vitruvius 2, 9.15 f.; Tacitus, *Annals* 13, 31.1.
34 Scholiast to Juvenal 8, 207; *Historia Augusta*, Pertinax 8.4.
35 Scholiast to Juvenal 3, 158; Pliny NH 10.2.
36 Suetonius, *Domitian* 4.1; Cassius Dio 67, 8.4; Statius, *Silvae* 1, 6.51– 85 ff.
37 Lanuvium, ILS 2121; Pompeii, ILS 5653, pro lud[is] lum[ina]; there are other instances of donations 'instead of' games.
38 Pliny NH 35, 52. It is not clear to me why most commentators assume that the shrine referred to was the one at Nemi.
39 A. Barbet, 'La Representation des Gladiateurs dans la Peinture Murale Romaine', in *Les Gladiateurs* (Lattes/Toulouse exhibition catalogue, 1987), 69–74; La Liégeaud: AE 1984.639; the inscriptions read 'Romulus' and 'Vocati sunt'; N. Davey and R. Ling, *Wall Painting in Roman Britain* (*Britannia* Monograph 3, 1982), 99.
40 For trouble at Leptis, cf. Pliny NH 5, 38 and Tacitus, *Histories* 4, 50.
41 S. Aurigemma, 'I Mosaici di Zliten', *Africa Italiana* 2 (1926), ills. 77, 119 etc.; G. Ville, *La Mosaïque Gréco-Romaine* I (1965), 147 ff., ills. 17, 19; K.M.D. Dunbabin, *The Mosaics of Roman North Africa* (Oxford, 1978), chapter 5; chapter 2 p. 36; ill. 55; 78.
42 Dunbabin, plates 75 f.
43 D. French, 'Two gladiatorial texts from Claudiopolis/Bithynia', *Epigraphica Anatolica* (1981), 91. Scaurus: illustrations 20 and 21 in Hönle; for discussion, see Sabbatini-Tumolesi no. 29, R. Ling in JRS 1983, 209, and V. Kockel, *Die Grabbauten vor dem Herkulanertor in Pompeii* (1983), 79–83. Cirta: CIL VIII.6995.
44 Hönle, nos. 104–6.
45 This point was noted by M. Grant, *Gladiators*, p. 39 f., who ascribed it to 'a note of shame . . . on the grounds that the spilling of human blood in sport . . . was not actually something to boast about' (p. 40).
46 *De architectura* 10, praef.3: nec solum id vitium in aedificiis sed etiam in muneribus, quae a magistratibus foro gladiatorum scaenisque ludorum dantur, quibus nec mora neque exspectatio conceditur, sed necessitas finito tempore perficere cogit.
47 Tacitus, *Annals* 4, 62; ILS 5065. At Atina, one C. Obinius gave a *venatio* in an enclosure on the forum (in sa[epto foro], rather than in sa[cerdotio], since he is described as an aedile at the time): AE 1981.219.
48 Mommsen, *Chronica Minora* 1, 146; *Historia Augusta*, Antoninus 9.1.

49

49 Livy, epit. 48, 55–60.
50 Cicero, *De officiis* 2, 57 and *Pro Sestio* 116.
51 E.g., at Corfinium: AE 1983.318; Interpromium Paeligniorum (by a prefect of Germanicus), CIL IX.3044; Falerii, CIL XI.3112.
52 For a discussion with a plan, cf. Golvin and Landes, *Amphithéâtres et Gladiateurs*, 70.
53 Plutarch, *Gaius Gracchus* 12.3; Pliny NH 36, 117; Dio 43, 22.3; Vitruvius 1, 71.
54 Cassius Dio 66, 25; Suetonius, *Titus* 7, 3; *Liber spectaculorum* 1, 7–8.
55 Cf. the famous lines on the survival of the Colosseum, Rome, and the world, ascribed to Bede (*Patrologia Latina* 94, 543):

> Quamdiu stat Coliseus, stat et Roma.
> Quando cadet Coliseus, cadet et Roma.
> Quando cadet Roma, cadet et mundus.
> Quid stas, quid stupes, bos Britannice?

56 Mommsen, *Chronica Minora* 1, 146; AE 1979, no.33 is an epitaph commemorating two imperial slaves, presumably contemporaries, one manumitted by Tiberius and one in charge of gladiatorial equipment: Idumaeus Ti.Caesaris, Maternus a veste gladiat.
57 The *ludus* is depicted on the Severan plan of the city: cf. Jordan (ed.), *Forma Urbis Romae*, table I.4, and D-S II, figure 3571.
58 J.-C. Golvin, *L'Amphithéâtre Romain* (Paris, 1988), tables on pp. 275 ff.
59 Golvin, p. 287 n. 174; J.-C. Lachaux, *Théâtres et Amphithéâtres d'Afrique Proconsulaire* (Aix, 1979), 56, whose dimensions are 178 by 150 m.; P.J. Wilkins, 'Amphitheatres and Private Munificence in Roman Africa', ZPE 75 (1988), 216 ff.
60 Josephus, *Antiquities* 19.130.
61 Insignissimum spectaculum ac receptissimum, Tertullian, *De Spectaculis* 12.
62 Tacitus, *Dialogus* 29,3–4; Horace, *Satires* 2, 6.44; Cicero. *Ad Fam.* 2, 8.1.; Horace, *Epodes* 1, 18, 19.
63 Epictetus, *Discourses* 3, 15.6.
64 Cf. chapter 2, p. 56 f. For 'Libelli munerarii', see *Historia Augusta*, Claudius 5.5 – unfortunately not a reliable source.
65 Athenaeus 4, 153 ff. For such behaviour among the Campanians, cf. Strabo 5, 4.13; Livy 9, 40.17; Silius Italicus 11, 51 ff.
66 L. Berger and M. Joos, *Das Augster Gladiatorenmosaik* (Augst BL, 1971). Mosaics with possible gladiatorial motifs have been found in Britain at Eccles in Kent and (with cupids playing at gladiators) Bignor, I.o.W.
67 W. Helbig, *Führer durch die öffentlichen Sammlungen Klassischer Altertümer in Rom* (4th edn, 1966), 2, 711 ff.
68 M. Donderer, *Mosaïque. Receuil d'hommages à Henri Stern* (Paris, 1983), 125 f.
69 Pat Witts has drawn my attention to those at Cos and from Kourion, Cyprus. Hunting scenes (and the associated representations of Orpheus) are frequent in the east. D. Levi, *Antioch Mosaic*

Pavements (Princeton, 1947), vol. II; e.g. plates lii–lvii (Constantinian villa), lxxvii f., lxxxvi ff. (from a Christian context).

70 K. Parlasca, *Römische Mosaiken in Deutschland*, Römisch-Germanische Forschungen 23 (1959), 82 ff.; 88 ff.; L. Berger–M. Joos, *Das Augster Gladiatorenmosaik* (1971); H. Stern, *Receuil general des mosaïques de la Gaule* I.1 (1957), no. 38; II.1 (1967), no. 308.

71 D. von Boeselager, 'Das Gladiatorenmosaik in Köln und seine Restaurierung im 19. Jahrhundert', *Kölner Jahrbuch für Vor- und Frühgeschichte* 20 (1987), 111–128.

72 *Roman Inscriptions from Britain*, ed. S.S. Frere and R.S.O. Tomlin, II.2 (1991), nos. 2419, 18–35.

73 Crescens, ILS 5142 = CIL IV.4356; Celadus, suspirium/decus puellarum, CIL IV.4353, 4356.

74 Suetonius, *Augustus* 44.2: most of these regulations refer to *ludi*. Cf. E. Rawson, '*Discrimina Ordinum*: The *Lex Julia Theatralis*', *Roman Culture and Society* (Oxford, 1991), 508–45.

75 *Historia Augusta*, Marcus 19.7.

76 Juvenal 6, 110 ff.; Petronius 126.6 (women find the arena/muledrivers/actors sexually attractive).

77 See p. 29; *Historia Augusta*, Hadrian 18.8; Commodus 2.9. See C.H. Edwards, 'Unspeakable Professions: Public Performance and Prostitution in Ancient Rome' (forthcoming) and *The Politics of Immorality in Ancient Rome* (Cambridge, 1993), chapter 3: 'Playing Romans'.

78 K. Bradley, *Slavery and Rebellion in the Roman Empire* (London, 1989), chapter 5.

79 Tacitus, *Annals* 3.43; Tacitus, *Annals* 15.46.

80 Cassius Dio 39, 77, 1–3.

81 Cassius Dio 44, 16.2; Nicolaus of Damascus, *Augustus* 25, 26a; Tacitus, *Histories* 2, 34–6.

82 Apuleius, *Apology* 98.7. Cf. A.A. Imholz, 'Gladiatorial Metaphors in Cicero's *Pro Sex.Roscio Amerino*', *Classical World* 65 (1972), 228–30; Martial 11, 66.

83 Seneca, *Letters* 87.9; 99.12 f. Cf. Tacitus, *Dialogus* 29.3 f.

84 *De spectaculis* 22.3.

85 Text: E.H. Warmington, *Remains of Old Latin* IV, 316 ff.; A.H.J. Greenidge, *Infamia* (Oxford, 1894), 69 f.

86 quive lanisturam artemve ludicram fecit fecerit, ILS 6085 l.123.

87 B. Levick, 'The Senatusconsultum from Larinum', JRS 73 (1983), 97 ff.

88 *Digest* 38, 1.37 pr., Paulus.

89 See p. 198 below: *Tabula Italica* line 7, ILS 5163 = CIL II.6278.

90 ILS 7846: for a discussion of the vulgarity of suicide by hanging as opposed to the use of a sword, cf. Van Hooff, *Autothanasia* (London, 1991), 65 ff; J.-L. Voisin, 'Apicata, Antinous, et quelques autres', *Mélanges Ecole Français à Rome* 99.1 (1987), 257–80.

91 Cyprian, *Ad Donatum* 7. Cyprian's *harenarii* should be understood to include gladiators.

92 Cassius Dio 72, 22.2; Seneca, *Controversia* 3, praef. 10: quidam sic

cum scaeva componi cupiunt quomodo alii timent; Lyco, murmillo
scaeva: ILS 5105.
93 παρὰ τυρρηνῶν παραλαβόντες τὸ ἔθος: 4, 153 f.
94 Isidore, *Origines* 10, 247; he may have been right. Tertullian, *Ad
nationes* 1, 10.47 and *Apologeticum* 15, 5; for Charon as Mercury, cf.
Cassius Dio 72, 19.4.
95 Tombs of the Augurs, of Pulcinella, and of the Olympiads at
Tarquinia. Critique in Ville, pp. 4 ff.
96 The customs of Swiss mountain cantons remain remarkably under-
studied. I am grateful to W. Beinart for drawing my attention to
parallels with violence among male migrant workers in South
Africa; see *Journal of Southern African Studies* 18, 3 (1992).
Procopius: *Histories* 5, 20.1–4.
97 Herodotus 1, 94.
98 The Etruscan question especially interested the Nazi theoretician
Alfred Rosenberg (in the context of Catholic opposition to the
Nazis): cf. V. Losemann, *Nationalsozialismus und Antike* (Hamburg,
1977), esp. pp. 140 f.
99 N. Spivey and S. Stoddart, *Etruscan Italy: an archaeological survey*
(London, 1990). In antiquity, Dionysius of Halicarnassus believed
that the Etruscans were autochthonous (1, 28.2 ff), but that was
because he wanted to persuade his readers that all Italians were
virtuous Europeans: E. Gabba, *Dionysius* (U. California Press,
1991), 112 f.
100 Strabo 5, 2.2.
101 F. Dupont, *L'Acteur Roi* (Paris, 1985).
102 Livy 9, 40.17: et Romani quidem ad honorem deum insignibus
armis hostium usi sunt; Campani ad superbiam et odio Samnitium
gladiatores, quod spectaculum inter epulas erat, eo ornatu armar-
unt Samnitiumque nomine compellarunt.
103 *De spectaculis* 12; cf. p. 151 f.
104 *Iliad* 23.175 ff.; Herodotus 6, 71 f.; Suetonius, *Augustus* 15.
105 S. Weinstock 'Saturnalien und Neujahrsfest in den Märtyreracten'
in A. Stuiber and A. Hermann (eds), *Mullus. Festschrift Theodor
Klauser*. JAC Ergänzungsband 1 (1964), 391–400.
106 Suetonius, *Claudius* 21.6.
107 J. Vogt, 'Der sterbende Sklave. Vorbild menschlicher Vollendung',
Sklaverei und Humanität. Ergänzungsheft (Wiesbaden, 1983), 6–16,
written when Vogt was already in his seventies.
108 V. Maxfield, *Military Decorations of the Roman Army* (London, 1981);
generally, K. Hopkins, *Conquerors and Slaves* (Cambridge, 1978);
W.V. Harris, *War and Imperialism in Republican Rome* (Oxford,
1979).
109 Pliny NH 7, 43/139.
110 Lack of scope for individual acts of bravery in the Greek phalanx:
Aristodemus 'acted like a madman in leaving the battle-line' (Herodotus 9. 71.3). Cf. J. Lazenby, 'The Killing Zone', in V.D. Hanson
(ed.), *Hoplites. The Classical Greek Battle Experience* (London, 1991),
esp. p. 103; on the inconclusive nature of our evidence about

phalanx warfare in Italy, cf. Bruno d'Agostino, 'Military Organization and Social Structure in Archaic Etruria' in O. Murray and S. Price (eds), *The Greek City* (Oxford, 1990), 59 ff. Aemilius Lepidus: Valerius Maximus 3, 1.1; the same event is commemorated on a coin, T. Mommsen, *Geschichte des römischen Münzwesens* (Munich, 1856), 634. Cf. J. Fries, *Der Zweikampf bei T. Livius* (Meisenheim, 1985).

111 Sallust, *Catilina* 51: memor generis atque pristinae suae dignitatis in confertissumos hostis incurrit ibique pugnans confoditur.

112 Livy 28.21: 206 BC. Scipio Carthaginem ad vota solvenda dis munusque gladiatorium, quod mortis causa patris patruique paraverat, edendum rediit. Gladiatorum spectaculum fuit non ex eo genere hominum ex quo lanistis comparare mos est, servorum de catasta ac liberorum qui venalem sanguinem habent: voluntaria omnis et gratuita opera pugnantium fuit. Nam alii missi ab regulis sunt ad specimen insitae genti virtutis ostendendum, alii ipsi professi se pugnaturos in gratiam ducis . . . .

113 Horace, *Satires* 2, 6.44.

114 Cicero, *Tusculans*, 2, 17.41.

115 Pliny, *Panegyric* 33.1 f.

116 Libanius, *Oration* 1.5.

117 C.M. Robertson, *History of Greek Art* (Oxford, 1975), 392, 551. It is conceivable that the two gladiators represented on the Maastricht relief are intended to be women.

118 Valerius Maximus, 2, 3.2; *Historia Augusta*, Maximinus et Balbinus 8.7: alii hoc litteris tradunt, quod verisimilius credo, ituros ad bellum Romanos debuisse pugnas videre et vulnera et ferrum et nudos inter se coeuntes, ne in bello armatos hostes timerent aut vulnera et sanguinem perhorrescerent; Ennodius, *Panegyricus Theodorico* 85; E. Baltrusch, 'Die Verstaatlichung der Gladiatorenspiele', *Hermes* 116 (1988), 324 ff.

119 Nicely put as a function of *naumachiae* and chariot-races by Ausonius, *Eclogue* 23 ('On Roman Festivals'), 21 f.:

Festa haec navigiis aut quae celebrata quadrigis
iungunt Romanos finitimosque duces.

For *naumachiae*, see p. 89 f.

120 See Glossary; references can be found in Daremberg-Saglio.

121 J. D'Arms, *The Ancient Historian and his Materials* (London, 1975), 155–65.

122 Tacitus, *Annals* 14, 17.

123 Pliny NH 3, 66; Tacitus, *Histories* 2, 95.

124 *Liber spectaculorum* 2.11f. For the inauguration of the Colosseum by Titus, Dio 66, 25; Suetonius, *Divus Titus* 7.3; cf. p. 177 below.

125 T.E.J. Wiedemann, CAH X chapter 8; Cassius Dio 66, 10.3.

126 Polybius 30, 26.1–3; Diodorus 31, 16; Athenaeus 5, 194 A f.; Valerius Maximus 2, 7.13 f.; Livy 41, 20.11–13. Cf. L.M. Günther, 'Gladiatoren beim Fest Antiochos' IV. zu Daphne (166 v.Chr.)?', *Hermes* 117 (1989), 250–2.

127 Diodorus Siculus 33, frag. 21a.
128 Lyon inscription: D. Fishwick, *The Roman Imperial Cult* I (Leiden, etc., 1987), pl. XX; Tacitus, *Annals* 3, 43; AE 1980.624; CIL I.776a = XII.5695.1.
129 Tacitus, *Annals* 13, 31: it is not clear whether this ban was just for the one year, or intended to be permanent as Tacitus implies.
130 Plutarch, *Lucullus* 23.1.
131 *Life of Apollonius*, 4, 22.
132 Strabo 14, 639; 17, 795; OGIS 533; Boeckh CIG 3935.
133 J-C. Golvin and C. Landes, *Amphithéâtres et Gladiateurs* (CNRS, 1990).
134 S.R.F. Price, *Rituals and Power: the Roman Imperial Cult in Asia Minor* (Oxford, 1984); D. Fishwick, *The Roman Imperial Cult* I (Leiden, etc., 1987 and 1991).
135 Details in J-C. Golvin, *L'amphithéâtre Romain* (Paris, 1988), 284 ff. London Guildhall: sparse reports in *Britannia* 19 (1988), 461–2 and 20 (1989), 305; N. Bateman, 'The London Amphitheatre', *Current Archaeology* 137 (1994), 164–71.
136 Vitruvius 1, 7.1: Marti extra urbem sed ad campum. Cf. H. Devijver and F. van Wonterghem, 'Neue Belege zum Campus der römischen Städte in Italien und im Westen', ZPE 60 (1985), 147–58.
137 CIL XIII.8639; CIL VII.1335.3; the corresponding volume of RIB has not yet appeared. The connection between soldiers and gladiators has been taken for granted, e.g. by R.W. Davies, *Service in the Roman Army* (Edinburgh, 1989), with supporting literary sources on pp. 81 ff. and p. 256 n. 60.
138 Hönle and Henze, p. 157; D.L. Bomgardner, 'Amphitheatres on the Fringe', *Journal of Roman Archaeology* 4 (1991), 282 f.
139 Dio 54, 28: 11 BC; Ovid, *Fasti* 3, 811–13.
140 K. Latte, *Römische Religionsgeschichte* (Munich, 1960), with 'der römische Festkalender' on pp. 431 ff.
141 Ausonius, *Eclogue* 23, 33–37:

> et gladiatores funebria proelia notum
> decertasse foro: nunc sibi harena suos
> vindicat extremo qui iam sub fine Decembris
> falcigerum placant sanguine Caeligenam.

142 Pausanias 6, 16.4; Boeckh CIG 4472, line 16 ff., from Laodicea in Syria. I am assuming that πυγμη = Lat. *pugna*, gladiatorial contest, as is usual at that date, rather than the classical wrestling match, though that is not the most immediate interpretation.

2

THE CONTEXT

FIGHTING BEASTS

The difficulty of making sense of the ambivalent feelings revealed by the ancient evidence is reflected in the range of
different theories developed by scholars since modern scholarship began two centuries ago. The emotions with which ancient
writers express their feelings about these contests are too complex to be reduced to the simple opposites of 'approval' and
'opposition'. To understand how such contrasting emotions
could co-exist, it is pertinent to look at various aspects of the
contexts in which Romans experienced gladiatorial contests.
Originally, as we have seen, they were associated with the death
of a powerful public figure. Under Augustus, they became a
regular institution at Rome, coinciding with the Quinquatrus in
March and with the Saturnalia at the end of the year. From the
time of Augustus on we also find that the performance of
gladiatorial combats was usually preceded by two other kinds
of display, which originally had nothing to do with *munera*:
venationes, which took place in the mornings and involved the
display and, normally, slaughter of animals; and the public
execution of criminals of low status (*noxii, cruciarii*) at midday.
The *munus* itself followed during the afternoon. Where games
were arranged over a period of two or more days, it seems that
the same threefold pattern was followed on each.

The association of these three categories of spectacle can be
seen on mosaic representations and on painted inscriptions
advertising public shows, as well as in literary sources such
as the *Book of Spectacles* ascribed to Martial or Seneca's seventh
Letter to Lucilius. A visual record naturally has to depict activities that actually take place in sequence as though they are

simultaneous. The mosaic from Zliten in Libya (figure 5 and p. 15) may represent spectacles put on on two different days; the dates of the regular Roman December games show that these need not necessarily have been consecutive. The mosaic shows two cycles of *venationes*, in which horses, antelope, onyx, and wild boar are hunted and killed by hounds and *bestiarii* with spears, and a fight between a bear and a bull, chained together; three captives being mauled by leopards and a lion; and the *munus* proper, to the accompaniment of an orchestra. That the mosaic does not represent different shows, but different parts of a single spectacle, is proved by inscriptions, such as dozens of advertisements from Pompeii inviting the public to events which included both wild beast shows and gladiatorial combats, and sometimes executions. At the time when Pompeii was over-whelmed by the volcanic ash from the eruption of Vesuvius in AD 79, such advertisements (some of them many years out of date) could be read painted on to public buildings within the town and on tombs outside the city gates. One *quinquennalis* advertised a show including thirty pairs of gladiators and their substitutes, together with a *venatio*. A *Flamen* of the emperor Nero promised twenty pairs to appear together with ten pro-vided by his son, as well as a *venatio legitima*, over four days. That such a show might also include executions is shown by an adver-tisement which tells the prospective audience that a gladiatorial *munus* is to feature crucifixions and a beast-hunt. Just as such advertisements attract potential spectators by boasting of the number of pairs of gladiators, so they sometimes give additional details of the beasts that are to be displayed.[1]

These painted advertisements give us some other information about the conditions under which *munera* were held. The dates of shows, at least in the 60s and 70s AD, were significantly different from those at Rome – 24–26 November, 8–11 April, 6–8 May, 31 May.[2] This will have been because some of the personnel involved were drawn from the imperial *familia*, which would have been needed at Rome at these times of the year. The possibility of inclement weather might be taken into account – one notice contained the caveat, 'weather permitting', and several stated that the spectators would be protected from the elements by awnings. Another notice promised that the show would start punctually.[3]

That such advertisements were not peculiar to Pompeii is

suggested by the fact that on the road leading to Nuceria was found an advertisement for games to be held there.[4] Sporadic literary references confirm this; a letter of Cicero's says that there were notices which gave the order in which gladiators were going to fight.[5] This would suggest that such advertisements were to be found in all cities where games were held. The writer of the *Historia Augusta* envisages that at Rome supporters could obtain programmes (*libelli munerarii*) with details of the individual gladiators' past performance, copied down from the advertisements.[6] Inscriptions commemorating the achievements of individual gladiators and of groups belonging to the same trainer (see p. 120 f.) show that there was a series of conventional symbols which served the purpose of score-cards, allowing supporters to see at a glance how many times a particular gladiator had defeated his opponent (V = victor) or had fought well enough to be allowed to leave the arena alive (M = missus). The Greek letter *theta* served to mark those who had lost their lives.

While *venationes* and gladiatorial *munera* were put on in the same place on the same occasion, their different origins and the different skills required by the participants can be seen from the existence of different training institutions and organisations, both at Rome and in the provinces. Alongside the three imperial gladiatorial *ludi*, the emperors also maintained a *ludus matutinus* near the Colosseum in which the *bestiarii* were trained; the word *matutinus* refers to the fact that *venationes* took place in the mornings. *Bestiarii* appeared in their own regular troupes; the mid-third-century mosaic from Smirat in Tunisia (p. 16) shows that the *editor* Magerius hired professional *bestiarii* from a *familia* called the Telegonii (and celebrates his liberality in paying them twice the prize-money of 500 *denarii* demanded on their behalf by the acclamations of the spectators).[7]

Visual representations of *venationes* were much more frequent than of gladiators. They give us some idea of how the *bestiarii* were fitted out, and what kinds of animals were slaughtered. A marble relief in the Museo Torlonia at Rome shows five *bestiarii* fighting three rampant beasts: a lion, a hound, and a bear. The men all have swords and helmets, and one a rectangular shield; another, who has sunk to the ground underneath the lion, holds a round shield and wears a suit of chain mail. In the background is a circular building, presumably to show that the *venatio* represented took place in the Colosseum. Pre-Flavian *venationes* at Rome took place in the Circus; one such appears on a terracotta plaque in the Museo Nazionale Romana. The plaque shows that even when no gladiatorial combats are evident, a show with wild beasts was a suitable occasion for including the execution of criminals: there is a naked man lying on the ground, while elsewhere a *bestiarius* holding a shield and wearing a helmet is attacked by a leopard from his left side, and a lion from the right; the lion appears to be being goaded to enter the Circus through a gate by a man in a tunic prodding it with a spear. On our left, the audience (represented by two figures) is shown high up on a platform supported by columns, with crenellations above. Centuries later, the ivory diptychs which fifth- and sixth-century consuls used in order to invite selected guests to their games depict essentially identical scenes. There is one dating to AD 506, now in Zurich, which shows several acrobats performing with bears on one leaf, and four men with spears fighting lions on the other (figure 8). There is some consistency in how *bestiarii* are represented; the Villa Borghese mosaic is the most typical example. They are dressed in finely decorated tunics and use spears as their weapons, but unlike gladiators have no defensive armour of any kind. The killing might be done by other animals, such as hunting dogs; a terra sigillata beaker at Colchester shows the *bestiarius* controlling a hound by means of a whip. Whips are also used to control animals as they fight each other on the Villa Borghese and Zliten mosaics. The Zurich diptych also shows an attendant wielding a lasso to control a bear.

Inscriptions with advertisements or commemorations of particular events give details of the numbers and types of animals put on show. As we have already seen from the advertisements for Pompeian spectacles, not all of these animals were foreign to the place where they were displayed, and not all of them were either wild as opposed to domesticated, or ferocious. The Pompeian *quinquennalis* Flaccus' games starred bulls, wild boar, and bears; only the latter would have had to be imported from outside Italy. A show at Beneventum distinguished bears from 'ferae'; there were sixteen of the former, four of the latter, presumably panthers or other large cats. A similar distinction is made on an inscription of unknown Italian provenance: it is between herbivorous animals and *ferae dentatae*, wild beasts with teeth. An inscription from Minturnae commemorates games given by one Baebius Justus in AD 249 after he had been honoured with the duumvirate. It distinguishes bears and herbivores (*cum ursis [. . .] herban.*) and goes on to give further details: the games took place over four days and included eleven pairs of gladiators; eleven gladiators of the first ('Campanian') class had been killed, as had ten cruel bears: 'and you yourselves remember, excellent citizens, that on each of the four days all the herbivores were killed'. It was clearly important to list a hierarchy of beasts in the order of dangerousness: four days of games at Beneventum starred 'four wild cats, sixteen bears, four other dangerous animals the rest being herbivores' ('feris n[umero] IIII, ursis XVI, noxeis IIII et ceteris herbariis'). Other inscriptions specify 'oriental' and 'African' or (possibly) 'Libyan' beasts.[8]

These advertisements clearly illustrate one aspect of the public display of beasts: such display was a function of the competition within Italian and provincial elites. As in similar ceremonies in other cultures requiring the public destruction of objects of value, men of high status proved that they were wealthy as well as virtuous by providing their communities with the spectacle of rare and expensive animals being destroyed. Hence the emphasis that games were given *suo impenso*, entirely at the expense of the *editor*, and hence also the imperative to provide games that went on over an increasing number of days: four days are mentioned at Minturnae, Puteoli, Pompeii, Beneventum, Carthage and elsewhere; a *munus* at Theveste in Africa went on for five days.[9] Animals of distant origin were particularly suitable: they symbolised not just the wealth of the *editor* (because of their rarity), but also his social power in having exceptionally good access to the overseas sources which could provide him with them. This was one reason why the Roman elite displayed lions and leopards; they were first shown to the people, and slaughtered, in 186 BC by M. Fulvius Nobilior.[10]

During the republican period, these *venationes* were not usually given in the context of gladiatorial *munera*, but on special occasions such as the celebration of a triumph. Nevertheless they set precedents for what the Roman people expected, once *venationes* had come to be regularly associated with gladiatorial contests from Augustus' time on. Competition required that the numbers of beasts slaughtered be constantly increased; the curule aediles of 169 BC gave games in the Circus Maximus which were said to have included 63 'Africanae bestia', 40 bears, and some elephants.[11] Male adult lions (*jubati*) were particularly prized; Pliny the Elder has a section listing particularly memorable occasions on which they were displayed, such as by the aediles of 104 BC, L. Licinius Crassus and Q. Mucius Scaevola; Sulla had produced no fewer than 100 such lions from the Mauretanian king Bocchus in the aftermath of the war against Jugurtha.[12] A *venatio* put on by Marcus Scaurus in 58 BC included 150 leopards (*variae*), a hippopotamus, and 5 crocodiles.[13] The late republican dynasts used *venationes* to demonstrate both how unchallengeable their power was, and the geographical extent of their conquests. The games which Pompey put on during his second consulship in 55 BC became particularly famous (partly because Cicero wrote a letter to a friend whose health prevented him from attending, consoling him for having missed only trifles). Pompey's games included the slaughter of 20 elephants, 600 lions, 410 leopards, various apes, the first north-European lynx to be seen at Rome, and the first rhinoceros. The sympathy which the crowd reportedly showed for the elephants as they were put to death in the arena became notorious – not, as some modern scholars would have it, because it proved that Romans could express sympathy for animals, but as an example of misplaced sympathy. Pompey's rival Julius Caesar had to exercise munificence on the same scale; the series of four triumphs he held in 46 BC included elephants, 400 lions, Thessalian bulls, and a giraffe. Pompey and Caesar set the scale for *venationes* that Augustus and his imperial successors were expected to live up to. On particular occasions, Augustus' games were said to have featured the slaughter of 420 leopards, dozens of elephants, and up to 400 bears and 300 lions. In the *Res gestae*, Augustus boasts of the cumulative total of 3,500 animals slaughtered in the various *venationes bestiarum Africanarum* he had provided for the Roman people. Cassius Dio gives statistics for the numbers which were killed on particular occasions: 600 in 13 BC, 260 lions and 36 crocodiles in 2 BC (in honour of Augustus' grandsons), 200 lions in AD 12. One of Caligula's shows included the killing of 400 bears and 400 *lybicae*. Nero had 400 bears and 300 lions killed on one occasion. And at the inauguration of the Colosseum under Titus, 9,000 beasts were slaughtered. The largest number of slaughtered animals for which there is reliable evidence is

11,000 (dangerous and herbivorous) during Trajan's triumph after his second Dacian war.[14]

The imperative to compete in terms of the sheer number of animals killed had reached such a stage that later emperors preferred to emulate their predecessors by displaying new varieties. The *venationes* which Antoninus Pius recorded for posterity on his series of MUNIFICENTIA coin issues from AD 149 onwards included elephants, hyenas, lions, tigers, rhinoceroses, crocodiles, and hippopotamuses. There were other ways of introducing variety and novelty, culminating in the appearance of the emperor himself as a *venator*, in the person of Commodus (see Chapter 5). During the secular games of AD 204, Septimius Severus arranged a *venatio*, probably in the Circus Maximus, which consisted of a ship which fell apart to release bears, lions and lionesses, leopards, ostriches, wild asses, and bison. As late as the third century, it was still possible to exhibit novel species of fauna to the Roman people; according to the *Historia Augusta*, Gordian as aedile under Septimius exhibited 100 *ferae libycae*, 100 bears, 200 stags from Britain and elsewhere, 30 wild horses, 100 wild sheep, 10 elks, 100 Cypriot bulls, 300 ostriches with reddened feathers (*miniati*), 30 wild asses, 150 boars, 200 ibexes and 200 *dammae* (probably gazelles). The list may well be fictitious, but it shows what a late Roman author thought a future emperor's exhibition would be like. The author's account of the triumph of the emperor Probus in the Circus Maximus in AD 281 is certainly fictitious – 1,000 ostriches, 1,000 stags, 100 boars, gazelles and ibexes as well as *herbatica animalia*. The author goes on to make the point that the 100 maned lions refused to fight: 'they did not present much of a spectacle in getting killed', *non magnum praebentes spectaculum quo occidebantur.*[15]

Apart from increasing the numbers of animals and finding new and exotic species to display, one strategy followed by emperors in order to compete with their predecessors was to think of novel combinations of animals which were set to fight each other. Seneca mentions a bear being chained to a bull, the surviving beast then being despatched by a *bestiarius*; a similar contest between a bull and a bear is depicted on the Zliten mosaic (figure 5; cf. figure 6). The *Book of Spectacles* mentions tigers being set against lions, and elephants against bulls. Comparable attempts to add novelty by making different categories of human beings fight against each other as gladiators are reported from the reign of Domitian. Generally it was the kill that provided the climax of the spectacle, though occasionally something else might be put on to provide an unusual sight: during Titus' games, a female beast was induced to give birth in the arena.[16]

The actual killing of the animals was as significant an aspect of the *venatio* as the display of the *editor*'s wealth, or the proof of his and the Roman people's political authority in being able to obtain animals from far distant places. Notwithstanding the recent philosophical fashion to ascribe certain inalienable 'rights' to animals, social anthropologists have long recognised that the characteristics (including 'rights') which different societies assign to various animal species are indications of the way in which these societies regard and evaluate the characteristics of their human members.[17] Pre-industrial societies cannot afford to be squeamish about the slaughter of animals, either domestic or wild. The sacrifice of animals on important occasions, domestic as well as public, was something that everyone had experienced from their earliest years. The proper relationship between human beings and animals was one of domination; in Greek thought, with its emphasis on reason (*logos*) as the distinguishing characteristic of the Greek-speaking adult male citizen, force (*bia*) was thought to be a necessary component of the relationship between rational beings and those with whom one could not reason, including slaves, barbarians and children as well as animals, and this view is also expressed by Latin writers such as Seneca.

> Children and adults are alike deceived, but adults in different and more important things. Therefore the wise man will treat an insult from such a foolish person as a joke, and sometimes, as if they were children, he would tell them off and inflict humiliation and punishment on them, not because he has received an injury, but because they have tried to do one, and to deter them in future. That is the way we deal with animals, using the whip . . .[18]

Domination over animals is thus parallel to, and can be used to symbolise, social domination: most obviously in the ritual of the hunt, as practised by the ancient Near Eastern rulers who sought to give their kingship permanence by recording their success in hunting lions (the 'dominant' beast) on the reliefs that decorated Assyrian palaces and Mycenean daggers. The lion holds a special place amongst those carnivores whose speed and the strength of whose jaws makes survival unlikely for any unprotected human being who should happen to disturb them; consequently the lion appears on Roman sarcophagi as a symbol of all-powerful death.[19] Such animals are as 'cruel' as the death they inflict on humans, and their killing is hardly a moral problem: the inscription commemorating games given at Minturnae in AD 249 does not celebrate sadism by boasting that ten bears were killed 'cruelly' (reading *crudel[iter]* with Hopkins, 'Murderous Games' p. 26), but rather that the world was rid of ten cruel bears (*ursos crudel[es]*): savage bears deserved to be killed. The danger which such savagery represents to human beings may come from domesticated animals, of which the bull (even if not bred specifically for the corrida) has been the most widespread exemplar in Mediterranean cultures for many thousands of years. No matter how gentle a beast may normally be, its very size and power can be deadly. An elephant-keeper was killed in a zoo at Twycross in Leicestershire in August 1991.[20] The appearance of elephants as the largest land animals in shows such as Pompey's was appropriate not only because Pompey was 'the Great' and because Rome's was the greatest empire, but also because the killing of elephants reassured the Roman people that it was in control of even the greatest of beasts. Whether or not the reported sympathy of the crowd on that occasion diminished the effectiveness of the symbol, elephants sometimes continued to be put to death, though other symbols of domination over the elephant might be employed than mere killing. The 25-year-old Pompey is said to have wanted to celebrate his African victory by entering Rome in an elephant-drawn chariot; at the later emperor Galba's praetorian games at the Floralia (ca. AD 30) an elephant is said to have been made to walk the tightrope; and at the inauguration of the Colosseum, an elephant displayed its, and the world's, submission to Titus by kneeling before him.[21]

Less immediate dangers from smaller or less violent animals may be just as real for the human population. Deer and antelope compete with man in exploiting the plant environment, just as wolves and foxes live off the domestic animals man has reserved to his own use. Where resources are scarce, these competitors have to be destroyed, even if they cause a physical threat to human beings only in the rarest circumstances, if at all. The fox-hunt survives in England today. Apart from any practical function it may have in controlling the numbers of foxes, it serves as a symbol of property-owners' dominance over the countryside (and consequently provokes hostility on masked political, as well as overt environmental, grounds). Such hunting should not of course be reduced to nothing more than an artifice to make the dominance of the elite manifest and ensure that it has to be recognised by the rest of society: in a pre-industrial world, any sign of control over the natural world is reassuring to society at large. Uncontrolled carnivores may represent a real danger to the survival of entire communities, as the role played by the much-maligned wolf in European fairy-tale shows. Communities whose experience of state power was minimal, such as many Balkan and Eastern European villages until early in this century, needed to employ professional hunters to deal with such a menace when it became intolerable; but where force is effectively monopolised by the state, the community turns to those who wield political power for action against uncontrolled and dangerous animals (cf. the pressure on the United Kingdom government to introduce legislation to control dangerous domestic dogs). In the Roman world, the elimination of such threats was thought to be one of the duties of an emperor. In the fourth century, Ausonius wrote some lines celebrating the slaying of a lion by the young Gratian (AD 359–83), to go with a painting of the achievement: 'The death which the lion suffered from such a frail arrow was the result, not of the arrow's power, but of the bowman's.'[22] A poem in the Greek Anthology praises the Roman government for allowing the Nasamonians to pasture their flocks without fear of attack by lions. Caesar has entirely eradicated all hostile wildlife:

> Borders of the Libyan Nasamonians, your plains are no longer impassable because of the races of wild beasts; no longer will you echo to the roaring of lions in the desert, way beyond the sands which belong to the Nomads, since the lad Caesar has captured a group without number and made them all face his fighters. The mountains which were once home to wild beasts now provide cattle-pasturage for men.[23]

But while the Roman world was an agrarian world, where fear

64

of the danger of the wild was as real as in any other pre-industrial village community, its culture was an urban culture. Hunting was not traditionally one of the pastimes of the Roman landed elite (some agricultural writers, including Columella, even go so far as to condemn it). In some other parts of the Mediterranean, hunting had been a major activity of pre-Roman elites: we are told that one of the proofs of Jugurtha's suitability for kingship over Numidia was his skill in hunting lions.[24] Hunting as a pastime increased in popularity in Italy itself from the first century AD on. But it was not by hunting that emperors symbolically fulfilled their duty to control the wild, but by presiding over the artificial *venatio* in the arena. As late as the sixth century AD, the arena was still the proper place for society to be reassured that the natural world was under control: many of the Latin poems from Vandal-ruled North Africa preserved in the Codex Salmasianus acclaim performers who kill or simply demonstrate their control over animals. Two poems referring to an elephant, said to be Indian, celebrate the fact that 'human power can control the fury of wild beasts – the great monster fears a tiny human', and that after it has been killed in a fight with another animal, its ivory can be used to make various objects used in human cultural activities, from the magistrate's staff to dice: 'What was previously a source of fear turns into a game when it dies.' These lines are packed with the associations that gave meaning to what Romans experienced during a *venatio*: the real fear (*pavor*) of the animal world, dangerous because of size and lack of reason (*rabies*), the idea that force (*vis humana*) should be used to make the animal afraid of man (*timet hominem*) instead of vice versa, the idea that its actual death is a symbol of the dominance of the state (the magistrate's rod, *consulibus sceptrum*), and the fact (symbolised by ivory dice) that this entire process can be turned into a source of enjoyment (*ludus*).[25]

The ancient Mediterranean may present us with some very vivid examples of the exhibition of animals as symbols both of man's control over nature, and of a particular state's power over the world, but such symbolism is not peculiar to antiquity. The zoological museums which Europeans developed in the early nineteenth century had similar political functions. R. Owen, the spirit behind London's Natural History Museum, explicitly expressed his intention that zoology should become 'worthy of this great Empire'.[26] European zoos had the same purpose, although not all of them symbolised as clearly as did Raffles' London Zoo both the scientist's control over nature by means of the tools of botany and zoology, and the British Empire's world hegemony in providing Regent's Park with exotic flora and fauna for the delectation (and improvement) of the people of the imperial capital. The 'park' had been associated with sovereign power by the Persian kings (and hence, in *Genesis*, with the divine paradise). Some hellenistic rulers stocked their parks with animals from around the world: Ptolemy II's menagerie at Alexandria was particularly famous. Roman emperors followed their lead: when Nero exploited the opportunity presented by the destruction of the centre of Rome by the great fire of AD 64 to build his 'Golden House', he filled the gardens 'with a multitude of every kind of cattle and wild beast'. Although Nero was reviled as a tyrant after his fall, and his palace and park were replaced by the Colosseum, where domination over the animal world was more directly enacted, later emperors too were thought to have surrounded themselves with every variety of animal.[27]

Within their mansions, too, both the rich and the not-so-rich needed to be reminded of the power of nature, and reassured that they ultimately dominated that nature. From the third century AD on, hunting mosaics become common throughout the empire; the spectacular coloured mosaic at Piazza Armerina in Sicily visually expresses the power of its imperial owner by depicting both the killing of beasts, and their capture and transportation to Rome from overseas provinces. Even in moderate provincial town houses, diners would be reminded of the savagery of nature as they tucked into their meat: the theme of the lion devouring a deer or gazelle is widespread (a well-known British example is in the Verulamium Museum). The domination of nature may be realistically represented by the hunter, or mythically by a figure such as Orpheus, who dominates the wild beasts through the magic of his music. A number of mosaics representing Orpheus in the context of wild beasts have been found in Britain, including those at Horkstow, Lincs; Withington, Cirencester, and Woodchester, Glos. Apart from being pictorially represented, the Orpheus myth could be enacted at the parties of the rich by slave actors: we are told by Varro that in the first century BC the guests of Quintus Hortensius were regaled with the spectacle of Orpheus summoning by his horn different animals in his game park

(Hortensius insisted on using the Greek word *therotrophium* instead of the pedestrian Latin *leporarium*). One of the interlocutors comments, 'It seemed to me no less lovely a show (*formosum spectaculum*) than those of the aediles in the Circus Maximus when there are *venationes* – though without any African beasts.' Another mythical huntsman was Hercules, the symbolism of whom will be examined in chapter 5.[28]

We have considered the display and slaughter of animals at some length because, although such shows were originally unconnected with gladiatorial *munera*, by the first century AD the two spectacles clearly formed complementary parts of the same cycle of entertainment, the *venatio* in the morning and the *munus* in the afternoon. Between these two spectacles something else took place which was not organically related to either, but which forms part of the same experience: the public execution of prisoners of low status. The reasons why this too came to form part of the same cycle of activities may originally have been to some extent practical. One of the Roman forms of execution was by throwing convicted criminals to wild beasts (*ad bestias*). Because it was the site for *venationes*, the amphitheatre provided a place where such beasts could be safely kept. Furthermore public executions naturally required a public, and the popularity of the games meant that the public was already there. But executions also took place elsewhere, and the audience was not required to stay and watch. When Seneca criticises those who stayed to watch such executions during the lunch-break on the grounds that no skill was involved in simply putting a person to death,[29] he pretends that he had not hitherto been aware of what the experience felt like; the implication is that the educated classes were free to leave after the *venatio* to take their lunch and their siesta before the gladiators appeared in the afternoon. He is also expressing criticism of Nero's predecessor Claudius, who enjoyed the morning and midday spectacle of animals and men being put to death to such an extent that, as Suetonius says, 'he would get to the amphitheatre at dawn, and he would stay in his seat while the audience went off to lunch'. Again, the implication is that educated people ought to prefer watching gladiators fight to watching animals or criminals being killed.[30]

EXECUTING CRIMINALS[31]

The cruelty of Roman methods of execution, at least of persons of low status, evokes as much revulsion in modern scholarship as does the killing of animals as a symbol of domination, or the mutual slaughter of gladiators. In late republican Italy, the execution of convicted criminals of citizen status is generally held to have been replaced by exile; but this amelioration is more apparent than real. Offences committed by very large sections of the population who were not citizens were not subject to regulation by public law at all. Within Italy, non-citizens were subject to magisterial coercion, and the punishment of slaves was (under the republic) normally a matter left to their masters. Non-citizens of low status (slaves or *dediticii*, members of defeated communities which had surrendered unconditionally to the power of Rome) were always liable to execution by crucifixion. Ouiside Italy, the authority of a Roman governor within his province was so absolute that no one could effectively challenge his decision to punish anyone in any way he decided, whatever the formal legal rights of the accused. Cicero's invective against Verres shows how weak the protection theoretically provided by citizen status might in fact be against the whims of a governor, particularly for members of local provincial communities who did not have powerful links of patronage with Rome; and the anecdotes recounted by Suetonius about some of Galba's judicial decisions while governor in Spain, whether true or not, show that even a century after Augustus had imposed some degree of central control over provincial governors, it could still be taken for granted that their word could set aside any legal rights: when a man sentenced to crucifixion protested that he was a Roman citizen, Galba ordered him to be hung on a higher cross than other criminals. Nor did central control make the exercise of judicial power any less severe. In the aftermath of the civil wars, there were no longer any inhibitions about inflicting the death penalty on citizens within Italy, or even on members of the elite (though voluntary exile and, increasingly, suicide might be sanctioned as ways of avoiding execution).

Whether judicial penalties in fact became increasingly savage over the course of the centuries is not as clear as it has seemed to some.[32] Certainly the number of offences for which the death penalty was prescribed increased over the centuries, but that may be a function of emperors' desire to be seen to be ever more active in upholding law and order. It may also be the case that emperors deliberately promulgated penalties which were harsher than those that they intended to apply, in order to give themselves scope to exercise the imperial virtue of clemency on those so convicted.

What is certainly the case is that as the distinction between Roman citizens and others ceased to be significant, particularly after the granting of citizenship to all free persons throughout the empire by the *Constitutio Antoniniana* of AD 212, a new definition of status came to prescribe the mode of execution for convicted criminals. Beheading by the sword came to be a privilege reserved only for the so-called *honestiores* (senators, soldiers and others in the emperor's service, and members of municipal councils, with their families). If competently carried out by an expert executioner, decapitation was swift and inflicted a minimum of physical pain. It continued to be a privilege reserved to the nobility in European states in the Roman law tradition until the French revolution assigned such privileges to every citizen, requiring the introduction in 1791 of the new technology developed by Dr Guillotine to make good the ensuing shortfall in trained executioners. But the rest of the population (the *humiliores*) found themselves subject in late antiquity to the forms of the death penalty to which only non-citizens had been liable in earlier centuries. These were: crucifixion, being torn to death by animals (*ad bestias*), and being burnt to death (*ad flammas* or *crematio*) – the first two perhaps borrowed from Carthaginian military practice at the time of the first Punic war.[33]

In the context of the European world since the Enlightenment, such penalties count not just as 'cruel and unusual' but as sadistic; they intentionally inflict on the convicted criminal pain which is not required to kill him. But to categorise behaviour as sadistic only makes sense in a culture where humanitarian sensibilities are taken as the norm; the Marquis de Sade's advocacy of the infliction of pain as a 'natural' human desire could only be an expression of perversity in an Enlightenment world in which it was taken for granted that such infliction of pain was indeed unnatural. If we are to try to understand the attitudes of any pre-Enlightenment society towards the imposition of cruel punishments on evil-doers, we have to set aside our perception that such punishments would be categorised as sadistic in our own culture. To some extent, this is a function of the very different levels of pain to which people were inured in pre-industrial societies: the development of anaesthetics and tranquillisers, and their widespread availability in the modern western world, has reduced the frequency with which people encounter severe and long-lasting pain (e.g. toothache), and consequently has also made it necessary to eliminate such pain as soon as possible once it does occur. But it would be naive to think that the pre-industrial world's preparedness to inflict pain on criminals was simply a function of the presence of quantitatively 'more' pain in general, just as the presence of quantitatively more violence, or quantitatively earlier mortality, in antiquity is not in itself an explanation for the feeling of satisfaction experienced by Romans when watching the events in the arena.

The infliction of pain was an essential element in dealing with criminals. This applies both to the death penalty and to other punishments: the most notorious is Constantine's decree that those assisting in the abduction of a virgin should have molten lead poured down their throats. It has been pointed out that condemnation to the mines was inflicted not just because emperors needed more mineworkers than a free system would provide, but because mining was perceived to be degrading and dangerous to life.[34] The execution of Christian martyrs and displaying of their corpses was intended as a cruel and perverse punishment, and so perceived by Christians.[35]

But this pain was not inflicted randomly or because it was enjoyed for its own sake, and therefore it is not appropriate to describe it as sadistic. Maximum cruelty was not exercised on every possible occasion; rather, the pain inflicted had to be commensurate with the suffering the criminal had caused, or might have caused, to others. A clear example is the burning alive of an adult convicted of setting fire to a temple or to a store of grain, already prescribed in the Law of the Twelve Tables.[36] The jurist Ulpian says that *crematio* applies to those guilty of sacrilege, as well as rebels and deserters.[37] The punishment might be inflicted on the part of the body through which the crime had been committed: as governor of Tarraconensis, Galba punished a fraudulent money-lender by amputating his hands and nailing him to his banker's table.[38] Caligula paraded a criminal whose hands had been amputated through the city with a placard stating what his crime had been. The physical pain inflicted on the criminal was also intended to degrade him. An evil-doer may be perceived as someone who arrogates to himself certain rights which he does not have (rights to appropriate property belonging to another, for example, or the right to inflict harm on another person). In a society based on status differentiation, such an arrogation of rights is perceived as claiming a status to which the accused has no claim. His action thus overturns the proper hierarchy of statuses public recognition of which is essential if society is to function smoothly. The public humiliation of the criminal re-establishes social order by cancelling the criminal's exercise of rights which he did not have. The gospel narrative of the crucifixion provides a characteristic example: having been found guilty of claiming the status of king of the Jews, Jesus was humiliated by being dressed up as king in a cloak and crowned with a diadem of thorns.

The punishment of criminals does not simply concern the convict, his victims, and the state, but all those who share a particular society's perceptions of what constitutes unacceptable behaviour subject to publicly proclaimed legal penalties. For the public to be reassured that the proper social order is indeed being restored by means of the inflicting of appropriate penalties, punishment needs to be made public in some way: in our own society, the media broadcast sufficient information about the activities of the police and the courts to give the general public at least some certainty that convicted criminals are being punished. Since the early nineteenth century, the industrial state has had the fiscal and human resources to provide a framework of overt and covert policing in even the least accessible parts of its territory, one of the effects of which is that it can be assumed, rightly or wrongly, that those who commit crimes will have to face a court of justice. The modern state also has the technical resources to maintain prisons that are at least reasonably escape-proof. Once someone has been convicted of a serious crime, there is considerable certainty that he will suffer deprivation of liberty on a scale thought to be roughly commensurate with the social harm he has done. The policeman and the prison are two visible factors that reassure a modern society that legal (if not moral) norms have more than just a theoretical role, and that ordinary people may carry on their lives on the assumption that those norms will be adhered to. When that reassurance is shattered as the result of a miscarriage of justice or an escape or threats by terrorists to commit further crimes unless a convicted associate is prematurely released from his punishment, then the reaction of the public is sometimes out of all proportion to the danger to public order which the particular incident itself poses. The focus of reassurance today is the trial; by contrast, the actual punishment has become almost a secret.[39]

Pre-industrial states could rely on neither a reliable police force nor secure prisons to provide their populations with such public reassurance. That reassurance had instead to be provided by the punishment itself; and that explains why punishment normally had to be both cruel and public. It had to be public not only to provide the publicity which newspapers and other media provide today, but also to show that the restoration of proper order concerned every status-group within society. As at every public event in a status-conscious society, the presence of persons of high status obviously also fulfilled the function of visibly reminding those present that the proper order included status distinctions, but it would be perverse to suggest that these reasons alone were why executions were public. After the execution, the body of the criminal would be openly displayed, with a tablet stating what he had been guilty of: the notice nailed to Jesus' cross stating his crime, that he had claimed to be king of the Jews, was a perfectly standard way of ensuring publicity. Publicity and reassurance were closely associated, as a passage from the early third-century jurist Callistratus suggests:

> The practice approved by most authorities has been to hang notorious brigands on a gallows in the place which they used to haunt, so that by the spectacle others may be deterred from the same crimes, and so that it may, when the penalty has been carried out, bring comfort to the relatives and kin of those killed in that place where the brigands committed their murders.[40]

That text, like others, also emphasises the deterrent value of publicity. A first-century AD declamation takes it as axiomatic that 'Whenever we crucify criminals, the most frequented highways are chosen, where the greatest number of onlookers can watch, and be persuaded by this warning.'[41]

Apart from reassuring the public, theorists in antiquity as today justified punishment both as a deterrent and as a way of reforming the criminal. Seneca cites all three reasons: 'The law has three aims in punishing injuries (and the emperor should have the same three aims): either to reform the person being punished, or to make others behave better as a result of his punishment [i.e., deter them], or so that the rest of us can lead our lives more securely with evil-doers eliminated.'[42] The idea of correction as a (perhaps the only) proper function of punishment goes back to Plato;[43] whether it was thought important outside limited philosophical circles may be doubted.

Gladiatorial spectacles were not introduced to Rome in order to provide a context for public executions. Nor were amphitheatres designed primarily for executions. Executions originally took place in other public places such as the Forum (such as that of the bandit Selouros under Augustus: Strabo 6.273 = p. 78 f.), and on other public occasions where large crowds gathered such as *ludi*. Valerius Maximus tells us how he imagined public executions of slaves as having taken place in early Rome:

> At the Plebeian Games, a certain *paterfamilias* (head of household) had his slave brutally flogged and led him to execution, bearing the 'fork' [i.e., the cross-beam used for crucifixion], through the Circus Flaminius just before the sacred procession entered. Jupiter commanded Titus Latinius, an ordinary citizen, in a dream to tell the consuls that he had not been pleased with the warm-up act at the last Circus Games. Unless they expiated this by repeating the Games, no small danger to the state would ensue.[44]

The passage illustrates that the punishment of slaves, even by execution, was the responsibility of private individuals in the republican period. Perhaps that was a particular reason why, paradoxically, the executions of slaves had to be carried out publicly: not only did the republican state not have the means to police or imprison slaves, but that was not even seen as part of the responsibility of state magistrates. The slave-holding societies of the ancient world were by no means the prison camps that some scholars have depicted them, where the obedience of slaves could be achieved only by permanent terror. Nevertheless fear of misbehaviour by slaves, especially violent misbehaviour, was one of the concerns of citizen society, as illustrated by maxims such as 'there are as many enemies as slaves' (quoted with disapproval by Seneca) or Livy's report that, on occasion, every Roman feared an enemy within his own household.[45] But precisely because the punishment of slaves was the responsibility of those whose property they were, the rest of society could not be certain that criminal slaves were being punished as they deserved unless such punishment were public, and spectacularly so. That applied particularly to executions and corporal punishment, since it was not in a slave-owner's interest to destroy the value of his own property by inflicting such punishments.

It is hard to say just what level of severity was required by society from those who owned criminal slaves. Cato the Elder was acclaimed as an exemplar of traditional moral standards, but Plutarch's account of how he treated his slaves accuses him of uncharacteristic inhumanity: 'Those who had been accused of a crime which deserved the death-penalty were tried in the presence of his other dependants, and executed if they were found guilty.'[46] But there is no shortage of evidence that Roman masters had their slaves executed when convinced that that was necessary. Although condemned before the 'private' household *consilium*, the slave might then be executed in public. Few households will have been wealthy and powerful enough to have had the technical resources to carry out an execution themselves; the role of the executioner was assumed by municipal undertakers. An early first-century AD inscription from Puteoli shows that such public executions of slaves were frequent enough to require regulation by the civic authorities: the regulations, covering the activities of the town's firm of funeral contractors, contain the detail characteristic of Roman legislation.

(line 7) If anyone wishes to have a slave – male or female – punished privately, he who wishes to have the punishment inflicted shall do so as follows. If he wants to put the slave on the cross or fork, the contractor must supply the posts, chains, ropes for floggers, and the floggers themselves. The person having the punishment inflicted is to pay 4 sesterces for each of the operatives who carry the fork, and the same for the floggers and for the executioner.
(11) The magistrate shall give orders for such punishments as he exacts in his public capacity, and when orders are given, (the contractor) is to be ready to exact the punishment. He is to set up crosses and supply without charge nails, pitch, wax, tapers and anything else that is necessary

for this in order to deal with the condemned man. Again, if he is ordered to drag away the corpse with a hook, the work-gang is to be dressed in red and ring a bell while dragging away the body, or bodies if there are several.

If a commission is given [to remove] a hanged man, he (the contractor) is to see to its fulfilment and the removal (of the body) within the hour. If it is for a male or female slave, if the notification is received before the tenth hour, removal is to be effected the same day; if after the tenth hour, then before the second hour on the following day.

Similar regulations about executions have been found on a marble tablet discovered at Cumae in 1967. It apparently includes provisions for 'If the executioner (*carnifex*) acts in public or gives or wishes to give a spectacle'.[47]

Apart from crucifixion there were two other recognised ways by which the death penalty could be carried out: burning (*ad flammas*) and throwing the criminal to wild beasts (*ad bestias*). Perhaps the best-known tale of a slave thrown to the lions for having run away from his master is that of Androclus, as originally told by Apion and reported by Aulus Gellius in the middle of the second century AD. There are some ambiguities in his account: Androclus flees from his master in Africa, but, when he is recaptured and punished, his master happens to be the Urban Prefect, the emperor's representative responsible for upholding law and order in Rome. It is left unclear whether Androclus is punished by the Prefect in his official capacity, or as the fugitive slave's master.[48]

The severity of punishments against slaves is illustrated by some of the anecdotes related in imperial biographies. It was a characteristic of Julius Caesar's clemency that he did not torture a slave before putting him to death: 'When his secretary, the slave Philemon, promised his enemies to kill him by poison, he punished him by nothing more severe than a straightforward execution.'[49] Similarly Augustus:

> When a slave called Cosmus made serious accusations against him, his punishment went no further than shackling. When he went for a walk with his steward Diomedes and a wild boar suddenly attacked them, Diomedes left him in the lurch; but Augustus preferred to accuse him of cowardice than of a crime, and he made fun of an incident

that was extremely serious, since the slave had meant no harm. (2) But he also forced one of his favourite freedmen, Polus, to commit suicide when he was discovered to have been seducing married women; he broke the legs of his secretary Thallus for having betrayed the contents of a letter for 500 *denarii*; and he had the *paedagogi* and servants of his [adopted] son Gaius thrown into the river with heavy weights tied to their necks because of the insolence and greed with which they had behaved out in the province [Asia] at the time when Gaius was sick and dying.[50]

Our feelings about the degree of severity exercised should not let us lose sight of the fact that these slaves had committed serious crimes, with wide political implications as well as simply endangering life. The Caesars were of course unusual in that there was no effective restraint on the way in which they chose to punish miscreants within their households; other Roman masters were subject to the control, albeit informal, exercised by their friends assembled in the household *consilium*. Anecdotal evidence shows how the influence of a powerful friend might restrain undue harshness towards slaves. The most famous concerns Vedius Pollio, whom Augustus stopped from executing a slave who had broken a valuable goblet by throwing him to some man-eating fish: a perverse extension of the standard mode of execution *ad bestias*.[51]

Under the principate, imperial constitutions circumscribed the occasions and degree of the punishment a slave's master might inflict – not so much out of humanitarian motives, as to prevent the master from exercising powers which emperors increasingly wanted to reserve to the state. This did not of course mean slaves did not continue to be executed; but now that could only be done with the approval of a public court, rather than of the more amenable family council, as specified in legislation probably dating to the late first century AD:

Following the Lex Petronia and the recommendations of the Senate qualifying that law, the rights of slave-owners who wanted to give their slaves to fight wild beasts were taken away from them. But if the slave has been brought before a court, and the owner's complaint has been found to be justified, then he may be handed over for punishment.[52]

Later legislation confirmed this by forbidding slaves from being sold to those organising *venationes*: 'Owners may not sell their slaves to be made to fight wild beasts, even if they have a criminal character. This was stated in a rescript of the Divine Emperors' (sc. Marcus Aurelius and Lucius Verus).[53] In a rescript dated 11 May, AD 319, Constantine again explicitly reserved any such punishments to the state.

As well as implementing these forms of execution on behalf of the owner of a criminous slave, the state also used them to punish certain crimes against the community: typically arson and sacrilege. Martial talks of the penalty *ad bestias* as applying to a slave who has cut his master's throat with a sword, has been mad enough to rob a temple of the gold deposited there, or has set Rome on fire with destructive torches.[54] Public law therefore prescribed particular punishments for those whose crimes had set them outside the pale of civilised society: murderers and arsonists. Having rejected the rules of human society, such criminals no longer had any claim to the protection that society gives its members from the chaos of nature: and consequently they were abandoned to the appropriate natural forces – wild beasts or flames – *ad bestias, ad flammas*. The penalty had to be carried out within a year of sentence being passed.[55]

Humanitarian motives should not necessarily be excluded from explanations for the increasing control of the conditions under which slaves might be executed, but there were other reasons too. It was in the interests of all emperors to restrict the power to take life to state authorities which were under their own control, and to prevent members of the Roman elite from displaying their power over their households too publicly. It has also been suggested that the popularity of the games in the first century AD made it advisable to restrict public executions to particular times – the games – and preferably to Rome. Any criminal slaves executed privately by their owners would have detracted from the public spectacle. The jurist Modestinus tells us that condemned criminals were sent to Italy from every province throughout the empire.[56] A successful public spectacle like Claudius' naval battle on the Fucine lake in AD 52 required thousands of criminals; Tacitus claims 19,000. It is not surprising that Claudius is accused by our sources of having condemned men to death for crimes which did not formally warrant execution, such as fraud. Modestinus says that on occasion judges had condemned those found guilty of robbery to the beasts. It is a standard accusation against evil emperors that they had people executed in this way who were either completely innocent or whose crimes did not deserve the death penalty. Of course, as the Androclus story shows, there were occasions when the sentence might not actually result in death.[57]

Once these executions of non-citizens had come to be monopolised by the state, there was a gradual tendency to extend them even to citizens of low status (in late antiquity, technically known as *humiliores*), while the citizen's privilege of execution by being decapitated by a blow from a sword came to be reserved to persons of senatorial, equestrian or curial rank (*honestiores*). Constantine had crucifixion banned, as insulting to Christians, and it has consequently disappeared from most of the legal sources. In the fourth century AD, both legal and literary texts list the sword, burning, and the beasts together as the standard forms of the death penalty (e.g. Gregory of Nazianzen's invective against Julian). Beheading by the sword was reserved for the *honestiores*, the beasts for those of humble status.[58]

The state's monopolisation of executions coincided with the construction of amphitheatres, and, in addition to the more complex developments to do with the concentration of power in the hands of the emperor, there were as we have seen strong practical reasons for holding executions in an amphitheatre: it was a secure place in which to keep wild beasts. But the amphitheatre was only one possible site for executions. One spectacular execution of a violent criminal in the reign of Augustus took place in the Forum. It was described by Strabo, and reveals several common features of public executions in pre-industrial societies, and not just in the Roman world.

Recently, in my own experience (νεωστὶ δ'ἐφ' ἡμῶν) a certain Selouros, called 'the son of Etna' was sent to Rome because he had commanded an army and terrorised the area around Mount Etna for a long time with frequent raiding. I saw him torn to pieces by the beasts in the Forum while a contest of gladiators was being performed (ἐν τῇ ἀγορᾷ μονομάχων ἀγῶνος συνεστῶτος). He had been put on a high platform, as though on Mount Etna, and when the platform suddenly broke up and collapsed, he himself crashed down into wild-beast cages which easily broke open, placed beneath the platform in readiness for this purpose.[59]

The episode, discussed in detail by K. Coleman, illustrates the publicity which Roman executions required. A date in the 30s BC has been assumed for this episode, and possibly a connection with Octavian's highly publicised measures to bring to justice runaway slaves who had supported Sextus Pompeius; but banditry is notoriously endemic to Sicily, and Selourus' activites around Mount Etna need have no connection with any civil war (we need not make too much of the fact that we are told by Appian, *Civilia* 5. 131 that Octavian sent captured slaves back to their towns of origin for punishment: Selourus' case was clearly exceptional). But we cannot be certain that this execution antedates the completion of Taurus' amphitheatre simply because it was held in the Forum. Once amphitheatres had been constructed, they provided an obvious suitable site for public executions: but that was not what they were primarily intended for.

Accounts by Christian writers of the experiences of those condemned to death by fire or the beasts because they were found guilty of being Christians provide a particularly fertile source of information about Roman executions.[60] One interesting text is the *Epistle to the Romans* of St Ignatius of Antioch, since the writer had himself been condemned to the beasts, and his expectations of what that death would be like inform his account of his transportation to the Colosseum (§5):

I have already been finding myself in conflict with beasts of prey by land and by sea, by night and by day, the whole way from Syria to Rome: chained as I am to half-a-score of savage leopards [i.e., a detachment of soldiers], who only grow more insolent the more bribes they are given . . . How I look forward to the real lions that have been prepared for me! All I pray is that I will find them swift. I am going to make overtures to them, so that, unlike some other wretches whom they have been too spiritless to touch, they may devour me with all speed. And if they are reluctant, I shall have to use force on them . . . Fire, cross, beast-fighting, hacking and quartering, splintering of bone and mangling of limb, even the pulversising of my whole body – let every horrid and diabolical torment come upon me, provided only that I can win my way to Jesus Christ!

Although a literary account by an educated Greek (albeit not of Roman citizen status), Ignatius' use of the theme of the cruelty involved in punishments *ad bestias* is not a fiction. Other martyr-acts describe what happened with so much circumstantial detail that it is economic to assume that they depend on eyewitness accounts. Polycarp of Smyrna was burnt to death on a date stated to have been 23 February, probably in AD 155. His execution followed the arrest and condemnation of a number of other Christians in his community. In this text, as in the letter of Ignatius, we find the literary device of reversing the direction in which force is applied: the Christian Germanicus forces the beasts to attack him, instead of vice versa. The experience of pain inflicted on the condemned also comes through clearly in the account:

> (§2) It was the same with those who were condemned to the wild beasts. The pains they endured were horrible, for they were forced to lie on beds of spikes and subjected to other varied forms of torture, in the hope that these lingering agonies would enable the devil to extort a recantation from them; in fact, there was no end to the devices the devil employed against them.
>
> (§3) Thank God, however, all his efforts were unavailing. Germanicus, an example of true nobility, lent new strength to their failing spirits by his steadfast endurance. He confronted the savage beasts with exceptional manliness, and when the Governor attempted persuasion, urging him to have pity on his own youth, he even used force to drag the animal towards him, in his desire for a speedier release from that world of unjust and lawless men.

The martyr-acts reverse the Roman world's assumptions about justice and law: the execution of Christians shows that the executions carried out by the pagan world are the opposite of public guarantees of social order. The text goes on to describe how the people of Smyrna call for the arrest of Polycarp, the Christian bishop; he is induced to flee first to one country estate (suggesting that, notwithstanding the later mode of his execution, he was a person of considerable wealth and status: we are told in §13 that he was a man who had never before had to take off his own shoes), then to another. Municipal officials followed him to the first, where they routinely tortured two slaves to find out where he had gone. They arrested him late at night. He ordered his slaves to provide his captors with food and drink, and prayed (aloud) for two hours, on behalf of the Church throughout the world. Then he was taken to the Circus at Smyrna. On the way, his friend Herodes, the Eirenarch (the municipal official responsible for public order), tried to persuade him to sacrifice to Caesar. When he reached the Circus, the governor too asked him several times to swear by the Fortune (*Tyche*) of Caesar. There follows what appears to be a verbatim account of the interrogation:

> (§11) The governor then said, 'I have wild beasts here. Unless you change your mind, I shall have you thrown to them.'
>
> 'Why then, call them up,' said Polycarp, 'for it is out of the question for us to exchange a proper faith for a bad one. It would be a very creditable thing, though, to change over from the wrong to the right.'
>
> The other said again, 'If you do not recant, I will have you burnt to death, since you think so lightly of wild beasts.'
>
> Polycarp replied: 'The fire you threaten me with cannot go on burning for very long: after a while it goes out. But what you are unaware of is the flames of future judgement and everlasting torment which are in store for the ungodly. Why do you go on wasting time? Bring out whatever you have a mind to.'

The Roman governor ordered a herald to announce three times that 'Polycarp has admitted to being a Christian'. The assembled crowd in the Circus then shouted for the Asiarch Philip to find a lion to let loose at Polycarp. However, he replied that this would not be legal: the wild-beast fighting for which the Asiarch was responsible (presumably the annual games associated with the imperial cult) had been declared closed. Execution *ad bestias* was therefore not a legal possibility; whereupon the crowd set up a unanimous cry that he should have Polycarp burnt alive. When the fire took hold, it did not at first burn him (§15):

> There he was in the centre of it, not like a human being in

flames but like a loaf baking in the oven, or like a gold or silver ingot being refined in the furnace. And we became aware of a delicious fragrance, like the odour of incense or other precious gums,

and not like the smell of human flesh which witnesses to executions are likely to have experienced. Finally, when they realised that his body could not be destroyed by fire, they ordered one of the executioners (the Greek text uses the Latin word *confector*) to go up and stab him with his weapon.

Many other martyr-acts describe the cruelty of Roman executions. The penalties of *ad bestias* and *ad flammas* might be linked to crucifixion. Pionius was nailed to a cross, and then burnt. At Lyon in AD 177, the female martyr Blandina was hung upside down on a cross as bait for wild beasts.[61] Tacitus' account of how Nero executed Christians for arsonists after the great fire of AD 64 is famous: he had them covered in pitch and set fire to them to illuminate evening spectacles.[62] Such cruel modes of execution were not just literary fancies associated with evil pagans, or an evil tyrant. That convicted criminals really were executed in this way, with the excruciating suffering involved, is confirmed by visual evidence. A terracotta statuette from North Africa, now in the Louvre (figure 7), represents a woman naked but for a loin-cloth, astride a bull with her hands tied behind her back. The bull has fallen to its knees; the woman is being mauled by a leopard. Beneath the bull is a man armed with a shield (perhaps the *confector* or a *bestiarius*). The emotions which induced someone to keep such a terracotta model in his home are not ones that we can easily share, but they should not be dismissed as aberrant. It would have served as a powerful warning to any slave contemplating disobedience. The mosaic from Zliten (figure 5) has no inhibitions about showing in detail how executions *ad bestias* were made to take place. Two of the prisoners represented are tied to stakes fixed to small chariots, which are being wheeled forward towards the wild beasts by attendants; another prisoner is being pushed forward towards a leaping lion by an attendant wielding a whip. The attendants wear tunics, the prisoners are naked apart from a loin-cloth. The criminals' skin-colour differs from that of the other figures, leading to the assumption that they could have been non-Roman Garamantes captured in the course of a raid against Roman territory (see p. 15 f.); alternatively, their yellow/brown skin (in contrast to the pink/brown of the others) might be an attempt to depict the effect of incarceration. On the mosaic from the 'Domus Sollertiana' at El Djem, two criminals are pushed forward by guards wearing some kind of body armour. In both mosaics, the craftsman has tried to represent the terror of the condemned men as they are about to be lacerated. The face of one of the El Djem figures cannot be seen, as it is already being mauled by a leopard; the other is wide-eyed with terror. One of the Zliten figures is bending backwards, and trying to protect himself with his arms.

The account of Polycarp's martyrdom shows that, after they had suffered excruciatingly in full view, the criminals were given the *coup de grace* by an executioner (*confector*). Martyr-acts emphasise that, when this was done in a public place, it was in response to the demands of a hostile crowd, which implies that it normally took place out of sight of the crowd. In the *Passion of Perpetua and Felicity*, the crowd at Carthage demanded that the martyrs' bodies be brought into the centre of the arena, 'so that their eyes could participate in the killing as the sword entered their flesh'.[63]

Christians were of course by no means the only category of criminals humiliated in the arena. Apart from arsonists and murderers, we are told that the infamous informers who became rich under wicked emperors by accusing members of the elite of crimes against him were paraded when a good emperor succeeded. More interestingly, those who lost their social rank because they had wasted their property to the point of bankruptcy were also treated in this way. The (relatively reliable) life of Hadrian in the *Historia Augusta* says with approval that he 'ordered bankrupts to be thrashed in the amphitheatre and then let go', without further punishment. Social, as well as physical, death was imposed publicly in the arena.[64]

One of the most difficult features of Roman executions for modern sentiments to come to terms with was the well-attested practice of forcing the convicted criminal to act out the part of a figure from Greco-Roman mythology or a character in a popular mime who suffers death for his or her wickedness. The excellent discussion of this phenomenon within the general context of Roman judicial penalties by K. Coleman[65] makes it unnecessary to list exhaustive details. It is particularly necessary here for post-Enlightenment preconceptions to be set aside if we are to understand the meaning of such practices for ordinary people in the Roman world.

An example of the dramatic stories used as a framework for the execution of a criminal concerned a bandit chieftain called Laureolus; this was a traditional mime, at the end of which Laureolus got his just deserts. We happen to know about this mime because there was a performance of it just before Caligula was assassinated in AD 41; the coincidence was interpreted as an omen that he too would get what he deserved.[66] The mime is also referred to by Juvenal 8, 185 ff. and Tertullian, *Aduersus Valentinianos* 14.4. In Juvenal's lines, the satirist objects to a Roman equestrian appearing as Laureolus, and says that the equestrian deserves to be executed for such self-degradation. That seems to have been exactly what was intended when the Laureolus mime was turned into the setting for a public execution, as is described in a poem in the *Book of Spectacles*:[66a]

Just as Prometheus provided the unremitting vulture with food when he was chained to that rock in Scythia, so Laureolus offered his entrails to a Caledonian bear as he hung from a cross which was no stage-prop. Dripping with blood, his torn limbs continued to live, and there was no substance left in any part of his body.

In the end he suffered the punishment he deserved: the criminal had cut the throat of parent or master with a sword, or had plundered a temple of the gold entrusted to it, or had savagely set fire to you, Rome. His crime had exceeded those of ancient stories; what had been a play became this man's punishment.

The criminal destined to be executed did not merely act the part of Laureolus, he was hung on a real cross (*non falsa cruce*) where he was torn apart by a real bear from Scotland, beyond the borders of the empire. The poet does not state what his crime had actually been, but lists several for which Roman law prescribed execution *ad bestias*: the murder of a relative or (for a slave) master, robbing a temple, and arson (see p. 77 above). And in the first couplet, he puts this particular punishment, as exacted in the framework of a mime, into the even wider framework of myth: the sufferings of the the real criminal acting Laureolus are compared to those of Prometheus.

Elizabeth Rawson warned against the 'tendency these days to

believe that all that the Romans cared for in the theatre was the spectacular and the grotesque'.[67] Executions carried out within the framework of a Greek myth were certainly spectacular, grotesque, and sometimes titillating, like Roman comedy or mimes; but that does not mean that they did not have, or were not perceived by the audience as having, a moral or educative purpose. We have seen that Seneca considered public executions 'improving' by virtue of their deterrent function. If a dramatic representation of the conflict between good and evil performed on the stage could be perceived as morally improving, then such a performance in the arena, including the real execution of a real convicted criminal, was doubly so: the assembled audience would see that, if the myth depicted the triumph of virtue in an ideal world, the execution showed justice overcoming wickedness right in front of their eyes. The fact that the attendants at midday executions were dressed as Mercury, and that the mythical character Charon appeared to escort the corpses of the slain in gladiatorial contests,[68] whatever historical explanations they may have, will in the imperial period have had a similar symbolic function in placing what went on in the arena into a cosmic, universal context.

It is in the second half of the first century AD, from Nero's reign on, that the evidence for such patterns of public executions is particularly strong. Coleman suggests that real criminals were used in order to make death scenes in dramatic displays more realistic; the approach taken by some other scholars recently to the wider cultural changes brought about by the principate would suggest the converse, that it reflected an increasing 'unreality' in public life, a response to the contrast between the reality of the imperial monarchy and public professions about continuing republican liberty.[69] There may however have been a less sophisticated reason for the development: the imperative to keep the attention of the public. Just as with *venationes* and with *munera*, each generation of Romans felt the need to compete with its predecessors in offering the public innovations; and executions, as public spectacles, were not immune from this rule. We may recall that Seneca had expressed the view that the midday executions were unpleasant because they were simple killings without any embellishment, *sine arte*. Claudius had been criticised for his enthusiasm in watching such straightforward executions. Perhaps it was in response to this criticism that Nero and later emperors had criminals executed within the context of a dramatic performance. It is from Nero's reign that we have the first reference to an execution as part of a myth: an epigram attributed to Lucillius in the *Palatine Anthology* tells of a thief called Meniscus who was burnt alive for having stolen three golden apples (perhaps the apples were real ones, stolen from Nero's Golden House). In an execution by *crematio*, the criminal was wrapped in a tunic smeared with pitch (called the *tunica molesta*), which was then set alight; the poet compares this tunic to the coat which Deianeira gave to her husband Herakles, smeared with the blood of the centaur Nessus, which burnt him to death.[70]

Providing titillation for the audience in order to keep their attention during the lunch-break was undoubtedly a major reason for this innovation, but it had other functions too. Nero's artistic interests were exceptional: it is not fanciful to suppose that, by using mythological references, he was attempting to emphasise the value of high culture, which a shared knowledge of Greek mythology through the educational system represented. Mimes like that of Laureolus may have been a more direct part of the audience's cultural experience. For the less literate or less well-educated, another source of knowledge of Greek myths might be the displays of performing animals which constituted one of the elements of the morning's *venationes*. These were known as 'Pyrrichae' (though there had been other varieties of such *pyrrichae* since the fifth century BC). Some such performances were fairly straightforward, such as Galba's elephant trained to walk the tightrope, the elephant taught to kneel in submission before Titus, or the dancing elephants referred to by Pliny the Elder and Aelian. In one of the animal fables of the poet Babrius, a camel performs in one of these *pyrrichae*.[71] There are visual representations of dancing bears in the context of *venationes* and executions (figure 6). More sophisticated shows included representations of mythological tales, including fairly salacious ones such as those of Pasiphae and of Icarus: 'Amongst the themes of these *pyrrichae*, there was (as many of the onlookers were convinced) a bull having intercourse with Pasiphae, who was hidden in a wooden image of a cow; and during his first attempt to fly, Icarus crashed down next to the imperial box and spattered Nero himself with blood.'[72] In a *pyrricha*, the animals were real but the human actors simply actors: there was no question of their suffering a bloody accident by falling out of the sky unless something went wrong with the performance. But when these stories were used to provide a more artistic framework for the midday executions in response, perhaps, to Seneca's strictures, the convicted prisoners who were made to play certain of the characters were really meant to suffer and die cruelly. Plutarch mentions members of the audience who failed to understand the distinction between professional actors and criminals sentenced to death:

> Some people behave just like little children: when they see criminals in the theatre dressed in tunics of gold thread and purple cloaks and with crowns on their heads as if in a *pyrricha* (πυρριχίζοντας), the unlookers are full of awe and hail them as happy. But then they are seen being stabbed and whipped and burnt to death in all that beautiful multi-coloured clothing.[73]

These myths provided a framework for the executions of criminals, sometimes involving a perversion of the myth itself. The *Book of Spectacles* tells of a criminal being dressed up as Orpheus and chained to a rock in the Colosseum (21). Various animals were released into the arena (presumably in order to heighten the audience's suspense as to what would happen); finally a bear, instead of being tamed by the music of the mythical Orpheus' lyre, disrespectfully tore the prisoner apart (*ursus ingratus*). Another criminal killed by a bear was dressed up as Daedalus. Daedalus may have been an apposite mythical figure because he tried to escape from Crete, or because he tried to fly: Coleman suggests that he may have been lowered into the bear's enclosure by means of a flying machine.[74] The first letter of St Clement refers to Christian women having been executed wearing the costume of the Danaids and of Dirce. The mythical Dirce had been killed by her sons by being tied to a bull, and the fifty daughters of Danaus were presumably represented as trying to seek refuge from the beasts by fleeing around the arena.[75]

Dramatic representations may also have enabled judicial mutilations to be carried out with more artifice than by simply hacking off a limb as Galba had done. An epigram in the *Book of Spectacles* refers to someone 'in matutina harena' playing the role of a 'Mucius Scaevola', the Roman hero who proved his bravery in the presence of the Etruscan king Lars Porsenna by thrusting his right hand into the flame; this is said to have been an alternative to the *tunica molesta*. The phrase 'in matutina harena', i.e. as part of a *venatio*, suggests that the poet may be intending his story to be taken in a metaphorical sense – as an alternative to death by *crematio*, the criminal volunteered to fight as a left-handed *bestiarius* instead.[76] We are entitled to be sceptical about stories of the mutilation of criminals in public. Coleman has discussed the evidence for executions involving the mutilation of male or female sexual organs. Tertullian attacks pagan spectacles with the argument that 'We have often (*saepe*) seen the god Attis from Pessinus being castrated, and a man who was being burnt alive playing the role of Hercules.' But castration was forbidden by Roman law, and in classical literary invective punishments of this type were characteristically ascribed to tyrants. Some of the references to alleged punishments of this kind therefore have to be understood in that context, and rejected as unhistorical: for instance, Domitian 'tortured people by applying fire to their genitals'.[77] Although it is hard for us to believe that a Roman audience could stomach a criminal being castrated before their eyes, this should not be ruled out: in the sixth century, Justinian indeed decreed castration as a punishment for sexual delicts; as with other extreme punishments, the intention may have been to give scope to the exercise of the imperial virtue of clemency by not imposing the punishment in practice. Coleman assembles the evidence in her discussion of the Tertullian passage, and suggests that criminals might be offered self-castration as an alternative to execution. Evidence from other historical epochs confirms that the judicial process is sometimes able to persuade criminals of the heinousness of their behaviour so effectively that they are prepared to carry out any act of self-abasement and self-torture that the court prescribes (one thinks of Stalinist show-trials).

Nor should the possibility be excluded that the kind of perverse punishment of a female criminal described in Apuleius' *Metamorphoses* was an actual practice and not just a literary fancy.[78] A poem in the *Book of Spectacles* describes a criminal (presumably condemned for a sexual crime) forced to act the role of the mythical Pasiphae, whose lack of sexual self-control induced her to have intercourse with a bull.[79] With deliberate ambiguity, the poet says 'Iunctam tauro' (tied to a bull, as depicted by the Louvre terracotta of a woman being executed *ad bestias*: figure 7); the Latin could mean, and was meant by the poet to be taken to mean, sexually penetrated by the bull. We may note that a series of terracotta lamps with scenes from the arena found at Athens includes several scenes of an animal having intercourse with a woman. The public destruction of a woman in the arena as she was dragged along by the bull would have provided quite enough scope for any members of the audience so inclined to supply the rest.[80]

The uncertainty as to the actual behaviour of the animals involved made *ad bestias* a far more exciting mode of execution for the audience than *crematio*. Sometimes – as in the story of St Polycarp, or more famously of Androclus and his lion – the beast might refrain from attacking the criminal at all; this became a commonplace in Christian writing, which made the beasts' unwillingness to attack martyrs a sign of the martyr's innocence. The theme went back to that of Daniel in the lions' den: Josephus explicitly says that God only allows beasts to execute the guilty.[81] The beast might kill one of the attendants instead of the condemned criminal: in the *Passion of SS. Perpetua and Felicity*, this happened to the Christian Saturus, who had been tied to a boar which dragged him along the ground and gored the *bestiarus*. A second attempt to execute Saturus failed when a bear refused to attack him as he was tied to a scaffold. The third attack, by a leopard, achieved its objective.[82] The cruelty inflicted on the criminal by a drawn-out execution (both psychological and physical) was also a factor; a Roman lamp shows the victim placed at the top of a platform out of reach of the beasts, while a lion has to climb a ramp to get at him; this will partly have been to enrage the beast further, and partly to increase the terror of anticipation suffered by the criminal.[83]

Another way of heightening the excitement felt by the audience, which predates such 'charades', lay in the mass-slaughter of prisoners acting out full-scale battles, especially naval battles, staged by a number of emperors from Caesar on. Such battles were often staged in connection with exceptional events such as imperial triumphs rather than the regular *munera*, and they ought to be distinguished from gladiatorial combat, even though they have some features in common: those in-volved in both categories might include prisoners of war. But gladiators were trained to fight in accordance with certain con-ventions and with certain traditional types of weapons; and, if they were criminals, their punishment was not considered to be capital. Those forced to take part in enactments of battles by contrast received no special training, and *naumachiae* should be seen as mass-executions of rebellious enemies rather than gladiatorial contests. In fact, the first recorded *naumachia* of this kind in 46 BC involved soldiers, not criminals at all: Julius Caesar's triumphal games, held in the Circus, featured 500 infantry, 300 cavalry, and twenty elephants carrying towers on their backs on each side. On another occasion, Caesar made 2,000 soldiers demonstrate their skill by fighting as Tyrians and Egyptians.[84] As part of the *ludi* celebrating the entry of his grandsons into public life, Augustus put on a naval battle in the Circus Flaminius between Athenians and Persians in 2 BC.[85] Claudius was the first who certainly used criminals to man the two fleets in his *naumachia*, representing Sicilians versus Rhodians; many of the 19,000 who took part were reprieved as a reward for their bravery. After his conquest of Britain, he also presented a spectacle in the Campus Martius showing the sacking of a British city.[86] Nero staged a naval battle featuring Athenians and Persians at the inauguration of his new amphitheatre in AD 57; it is interesting that, after the battle had ended, the water was drained away, and there followed a gladiatorial show held on dry land.[87] At the inauguration of the Colosseum, Titus had water pour into the arena; the various animals who were in it had all been taught to swim. There followed a battle between Corcyreans and Corinthians. On another occasion Titus had Athenians fight Syracusans; both sets re-enacted battles of the Peloponnesian war as described by Thucydides. It was thought worthy of note that, in the *naumachia* which Domitian held in the Circus to celebrate a German triumph, most of the participants lost their lives as the result of a sudden storm.[88]

What the public had watched in the arena before the gladiatorial duels began in the afternoon was the killing, with a lesser or greater degree of artifice, of beasts and of criminals or prisoners-of-war. The arena was the place were these categories of threats to civilised life were destroyed – not just symbolically, but in actual fact. To kill dangerous beasts was to protect mankind, either from direct attack (even from domesticated creatures such as bulls and hounds), or from those who competed with the human community for scarce resources. The culture of the Roman empire may have been an urban culture, but many of those watching will have come to the city from their rural homes specially for these regular but infrequent displays; and all the onlookers will have been aware that their lives depended directly on success in the constant struggle against the natural world, to a much greater extent than any urban crowd today.

As the place where the conflict between man and beast was enacted, the arena thus symbolised the margin between culture and the wild. It was also the place where beasts and criminals were transferred from life to death. That the passage from life to death of another human being (and to some extent even of an animal) is a major source of anxiety in any culture goes without saying: it reminds the human spectator all too clearly of his own mortality. The execution of criminals necessarily evokes highly ambiguous emotions and responses, in antiquity no less than today. Crime must in some sense be punished if people are to believe that civilised life as they know it will go on; but taking the life of another person is not something that people are prepared to do lightly. It can best be done if the victim is not perceived as a person at all, but as 'foreign' or sub- or non-human or simply (as in modern warfare) as a target whose destruction is a technical and not a moral problem. Symmachus' callous remark about the suicide of twenty Saxon prisoners[89] is not the only indication that a Roman needed to have no uneasy conscience about the elimination of those who resisted the empire. Criminals are in a different category. They originate within one's own society, and may be perceived as traitors to the rules by which that society functions. Different cultures have evolved different ways of avoiding the unease involved in their physical destruction. The execution may be carried out by the community as a whole, or by several people at the same time (stoning, the firing squad); the criminal himself may be forced to perform the act from which his death results (the Athenian penalty of execution by drinking hemlock). Frequently the criminal is in some sense ejected from the community and left to try to resist the forces of nature on his own, without any of the help with which human society provides its members. The community does not directly take away the criminal's life: but it no longer protects him from the power of nature. The traditional Germanic method of execution was to leave the criminal hanging from an oak tree, sacred to Wodan, and letting nature take its course. While modern English law provides for the extreme penalty (now limited to very exceptional circumstances) to be carried out swiftly and with a minimum of physical suffering, the judge's sentence continues to be a reminder of earlier times: that the convicted criminal 'be hanged by the neck until he be dead'.

The punishment of criminals at Rome by throwing them to the wild beasts, tying them to a cross, or leaving them to burn, followed the same principle. Heinous crimes like murder or arson excluded their perpetrators from any claim to the protection of human society. Those whom a court of law had found guilty of the violence of beasts, or of endangering the lives of others through arson, were surrendered to the appropriate natural forces. Once condemned, they were physically still alive: but socially already dead. As with any criminal sentenced to death, only a formal reprieve could set aside the certainty of execution. The convicts whom Claudius forced to fight in a *naumachia* at the inauguration of his tunnelling work at the Fucine lake saluted him with the phrase 'We who are about to die salute you'; when Claudius quipped 'Or not', they took the emperor's words as such a reprieve, and refused to fight on the grounds that they had been pardoned.[90]

Famous though that phrase is, there is little to warrant the belief that it was used by gladiators. The beasts and the criminals had to die, if civilisation was to continue. That necessarily elicited anxieties about death amongst the onlookers. What the crowd came to see during the last part of the day, when the gladiators fought in the arena, was not just the destruction of yet more life (even if guilty, or at least 'unworthy'); it was the possibility of the dead coming alive again. A gladiator who demonstrated sufficient *virtus* as he fought in the arena – even if he was defeated by his opponent – might impress the assembled onlookers enough for them to give him his life back, by demanding that the giver of the games grant him his *missio*. If in the morning's *venatio* and executions the spectators saw two instances of the passage from life to death, the afternoon's gladiatorial *munus* enacted the passage from death to life: a brave fighter might rise from the socially dead, and re-join the society of the living.

What we know about the actual sequence of events that constituted the *munus* during the afternoon is largely based on the visual evidence of mosaics, tombstones, and glass and pottery lamps and tableware with representations of pairs of gladiators in combat. The interpretation of such evidence is not always straightforward; for reasons of visual interest, representations generally show different types of fighters. Like modern visual reportage, they also concentrate on what exercised people's imaginations and emotions most, especially the moment of decision. The moment when one of the gladiators was face-to-face with death was not only visually spectacular, it was also the essential point of the display, the point where what went on the arena became the reality which every onlooker dreaded: confronting their own mortality. The skills demonstrated by the combatants were far from uninteresting, because it was on them that the defeated gladiator's chances of escaping death depended; but scholars are imposing their own moral presuppositions when they imagine that the audience came simply to watch a dangerous sport like motor-racing. They came to see how men faced the necessity of dying.

There are other problems with visual evidence. It is sometimes difficult to judge whether a sequence of figures represents things going on at the same time, or in chronological succession. Only occasionally do representations (principally mosaics) give the Latin technical terms for various aspects of the activities, or report the words or sounds made by the crowd or individual participants; for that we have to rely on literary descriptions, and, as with all reporting in classical texts, we can never be certain just how typical particular evidence is. Rather less is consequently known about what actually went on in the arena than some modern accounts would suggest. That the phrase 'We who are going to die salute you' does not refer to gladiators has already been mentioned. We cannot be sure how universal the cry 'Habet, hoc habet' was when a gladiator fell to the ground.[91] Graffiti are likely to be more reliable: a wall at Beneventum has the words *Missos, missos; iug[u]la, iug[u]la*.[92] Literary references are often interested only in particular details of the show, generally without giving us any meaningful context and sometimes in order to exploit them as elements in a quite different argument.

As we have seen, some mosaics represent *venationes* together with gladiatorial combats. A Pompeian tomb relief now at Naples (figure 14) begins with a ceremonial procession, the *pompa*; that this introduced the afternoon's events is confirmed by a literary source, a Quintilianic declamation. As inscriptions show, the *pompa* was an essential part of funeral games, even when no gladiators appeared.[93] Although not all the details on this Pompeian relief are well-enough preserved to be identified by themselves, many can be reconstructed from parallels on other reliefs or on mosaics; and many of the activities and paraphernalia can be labelled with Latin technical terms supplied from literary sources. The head of the procession, on the right, is led by two lictors in togas carrying their *fasces*; the games depicted were therefore given by men who held public office as *duoviri*. Next come three figures wearing cloaks blowing the long military trumpet, the *tuba*. Mosaics tell us more about the musical instruments used in the arena: a water organ appears at Nennig and Zliten, as well as on a bronze vase found at Reims, now in the Musée du Petit Palais, Paris. Literary texts confirm the use of musical instruments: Petronius mentions the water-organ, a Quintilianic declamation the *tuba*, and Juvenal has trumpets, flutes, and pipes.[94] These similarities between literary and visual descriptions from different parts of the Roman world are significant. The rituals in the arena represent a common culture uniting Italy, Africa and the Celtic provinces in their Romanness.

The *pompa* continues with a group of four men wearing tunics who bear aloft a litter or bier with two small figures on it, possibly representing the ghosts (*manes*) of the deceased (p. 33 above; there are other, less likely, interpretations). Two further attendants in tunics are followed by an expansive figure in a toga, who can be identified as the *editor*. Next come six men carrying helmets, who may or may not be the gladiators themselves. The first two also carry small round shields used by those who fought from horseback (*equites*). There follow two men blowing horns (the *cornu*). The rear of the procession is brought up by two men leading the horses for the combat on horseback with which the fighting often began.

The actual combats are represented on the middle frieze, which is also the widest (not illustrated here). On the left, the first duel has already been decided: one of the *equites* stands with his shield raised in his left hand as a gesture of victory and a short sword in his right. His opponent lies on the ground (though he is still alive, as his head is raised). To their right, a gladiator armed in the Thracian style holds up his sword in the presence of a man with a rod, probably the umpire; men wearing tunics and holding rods are shown as umpires elsewhere,

94

e.g. on the panel representing a combat between a Thracian and a *retiarius* on the Nennig mosaic, on the Zliten mosaic, and on an oil lamp in the Musée Archéologique at Nimes. Next to them is a group of five smaller figures. It is not easy to be certain just what they are doing, but four of them are wearing tunics while the fifth, another Thracian with helmet and loincloth, is kneeling down. Perhaps the four assistants are helping the first Thracian's wounded and defeated opponent out of the arena. In the centre of the frieze there is another pair; the one on the right has been forced on to one knee, and appears to be appealing for his life by raising the digit finger of his left hand. The same gesture can also be seen on a number of terracotta oil-lamps, including one in the British Museum (figure 3), a terra sigillata beaker from Colchester (figure 12), a relief in Maastricht, the Zliten mosaic, and on Mazois' drawing of the 'tomb of Umbricius Scaurus' at Pompeii. On some representations, including the Maastricht relief, the defeated gladiator has put his shield on the ground to show that he is too exhausted to fight any more (see p. 38 f. above for his emasculated stance and figure 11). None of these reliefs shows the crowd, so they cannot confirm the widespread modern belief in the gesture of 'thumbs up' or 'thumbs down' to give expression to the audience's view as to whether the defeated gladiator should be killed or not. Indeed no visual evidence supports this belief, which is based on literary sources: Juvenal, Prudentius, and the *Anthologia Latina*: 'Even a gladiator who has been defeated in the savage arena continues to hope, although the crowd threatens him with hostile thumb.'[95] But a Munich relief shows a different symbol of reprieve at the moment when the crowd decides the fate of the defeated gladiator (figure 13). While trumpets are shown sounding in the background, he squats on the ground while his accomplice holds his sword above his head, ready to strike. Round shields and chain mail suggest that the two fighters are *equites*. From behind the trumpeters, a hand stretches out: it holds two fingers out, the sign of blessing for pagans as for Christians. The gladiator will be reprieved. Although defeated, he had demonstrated enough *virtus* to win salvation.

Other gladiators won no such blessing. Visual representations are keen to show the *coup de grace*. On the badly preserved second panel of the Pompeian relief in Naples, the defeated gladiator grasps the left knee of his victorious opponent, who thrusts his sword into his throat, possibly after having removed his helmet with his left hand. Five other figures are shown standing by, presumably the umpire and his four attendants shown before. The same mode of execution, except with the victor holding his opponent's helmet in his right hand and burying his sword in his throat with the left, is shown in Mazois' drawing (left-handed gladiators were particularly fearsome: see index). Something very similar can also be seen on a relief at Rome depicting a number of victorious combats apparently by the same man (figure 15); three of the men are kneeling in defeat, in two cases clearly grasping the heel or lower leg of the victor, who in two of the three cases clearly holds his defeated opponent by the top of the helmet before plunging his sword into his neck. On the vignette immediately above, the same man (labelled 'eundem' below) is shown raising his right digit in an appeal for mercy. Other reliefs, from Venafrum and in Bologna, show a different ritual of execution: the defeated gladiator stands or kneels quietly with his hands behind his back awaiting the victor's sword. Not all mosaics depict the same degree of orderliness in their representations of killing. An unorthodox *coup de grace* is shown on a relief from Dorres, where one *secutor* plunges his sword into the back of another, pushing it in with both hands. Knifing in the back also figures in the Villa Borghese mosaic. The disorder and confusion of the duels depicted on that mosaic is exceptional (a 'supreme monument of bad taste', in Grant's words). Most representations of death show the killer and his victim as accomplices in a ritual in which each had a prescribed role to play. Of course, a gladiator who failed to accept his execution heroically would hardly have been remembered on a relief glorifying the generosity of the *editor*. Nevertheless these representations confirm the assertions found in writers like Cicero and Pliny about the bravery which the Roman public expected of a gladiator.[96]

The successful gladiator raises his right arm, holding his sword, as a sign of his victory over death; the theme was particularly suitable for funerary reliefs, such as one of a *secutor* in the Museo d'Arte Antica in Milan (with his pet dog – a symbol of death – by his heel). Other examples are on the Villa Borghese mosaic, and that at Augst in Switzerland (figure 9b), where the gladiator is left-handed. Earlier in the day, the audience had seen the elimination of evil enacted in the victory of man over nature in the *venatio*, and the very much more problematic elimination of evil in the execution of the traitors and enemies of Roman society at midday. It could leave the arena in the evening after having seen examples of the triumph of human virtue over death. Everyone had been reminded of their mortality: but whether a particular gladiator had won or lost, had fought bravely enough to be reprieved or had met the death that everyone had to face, the ritualisation of the encounter with death had put death in its place.

NOTES

1 P. Sabbatini-Tumolesi, *Gladiatorum Paria. Annunci di spettacoli gladiatorii a Pompeii* (Rome, 1980). ILS 5143: gl.par.XXX et eor.supp. pugn.pompeis . . . ven[atio] erit.; ILS 5145: venatio legitima; CIL IV.9983a: Cruciarii ven[atio] et vela er[unt]; cf. AE 1975.256: an honorific inscription from Paestum was erected 'Because he put on twenty pairs of gladiators as well as a *venatio*, which he adorned by providing convicts' (this *editor* also won the favour of the city councillors by providing each one with a gift of 20 HS): Quot viginti paria gladiatorum edidit adiecta venatione . . . quam . . . noxeorum comparatione adornavit. Lists of animals: ILS 5053 (p. 9 above), CIL IV.1190 and 1184.
2 Sabbatini-Tumolesi, *Gladiatorum Paria*.
3 CIL IV.1181; ILS 5143, ILS 5154: vela erunt; CIL IV.1180.
4 ILS 5146.
5 Cicero, *Ad Fam*. 2, 8.1.
6 *Historia Augusta*, Claudius Gothicus 5.5.
7 K. Dunbabin *Mosaics*, 67–9 and pls. 52 f.; A.Beschaouch, 'La mosaique de chasse à l'amphithéâtre découverte à Smirat en Tunesie', CRAI (1966), 134–57.
8 CIL X, 1074. Beneventum: ILS 5063a. ferae dentatae: ILS 5054. Minturnae: ILS 5062; orientales: ILS 5055; Africanae: ILS 5059, also Pliny, *Letters* 6, 34.3; Libycae: 5060 and 5061.
9 ILS 5062; 6333; 5146; 5063a; ILS 9406; AE 1977.859 = CIL VIII.1887/16510. The five days at Praeneste (ILS 6256) are *ludi*, not a *munus*.
10 Livy 39, 22.1–2.
11 Livy 44, 18.8.
12 Pliny NH 8, 20/53; cf. Seneca, *De brevitate vitae* 13.6.
13 Pliny NH 8, 24/64 and 40/96.
14 Pompey: Pliny NH 8, 2/4; 7/20, 21; 20/53; 24/64; 28/70; 29/71; Cassius Dio 39, 38.2–5; Cicero, *Ad Fam*. 7, 1.3. Caesar: Pliny NH 8, 20/53; 70/182; Suetonius, *Julius* 37.2; Cassius Dio 43, 22.23. Augustus: Pliny NH 8, 24/64; *Res gestae* 22; Cassius Dio 61, 9.1. 13 BC: 54, 26.1. 2 BC: 55, 10.7/8. AD 12: 56, 27.4/5. Caligula: 59, 7.3.

Nero: 60, 7.3; 61, 9.1. Titus: 66, 25.1. Trajan: 68, 15. Further details in G. Jennison, *Animals for Show and Pleasure in Ancient Rome* (Manchester, 1937), and J.M.C. Toynbee, *Animals in Roman Life and Art* (London, 1973).

15 MUNIFICENTIA coins, *Coins of the Roman Empire in the British Museum* IV (1940), 300–1, nos. 1838–42, pl. 45, nos. 1, 2; 788, 794 n. 543, pl. 105, no. 13. Severus: Dio 76,1 (with coins, CREBM V (1950), plates 34.4 (Caracalla), 35.19 (Septimius), 39.6 (Geta); 40.17 (Caracalla)). *Historia Augusta*, Gordiani Tres 3, 6.7; Probus 19.

16 Seneca, *De ira* 3, 43.2; *Liber spectaculorum* 18 and 19; 12–14.

17 Notably in the work of C. Levi-Strauss; cf. K. Tester, *Animals and Society: the Humanity of Animal Rights* (Routledge, 1991).

18 *De Constantia Sapientis* 11 f.; T.E.J. Wiedemann, *Adults and Children in the Roman Empire* (London, 1989), 27–30. I am not persuaded by recent attempts to minimise the place of beating in adult–child relationships in antiquity.

19 Toynbee, pp. 60–9. For St Paul and the lion, see p. 154 f. below.

20 *The Times*, London, Monday 5 August 1991.

21 Plutarch, *Pompey* 14; Suetonius, *Galba* 6.1; *Liber spectaculorum* 1. For other performing elephants at Rome, cf. Aelian, *Historia Animalium* 2, 11.

22 Ausonius, *Epigrams* 30: pictura subditi ubi leo una sagitta a Gratiano occisus est.

> Quod leo tam tenui patitur sub arundine letum
> Non vires ferri, sed ferientis agunt.

23 *Anthologia Palatina* 7, 626 (Loeb, 2 p. 334 f.); cf. Strabo 2, 5.33.

24 Sallust, *Jugurtha* 6.1; J. Aymard, *Essai sur les chasses romaines des origines à la fin de la siècle des Antonins* (Paris, 1951); J.K. Anderson, *Hunting in the Ancient World* (Berkeley, 1985).

25 *Latin Anthology* 186. 7f. = p. 128 ed. Shackleton-Bailey:

> vis humana potest rabiem mutare ferinam;
> ecce hominem parvum belua magna timet . . .
> fit moriens ludus, qui fuit ante pavor.

26 J. Mackenzie, *The Empire of Nature* (Manchester, 1988), 37.

27 H.M. Hubbell, 'Ptolemy's Zoo', CJ 31 (1935); Athenaeus 5, 201; Suetonius, *Nero* 31.1: cum multitudine omnis generis pecudum et ferarum; *Historia Augusta*, Gordiani Tres 33,1.2.

28 Hunting mosaics: Toynbee, p. 25: esp. hunting for the games. 263–78; p. 292 on 59 Orpheus floor-mosaics. Varro, *De re rustica* 3, 13; cf. Pliny NH 8, 78/211.

29 *Letters* 7.5, sine arte . . . mera homicidia.

30 Suetonius, *Claudius* 34.2.

31 For an excellent recent study of some of the issues raised by this topic, see K.M. Coleman, 'Fatal Charades: Roman Executions Staged as Mythological Enactments', JRS 80 (1990), 44–73.

32 Cicero, II *Verrines* 5.163 ff.; 1, 13, 122; Suetonius, *Galba* 9.1; R. MacMullen, 'Judicial Savagery in the Late Empire', *Changes in the*

Roman Empire (Princeton, 1990), chapter 20.

33 For Carthaginian executions, cf. Polybius 1, 85 ff.

34 F. Millar, 'Condemnation to hard labour in the Roman empire', *Papers of the British School at Rome* 52 (1984), 124–47. Constantine: CTh. 9, 24.1 (1).

35 Καὶ ἦν ἡ θεὰ τῶν αἰκισμῶν ἐνηλλαγμένη, Eusebius, *Historia Ecclesiastica* 8.10 = PG 20.764; cf. Tertullian, *De spectaculis* 19: tam crudeliter impendatur.

36 *Digest* 47, 9.9; cf. T. Mayer-Maly, 'Vivicomburium', RE IX A.1, 497 f.

37 *Digest* 48, 13.7; 48, 19.8.2.

38 Suetonius, *Galba* 9.1.

39 These issues have been explored by M. Foucault, *Discipline and Punish: the birth of the prison* (Penguin, 1977) = *Surveiller et Punir* (Paris, 1975).

40 *Digest* 48. 19.28.15: solacio sit cognatis et adfinibus.

41 Pseudo-Quintilian, *Declamationes maiores* 274. 13 (Winterbottom).

42 Seneca, *De clementia* 1, 22.1: transeamus ad alienas iniurias, in quibus vindicandis haec tria lex secuta est, quae princeps quoque sequi debet: aut ut eum, quem punit, emendet, aut ut poena eius ceteros meliores reddat, aut ut sublatis malis securiores ceteri vivant.

43 *Gorgias* 525D, etc.

44 Valerius Maximus 1, 7.4.

45 Seneca, *Letters* 47.5; Livy 3, 16.3.

46 Plutarch, *Cato the Elder* 21.4.

47 Puteoli: AE 1971.88; full translation in J. Gardner and T. Wiedemann, *The Roman Household* (London, 1991), no. 22; Cumae: AE 1971.89 A II, l.3 f.

48 *Attic Nights* 5, 14.10; 17.27.

49 Suetonius, *Julius* 74.

50 Suetonius, *Augustus* 67.

51 Seneca, *De ira* 3, 40; Cassius Dio 54, 23.1 ff.

52 *Digest* 48, 8.11.2 (Modestinus).

53 CTh. 9, 12.1; Marcianus, *Digest* 18, 1.42.

54 *Liber spectaculorum* 7, 7–10. For the text, see p. 84.

55 *Sententiae Pauli* 5, 17.3; cf also Ulpian, *Collatio leg.Mos.* 11, 7.4; CTh. 9, 18.1; Ulpian, *Digest* 48, 19.8 §12; *Digest* 49, 18.3.

56 Modestinus, *Digest* 48, 19.31.

57 Tacitus, *Annals* 12, 56; Suetonius, *Claudius* 14.; *Digest* 48, 19.28 §15: nonnulli etiam ad bestias hos damnaverunt; Cassius Dio, 59, 10.1 and 3; Suetonius, *Nero* 12.1: neminem occidit, ne noxiorum quidem.

58 Eusebius, *Historia Ecclesiastica* 5, 1.47 = PG 82; Gregory of Nazianzen, *Oratio* 3, 69 and 71.

59 Strabo 6, 273.

60 The accounts of the sufferings of Ignatius and Polycarp are quoted by Eusebius, *Historia Ecclesiastica* 3, 36 and 4, 15. I have used the translation by M. Staniforth in the Penguin Classics *Early Christian*

Writings (Harmondsworth, 1968). For a discussion, see R. Lane Fox, *Pagans and Christians* (London, 1986), chapter 9.
61 Eusebius, *Historia Ecclesiastica* 5, 1.
62 Tacitus, *Annals* 15, 44.4.
63 Not 'solito loco', *Passion of Perpetua and Felicity* 21.7; see also p. 151 below. The bodies of those executed by crucifixion or burning could obviously not be removed from public gaze like this: p. 75 above.
64 Pliny, *Panegyric* 34 f. (Trajan); *Historia Augusta*, Hadrian 18.9.
65 K.M. Coleman, 'Fatal Charades: Roman executions staged as mythological enactments', JRS 80 (1990), 44–73.
66 Josephus, *Antiquities* 19.94, Suetonius, *Gaius* 56.2 f.; T.P. Wiseman, *Catullus and his World* (Cambridge, 1985), 258 f.

66a   Qualiter in Scythica religatus rupe Prometheus
      adsiduam nimio pectore pavit avem,
      Nuda caledonio sic viscera praebuit urso
      non falsa pendens in cruce Laureolus.
      Vivebant laceri membris stillantibus artus
      inque omni nusquam corpore corpus erat.
      denique supplicium [†dignum tulit; ille parentis†]
      vel domini iugulum foderat ense nocens,
      templa vel arcano demens spoliaverat auro,
      subdiderat saevas vel tibi, Roma, faces.
      vicerat antiquae sceleratus crimina famae,
      in quo, quae fuerat fabula, poena fuit.

67 'Speciosa Locis Morataque Recte', *Homo Viator* (1987) 80–8 = *Roman Culture and Society* (Oxford, 1991), p. 571.
68 Tertullian, *Apologeticum* 15.5; cf. *Ad nationes* 1, 10.47.
69 F. Dupont, *L'Acteur Roi* (Paris, 1985); C.A.Barton, 'The Scandal of the Arena', *Representations* 27 (1989), 1 ff.
70 *Anthologia Palatina* 2, 184; Coleman p. 60.
71 Pliny, *NH* 9, 4–5 and n. 21 above; Babrius 80, 3–4.
72 Suetonius, *Nero* 12.2.
73 Plutarch, *Moralia* 554B = *De ser. num. vindic.* 9.
74 *Liber spectaculorum* 8. Cf. R.K. Ehrman, *Mnemosyne* 40 (1987), 422–5; Coleman p. 63.
75 *First Epistle of Clement* §6.2; cf. Tertullian, *De Idololatria* = CSEL 20.39 ff; 40, 6.9 ff.
76 *Liber spectaculorum* 8.30.
77 Tertullian, *Ad nationes* 1, 10.47; Suetonius, *Domitian* 7.1; *Digest* 48, 8.4(2); Suetonius, *Domitian* 10.5; cf. T.E.J. Wiedemann, 'An Early Irish Eunuch?', *Liverpool Classical Monthly* 11.8 (October 1986), 139 f. with other examples.
78 Apuleius, *Metamorphoses* 10, 22; 29; 34.
79 *Liber spectaculorum* 5.
80 Coleman p. 64 and n. 173 on bestiality elsewhere: she concludes that Apuleius' account is 'less fanciful than is usually supposed'.
81 *Antiquities* 10, 1.6; cf. the three youths untouched by *crematio*, 10, 10.5. For ancient readings of the Daniel story, see P.R. Davies,

THE CONTEXT

'Daniel in the Lions' Den', in L. Alexander (ed.), *Images of Empire* (Sheffield, 1991), 160–78.

82 *Passion of Perpetua and Felicity* 19.5 f.

83 D-S I, 1574 fig. 2083; Coleman p. 59 n. 134.

84 Suetonius, *Julius* 39.4; Appian, *Civilia* 2, 102, who thought that they were criminals and prisoners taken in war; Cassius Dio 43, 23.3; Suetonius, *Julius* 39.3, Pliny NH 8, 22. On aquatic displays: K. Coleman, 'Launching into History: Aquatic Displays in the Early Empire', JRS 83 (1993), 48–74.

85 *Res gestae* 23, Dio 55.10.7.

86 Tacitus, *Annals* 12, 56; Suetonius, *Claudius* 21.6.

87 Tacitus, *Annals* 12.56; Dio 61.9.5.

88 Dio 66, 25.3; 66, 25.4; Dio 67.8.2.

89 *Letters* 2, 46.

90 Suetonius, *Claudius* 21.6.

91 Applied to the death of Hercules by Seneca, *Hercules Oeteus* 1472; Donatus, commentary on Terence's *Andria* 1,1.56.

92 ILS 5134.

93 Quintilian, *Declamationes maioree* 9,6; AE 1976.144 = 1947.53, from Herculaneum.

94 Petronius, *Satyricon* 36.6; Quintilian, *Declamationes* 9.6; Juvenal 3, 34.

95 Juvenal 3, 36; Prudentius *Contra Symmachum*, 2, 1099; *Anthologia Latina*: 415, 28 R.= p. 413 Shackleton-Bailey:

> sperat et in saeva victus gladiator harena
> sit licet infesto pollice turba minax.

96 Cicero, *Tusculans* 2, 17.41; p. 38 above.

Figure 1 The Corn Exchange, Leeds (1861–3); one of many nineteenth-century buildings whose form was inspired by that of Roman amphitheatres, even though this one was intended for quite different functions.

Figure 2 The Colosseum on a coin of Alexander Severus (AD 223).

Figure 3 Terracotta lamp with a representation of two gladiators, one raising his finger to admit defeat.

Figure 4 Terracotta lamp in the shape of a gladiator's helmet.

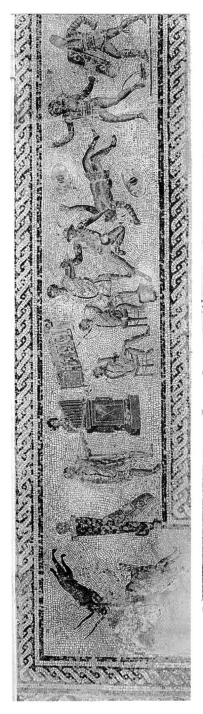

Figure 5 (a and b) Scenes from the 'Villa di Dar Buc Amméra' mosaic (Zliten, Libya), representing a *venatio*, executions and gladiators, with orchestral accompaniment.

Figure 5 (c and d) Scenes from the 'Villa di Dar Buc Amméra' mosaic.

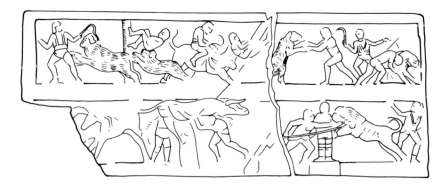

Figure 6 Relief from Apri (Thrace), representing a *venatio* with bull-
and bear-leaping, a *pyrricha* with a dancing bear, and an execution
(bottom right).

Figure 7 Execution scene: a woman tied onto a bull is mauled by a
leopard. The crouching figure holding a shield is presumably the
confector (executioner). Terracotta from Kalaa Scira, N. Africa.

Figure 8 Ivory diptych commemorating the consular games of Areobindus in AD 506, with acrobats and bears (bottom left) and *venatio* (right).

Figure 9a Two *equites* in combat.

9b A *secutor* raises his sword to claim victory over a *retiarius*.

9c A gladiator puts down his shield to admit defeat.

9d Murmillo strikes a *retiarius* in the thigh, while the *retiarius* deals a death-blow to his opponent's neck.

Figure 9 Four scenes from a mosaic representing a *munus* found at Augusta Raurica (Augst, near Basel, Switzerland) in 1971.

Figure 10 A gladiator puts down his shield to admit defeat. Wall-painting from Colchester (Britain).

Figure 11 Funerary relief showing a victorious and a defeated gladiator.

Figure 12 Terra sigillata beaker with a *secutor* and a *retiarius*, who holds up his finger in an appeal for mercy.

Figure 13 A defeated gladiator awaits the death-blow; the hand held
out in blessing on the left shows that he will be granted his life.

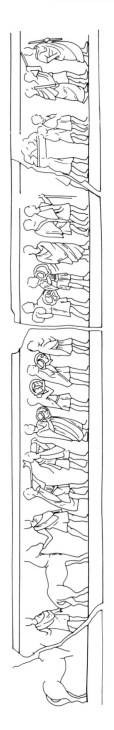

Figure 14 Funerary relief representing the *pompa* with which a gladiatorial *munus* began.

Figure 15 Gladiator's tombstone, depicting several of the combats in which he emerged victorious.

COMBAT OF
WOMEN GLADIATORS.

Figure 16 Two female gladiators, 'Amazonia', 'Achillia', said to have been 'given their freedom' (i.e. *missio*).

Figure 17 Tombstone of a gladiator bearing the victor's palm; the inscription, in Greek, reads 'The Familia [erected it] to Satornilos, to remember him'.

3

THE GLADIATORS:
BACKGROUND AND STATUS

One of the components of the ambivalent Roman attitude to gladiatorial contests is the frequency with which moralists both emphasise and express their revulsion at the tendency for free men, sometimes even free men of high status, to choose a career as a 'professional' gladiator. The fact that this expressed a moral attitude should warn us against assuming that it occurred as frequently in practice as it does in literature. In historical narratives too instances of free persons, especially if they were senators or equestrians, who chose to appear as gladiators are over-emphasised precisely because they were unusual. The gladiator's place at the furthest margin of the Roman social world implied that, if that world were properly ordered, such cases would not have existed at all. A person with standing in the community who wished to fight as a gladiator not out of necessity but for pleasure was openly and demonstratively threatening the status-distinctions on which Roman society was based, and claiming that he was beyond the reach of the laws with which successive emperors tried to codify these distinctions. Paradoxically it was those who held the imperial office who were the most tempted to demonstrate that they were above the laws applying to ordinary members of the elite by participating in gladiatorial contests. Very few of them went as far as Nero did, and broke the laws forbidding senators to appear on the stage as actors; but several appeared in the arena.

Whatever the numerical proportion of free men, including Roman citizens, who chose to make a career as professional gladiators, they were assimilated in status to the other categories of persons from whom gladiators were drawn: defeated enemies, and condemned criminals of servile status. While most defeated enemies were simply sold as slaves or executed, or forced to execute each other, some clearly received specific training in a Roman *ludus* before being forced to fight in the arena. They included Spartacus and the seventy-eight other gladiators who broke out from the *ludus* near Capua owned by Lentulus Batiatus. But we may note that Plutarch, writing at the end of the first century AD, was shocked that these trainee gladiators had not been sent to the *ludus* as a punishment for criminal behaviour, and that he refers to 'the wickedness of the man who had bought them'.[1] Plutarch seems to assume that in his own time most slaves who found their way into a gladiatorial *ludus* had been sent there by their masters as a punishment. This may reveal a difference between his own time and the late republic, when the high level of warfare throughout the Mediterranean and the consequent availability of prisoners-of-war made these the primary component amongst gladiators. Spartacus himself is said to have been captured in war and sold at Rome.[2] Cicero assumes that gladiators are bought from the *catasta*, the slave-dealer's platform, as does Livy,[3] though these references could be to troupes of ready-trained gladiators being sold by the *lanista* to the person who wished to provide the actual contest (the *editor*). Atticus is known to have bought a troupe of trained gladiators as a financial investment in 56 BC (the cost of the investment was repaid after just two matches).[4] While it is very likely that these men had at one point been captured enemies, we cannot tell how long that had been before they came to be trained as gladiators.

The marginal position of such captives in Roman eyes is clear. Defeated military opponents were enemies of the Romans who had refused to accept the benefits of subjection to Roman order. The Romans notoriously convinced themselves that no one might legitimately oppose their rule: to fight Rome was to rebel. Such rebels had forfeited any right to a place within Roman society: they had excluded themselves from the community of civilized peoples, and deserved death. Out of their clemency, the Romans might choose to give them a new life. They might 'save' them (*servare*) and make them slaves (*servi*): whatever the real etymology of the Latin word for slaves, Roman writers explicitly state that a slave is so-called because he has been 'saved' from the death he deserves.[5] This applied to whole peoples as well as individual soldiers: 'The nations which could safely be pardoned, I chose to save rather than to eradicate', boasts Augustus.[6] But if the enemy had behaved with atrocious barbarity, or perhaps was just too dangerous, the Romans had every right not to exercise such clemency. Three centuries later, having defeated the Germanic Bructeri, the emperor Constantine had those whose 'barbarism and treachery made them useless as slaves' executed in the arena, probably at Trier.[7]

Rebels deserved execution: that execution might be carried out by crucifixion, like that of Spartacus' defeated followers, or in the arena, like the killing of tens of thousands of Jewish prisoners of war in the shows organised by Titus and Vespasian in various provinces in the aftermath of the conquest of Jerusalem.[8] To make them fight as gladiators was actually to give these men the favour of winning back their lives by showing that they were exceptionally brave: occasionally we are told of war-captives who so impressed the Roman audience by their fighting spirit that they were granted their lives or even their freedom, such as some of the Britons captured by Claudius during his occupation of southern Britain in AD 43.[9]

Since a slave's physical survival was perceived as a favour granted initially by whoever had decided to let him live in the first place (whether the soldier who might have killed him in battle or the owner of his mother when he was born, who might have ordered him to be exposed), and thereafter constantly in the gift of the *paterfamilias* of the household, membership of which gave the slave access to shelter, food and clothing, it followed that Roman owners had the right to revoke that favour at any time if the slave did not constantly show his appreciation. There were no moral qualms about punishing slaves whose behaviour fell short of their owners' demands; the owners of such slaves might, for instance, take steps to ensure that such slaves would never be manumitted, even after the owner's death; clauses to this effect appear frequently in Roman wills.[10] Since the right to inflict punishment was derived from the principle that the slave owed his very life to his master, there was no question that such punishment might include execution. On occasions of civil unrest such as Spartacus' rebellion, Roman military commanders would take it upon themselves to crucify slaves who had deserted their masters; but if the slaves' legal owners could be found, the assumption was that the right to punish lay with them. Augustus claimed that after his campaign against Sextus Pompeius in 36 BC, 'I captured about thirty thousand of the slaves who had fled from their masters and taken up arms against the Republic and returned them to their masters for punishment.'[11]

Condemnation to crucifixion or to death by being thrown to wild beasts was perceived as the proper penalty for someone of servile status who had chosen to reject the rules of civilised Romans. The wicked and the rebellious had acted in a way that put them outside society. Some Christians, too, marked themselves out as not belonging to the cities of this world (only some, of course, and those often disowned as extremists by their bishops). These people had chosen to deny their social existence, and the community reacted accordingly. As Eusebius says of the Christians martyred in the arena: 'You [sc. the persecuting authorities] treat us as though we have no existence.'[12]

There was another penalty which a Roman judge could impose: condemnation to a gladiatorial school, *ad ludos*.[13] It may be worth repeating that, in comparison with the standard forms of execution, the punishment of handing one's slave over to a professional trainer, *lanista*, to become a gladiator, was lenient. There was a significant difference between condemning a criminal to the beasts or the flames, and to the gladiatorial school. The criminal condemned *ad ludos* was a socially 'dead man' who had a chance of coming alive again. The late Roman *Collatio Mosaicarum et Romanarum Legum*, citing Ulpian, envisages that a criminal condemned *ad ludos* would be allowed to retire from fighting after three years, and be granted his freedom again after five.[14] Of course that only applied if the gladiator survived: but in other categories of punishment, too, such as hard labour in the mines (*ad opus* or *ad metallum*), the chances of survival might be minimal. Pliny couples those condemned to forced labour with those condemned to train as gladiators when he reports to Trajan that many such convicts had in fact avoided undergoing the penalty to which they had been sentenced, presumably by Roman governors of Bithynia.[15] If a convict fought bravely enough, the community might be sufficiently impressed to be prepared to give him back his life. A brave fighter might rise from the dead, and re-join the society of the living. That was not in the gift of the president of the games, magistrate or even emperor, but in the gift of society as a whole: of the Roman people, present in the amphitheatre.

The penalty *ad ludos* does not therefore figure in lists of types of execution. Again, it seems to have been the right of every slave-owner up to the first century AD. Thus the later emperor Vitellius, angry with a favourite slave, handed him over to be punished in this way.[16] Augustus' legislation on manumission (in the *Lex Aelia Sentia*) specified that slaves who had been condemned *ad ludos* or *ad bestias* could never attain Roman citizenship on manumission – implying, of course, that some of them would be expected to survive.[17] As with other forms of public punishment, emperors imposed ever tighter controls over the years.

Regulations ascribed to Hadrian by the *Historia Augusta* forbade masters from executing their slaves and insisted that they had to be condemned by state judges, and also that 'Male or female slaves might not be sold to pimps or to trainers of gladiators unless due cause had been proved', implicitly before a court of law.[18] Unfortunately the legal texts preserved in the *Digest* and other parts of Justinian's *Corpus Juris* make virtually no reference to the penalty *ad ludos*. The reason why most such references made by earlier jurists will have been excised from Tribonian's compilation is presumably that, like crucifixion, *ad ludos* had ceased to be one of the penalties imposed by the state from the late fourth century AD on (see Chapter 4). Laws on *lanistae* do not survive, except when they coincidentally make an unconnected legal point: e.g. whether sale or hire was intended in an agreement that a gladiator who dies will have the owner compensated by 1,000 denarii, but only 20 if he survives the contest.[19]

It is hard to say from surviving legal texts (where references to *ad ludos* punishment have been erased) what condemnation *ad ludos* was thought in the pre-Constantinian period to have been an appropriate punishment for. Rhetorical writers associate it with murder, arson, and the sacrilegious crime of temple-robbery: 'I trained as a gladiator – I spent my time among the sacrilegious, arsonists, and murderers',[20] although legal texts and Martial's poem on the execution of the bandit Laureolus suggest that these crimes warranted the death-penalty.[21] Whether or not such condemned criminals constituted the great majority of gladiators, what they had in common with those gladiators of free birth was that they ought not to have existed.

Those who trained as gladiators included men of free birth who had chosen to take upon themselves the disciplines and dangers of living like condemned slaves. While epigraphical evidence cannot say anything about a man's motives for becoming a gladiator, it certainly confirms that the citizen who took the gladiator's oath was no literary fiction. Pompeian graffiti refer to men with names like Lucius Sempronius, Quintus Petillius, and Lucius Fabius as gladiators; these are the names of free-born Roman citizens. On a fragmentary list of the gladiatorial family of C. Salvius Capito from Venusia, at least nine of the twenty-eight names seem to be those of free men.[22] In the Greek world, too, Roman citizens are epigraphically attested as gladiators: a man buried at Patras in the second or third century AD who had fought as a 'Thracian' bore the three names of a Roman citizen.[23]

As we have seen, the literary sources heavily emphasise the utter degradation of the professional gladiator; such a man had freely chosen to assimilate himself to the groups that marked the limits of Roman society. Moralists and satirists tell us that he had to take an oath to accept forms of chastisement that the law otherwise only allowed to be inflicted on slaves. Seneca compares the binding power of the promise to follow Stoic moral teaching with the power of the gladiator's oath:

> The words of this most noble oath are the same as those of that most dishonourable one: to be burnt (i.e., branded), to be chained up, and to be killed by an iron weapon. A binding condition is imposed on those who hire their hands out to the arena and consume food and drink which they are to pay back in blood, that they should suffer such things even if they do not wish to.[24]

There seems to have been a standard formula for the words of the gladiator's oath. In the *Satyricon* (almost contemporary with Seneca's letters), Petronius describes how his anti-heroes Encolpius and Giton hope to escape detection by masquerading as gladiators:

> We swore the oath following Eumolpus' words: to be burnt, to be chained up, to be beaten, and to be killed by an iron weapon, and whatever else Eumolpus might have ordered. Just like real gladiators, we assigned our bodies and our souls to our master in the most formal way.[25]

That the Tribunes of the Plebs (who continued under the early principate to have the residual function of protecting ordinary citizens against abuses of power) exercised some formal control over the phrasing of the oath, at any rate by the early second century AD, is suggested by Juvenal's remark that he 'will write out the conditions and imperious words of the trainer without any Tribune objecting'.[26]

Those men of free birth – especially those who were Roman citizens – who chose to become gladiators abandoned the privileges and protection due to their status. Their motives for doing this are obscure. Ancient sources make several suggestions, some more rhetorically coloured than others. The Elder Seneca complains that the most suitable military material is stolen from the call-up in order to undergo gladiatorial instead of military training; the implication that some young men preferred risking a few years as a gladiator to the twenty or twenty-five years in distant provinces required by military service in the legions need not be as far-fetched as all that, but Seneca's point is really to emphasise the seriousness of military virtue, with the moral degradation of the gladiator mentioned as a contrast.[27] Poverty is mentioned as a motive by several writers; again, the literary context is frequently a rhetorical one, with gladiators being specified only because they emphasise the depth of degradation to which poverty may force a free man. Thus one of the rhetorical exercises ascribed to Quintilian talks of someone who took the gladiator's oath in order to earn the money to give his father a proper funeral. This theme does not appear only in the Latin world: the Syro-Greek satirist Lucian tells the story of a Scythian called Sisinnes, who volunteered to fight as a gladiator at Amastris on the Black Sea, in order to earn the ten thousand drachmae required to ransom a friend from captivity.[28] And the idea that poverty forces free men to sell themselves to the rich by fighting as gladiators occurs in Christian polemics against Graeco-Roman culture. In the second century AD, Tatian refers to 'men who are forced to sell themselves to be killed because of their lack of means; the poor man sells himself, and the rich man buys him to become a killer, so that he who is hungry kills in order to have something, while the rich man buys gladiators in order to have some killing'.[29]

But literary references to free men as gladiators are found in other contexts where they are not part of a moral invective against such spectacles. Two Atellan farces, of uncertain date but perhaps second century BC, bear the titles '*Pomponius auctoratus*' and '*Bucco auctoratus*'. More specific literary references to particular individuals who at some point in their lives trained or fought as gladiators are more difficult to interpret. When Cassius Dio discusses Septimius Severus' decision after having obtained power in AD 193 to recruit the Praetorian Guard from provincial legions rather than from Italians, his statement that 'this ruined the young people of Italy, who became bandits and gladiators instead of soldiers', contains a moral evaluation first and foremost, not an economic analysis.[30] References to free men as gladiators in rhetoric may be largely statements of moral disapproval, though presumably with some basis in fact. Cicero says that one of Catiline's associates, C. Marcellus, had gone to train as a gladiator at Capua.[31] Citizens may sometimes have received gladiatorial training for a period as young men, without subsequently earning their living as professionals: Cicero cites some words of Lucilius (mid-second century BC) about a Q. Velocius who as a 'boy' (*puer*) fought as a Samnite; Velocius may or may not have been a real person.[32] When Julius Caesar prepared a gladiatorial spectacle of unprecedented splendour to commemorate his daughter Julia, he asked both senators and equestrians who had experience of fighting to train some of the gladiators he had bought, as well as the usual professional *lanistae*; Suetonius states explicitly that autograph letters of Caesar's survived in which he requested these trainers to provide instruction.[33] This would seem to confirm that in the first century BC there were some equestrians and even senators who had undergone enough training themselves to train others.

The motive ascribed in literary sources to those free men of higher social status who chose to become gladiators tends to be moral rather than economic: a lust to do battle. When it became clear during the reign of Tiberius that Rome's military expansion was now at an end, the idea that men with an innate taste for fighting should choose to become gladiators so that they could find enemies to do battle with even in peacetime became a literary commonplace.[34] Christian critics of Roman culture took up the theme: for Tertullian, the fact that lust for fighting leads young men with leisure to become gladiators is an indication of the moral bankruptcy of the Roman elite.[35] Moralising passages of this sort do not of course support the view that the institution as such functioned as a replacement for aggression in battle (p. 39 above). Not all these free men who had some gladiatorial training should be categorised as professional gladiators. Some wanted a degree of training in handling weapons, others were rich men engaging in a private pastime. Both groups included emperors. Inscriptions attest the presence of *lanistae* in *juventus*-organisations; demonstration duels with weapons appear to have taken place at the annual *Juvenalia*.[36] The ascription of gladiatorial interests to emperors raises a number of particular issues which will be discussed in Chapter 5. There are occasions where hostile sources are simply uttering abuse at an unsuccessful or (in the eyes of the senatorial elite which created the historical tradition) unpopular emperor when they accuse him of having been a gladiator. A clear example is that of Macrinus, accused not just of having been a gladiator, but also a male prostitute (*prostibulus*).[37] A quarter of a century earlier, Commodus' wish to enter the consular office in AD 193 dressed as a gladiator was said to have led to his assassination.[38] Emperors, like gladiators, represented the limits of social existence. Like Hercules, Commodus wanted to do divine work on earth in order to achieve a place among the gods. Like Hercules, he was publicly reclassified as mad, but of course only after he had been assassinated.

Caligula's motives for appearing as a gladiator, over a century and a half earlier, may have been more like those of other members of the elite. Caligula enjoyed fighting as a Thracian, but we may note that he had not been allowed to have any military training under Tiberius.[39] Titus as a boy was said to have taken part in a pretend match in heavy armour at the *Juvenalia* in the region from which his father Vespasian's family came, against someone called Alienus. If this was supposed to have been Caecina Alienus, the consul of AD 69 and one of Vitellius' two senior generals, then the story is simply a symbolic premonition of the civil war between Vespasian and Vitellius. Under Titus' brother, Domitian, we are told about a senator who had previously fought in the arena, perhaps in a similar display.[40] The late antique *Historia Augusta* states that several 'good' as well as 'bad' emperors practised as gladiators; although the author, as a proponent of traditional (pagan) Roman practices, had strong reasons for supporting the authentically Roman nature of such games, his sources for the second-century emperors are reliable and there may be some basis for ascribing such practices to men who had had few opportunities to learn how to fight before they became commanders-in-chief of all Roman armies. They included Hadrian and Lucius Verus, when he was at Antioch in the AD 160s preparing to lead a Roman army against the Parthians.[41] The writer's view is that such training was entirely suitable for a young emperor, though not for someone who became emperor at an advanced age, like Didius Julianus. An independent source tells us that young princes such as Caracalla and Geta learnt both chariot-driving and fighting.[42]

Professional gladiators need to be distinguished from those who merely wanted some weapons-training. The reasons why a man of high-status background might wish to become a professional will have included some of those for joining the French Foreign Legion today. Apart from a desire to fight, the need to obtain a new identity looms large, in order to escape unbearable or dishonourable personal or financial circumstances. Cassius Dio suggests that, of the twenty-six equestrians formally condemned by the Senate to fight during the reign of Caligula, 'some had wasted their property, and others had practised as gladiators'.[43] For those who had been brought up to act the part of a rich man, there was very little they could do to earn a livelihood in the ancient world if they had the misfortune to lose their wealth, perhaps in an unsuccessful lawsuit or as a result of extravagance. Some became centurions, others schoolteachers. Some, like the famous Beirut *grammaticus* Marcus Probus, or the later emperor Pertinax, are said to have been both. Becoming a gladiator fell into the same category. One of the few other options open to a *déclassé* equestrian was to turn to crime, like highwaymen in early modern Europe, evoking many of the same ambivalent feelings of fascination and revulsion as gladiators. Gladiators, like highwaymen, symbolised the rejection of a normal, lawful, civilised life-style. But gladiators were more difficult to place. Bandits, highwaymen, and the French Foreign Legion all operate far away, at the geographical margins of society. Gladiators, like *déclassé* schoolteachers, appear (at least on certain occasions) in full view of the public, forced to make a living by demonstrating their accomplishments in fighting and the liberal arts respectively: skills which under ordinary circumstances were proper to the free Roman citizen of high status.

As a symbol of marginality, gladiatorial contests attracted many other kinds of marginal groups over the years; the wish of each emperor to compete with his predecessors by providing something more magnificent might lead not just to more spectacularity in terms of size or expense, but also in terms of making new and peculiar types of people fight. Such peculiarity or marginality might be quite different to that of criminals or *déclassé* senators. As early as the 40s BC, Cornelius Balbus had been accused of sentencing a Roman citizen to fight wild beasts because the man was physically handicapped. One category of gladiators was labelled *tunicati*, 'effeminates'. To impress the Armenian king Tiridates, Nero had his freedman Patrobius arrange a show at Puteoli in AD 66 in which all the fighters were African blacks; they included women and children as well as men. An inscription from Ostia honours the first man to make women fight (p. 10 above); and there are a number of visual representations of female gladiators, such as that of Amazonia and Achillia in the British Museum, and possibly those on the relief from Maastricht (figures 11 and 16). According to Tacitus, Roman women of high status, as well as male senators, fought for Nero at Rome in AD 63.[44] Domitian made women fight at night, by torchlight, and a contest of his in which women fought against dwarves was praised by Martial as winning the especial favour of the populace.[45] In this as in other matters, emperors were in an ambiguous position. They both wanted to use the shows to demonstrate through their provision of spectacles that their power was greater than that of any predecessor, and they also wished to represent themselves as upholding legality. As we have seen, a number of emperors had legislated to maintain proper distinctions between those who might and those who might not appear as gladiators. The fact that Septimius Severus banned the appearance of women at athletic contests 'in order to protect the honour of all women' suggests that it was not just under 'wicked' emperors like Nero and Domitian that some women were willing to appear in the arena. Paradoxically, the very fact that women were not expected to share male virtues enabled a female gladiator to symbolise that *virtus* as an abstract quality.[46]

That the conditions under which gladiators trained and lived – in terms of both material shortcomings and of a higher than average statistical risk of death – were not those that most people would choose today does not need to be said. Even by the standards of a pre-industrial society, they could be so unacceptable as to make those who had been forced to undergo them against their will rebel on occasion, or to commit suicide. In one of his moral letters, Seneca describes the suicides of two German prisoners-of-war; one of them choked himself to death in a lavatory with one of the sponges fixed to a sharp stick which the Romans used to clean themselves, another put his head between the moving spokes of the wheel of the cart taking him to the amphitheatre. But we may note that Seneca does not ascribe their despair to the material conditions of a *ludus*, but to their shame at being forced to appear in a public spectacle. Three centuries later Symmachus tells a similar story, except that on this occasion twenty captured German warriors killed each other while waiting to appear in a show; again, their despair is ascribed to shame, not the conditions under which they were being kept.[47] However appalled some modern scholars may affect to be at the material conditions of gladiators, slave or free – including their life-expectancy – we have to judge them by the material standards of other similar groups in the Roman world. The conditions leading to the break-out of Spartacus and seventy-eight fellow-gladiators from the *ludus* near Capua owned by Lentulus Batiatus were not typical, even of the late republic. As we have seen, Plutarch was shocked that these men had been sent to the *ludus* as a punishment for criminal behaviour, and he speaks of 'the wickedness of the man who had bought them'.[48]

The complete social deracination that went with their status as slaves was not the least of the factors that made the lives of slave gladiators miserable. Spartacus' fellow trainees included men of Celtic, Germanic and Thracian origin; as in any household containing large numbers of slaves (in antiquity or later), there was an intentional ethnic mix among the trainees in Batiatus' *ludus* in order to minimise the danger that they might develop any feeling of social cohesion amongst themselves which might free them from the slave's one formal social relationship, his absolute dependence on his master. What was curious about the gladiatorial *ludi* was that the social status of every trainee was assimilated to the absolute dependence of a slave. A free man who became a gladiator formally abjured any rights he had as a citizen.

Like the gladiator who was a bought slave, the free gladiator emphasised the fact that he was an outsider. Gladiators' tombstones frequently mention their ethnic origin ('*natione* . . . '), even where the gladiator in question was a Roman citizen and 'ethnicity' in fact simply meant the municipality of origin. Among the Roman citizens whose *natio* is referred to included in Dessau's *Inscriptiones Latinae Selectae* there is M. Antonius Exochus from Alexandria, who fought at Rome as a Thracian in Trajan's games (5088, cf. 5089, not a Roman citizen); a Tungrian called M. Ulpius Felix, buried at Rome by his freedwoman wife; at Nimes in southern France, a Spaniard and an Arab (5087, 5096) as well as a Greek who was not a Roman citizen, though presumably free since the woman who erected his tomb describes herself as his *coniunx* (5095; while the word *coniunx* is not always to be read as a technical term, we have no need to doubt that, like some other Greek gladiators, this man was married). Non-citizens include a Syrian *secutor* buried at Alicubi in Sicily (5113), a Bessian at Cadiz (5098), and a Thracian at Rome who fought as a Samnite, not as a Thracian: perhaps an example of double deracination (5085). The wish to claim a distinct ethnic background was so strong that we are told of one Pinnesis who fought as a Thracian at Bergamo in the time of the emperor Gordian that he originated from Rhaetia, which was as near to Bergamo as one could get without actually being an Italian. A *murmillo* buried at Nimes was identified by his wife as an Aeduan, a Gallic people whose territory was again not very distant; and a Florentine *secutor* was buried at Milan by his family (5115). Literary sources confirm the picture that some gladiatorial teams had no fixed base, but moved from place to place within Italy.[49] In time of famine or shortage, gladiators were among the categories of non-residents who were expelled from Rome, e.g. by Augustus during the grain crisis of AD 6–7.[50] Deracination was not just imposed upon gladiators by those in authority, it was something they could boast about. An advertisement at Pompeii emphasises the peripatetic nature of the troupe of N. Festus Ampliatus as 'famous throughout the world'.[51]

Inscriptions show that it was not just the extent of deracination with respect to place of origin that, for some at least, was apparent rather than real, but also with respect to what we would call family life. The *secutor* Urbicus from Florence was buried at the age of 22 leaving a 5-month-old daughter called

Olympias (who seems to have been looked after by a slave called Fortunensis) and his wife Laurica, with whom, the inscription states with characteristic Roman moral pride, he had lived for seven years (5115). Roman law specified restrictions on actors and professional *bestiarii* from attaining the legal privileges granted to the fathers of two legitimate children; that would only have been necessary if some such persons were assumed to have families.[52] A passage in one of Plutarch's *Moral Essays* is particularly interesting for the light it throws on assumptions about gladiators' domestic circumstances. In a discussion of the difference between the true Hellene, who acts rationally and responsibly, and the irrational barbarian, who is enslaved to the lower pleasures, Plutarch suddenly turns to the behaviour of gladiators on the evening before a mortal contest. A Greek gladiator, instead of enjoying his last supper, will be making provision for his wife and for the manumission of his slaves, presumably in his will. While this can hardly be taken as evidence that many of those who fought as gladiators, even in the Greek world, had wives and slaves depending upon them, its very irrelevance to Plutarch's argument shows that he assumed that such a domestic situation would occasion no surprise in the reader.[53] Inscriptions from Rome, Puteoli, Padua, Lyon, Nimes, Orange, Cadiz and Salonae in Dalmatia, were erected by gladiators' wives.[54] Other family members are mentioned: a *cursor* of the *ludus magnus* at Rome, Tigris, was buried by his brother Theonas. At Ostia, the *retiarius* Firmus was buried by his 'brothers' (since he had at least two names, he was presumably a citizen), though that relationship may have been metaphorical.[55] At Brixia, *amici* bury a gladiator; at Nimes, a fellow-gladiator who buried an *essedarius* made it explicit that the cost for the monument was borne by himself, *de suo*.[56]

If gladiators who were slaves could not enter into a marriage that would be recognised under Roman law, that was because the union of no slave could be recognised in the pre-Christian period as a valid marriage. That did not mean that, like other slaves, slave-gladiators could not enjoy a stable family relationship: an inscription from Nomentum refers to the 'consors' and son of a slave gladiator belonging to the imperial *ludus magnus*.[57] Spartacus himself is said to have lived with a woman from his own tribe.[58] Among the features found during the excavation of the gladiator's barracks at Pompeii in the last century was a burial jar containing the remains of a new-born infant, and the skeleton of a richly bejewelled woman who may have been the wife or lover of one of the gladiators. As for other slaves, the slave-group itself might provide the emotional bonds for those without a natural family. Prior, a *retiarius* of the *ludus magnus* at Rome, was buried by his 'convictor', the *murmillo* Juvenis. In Sicily, Flamma the Syrian was buried by his 'coarmio', Delicatus.[59]

The evidence of inscriptions is certainly not typical, since those who were commemorated were precisely those who had the social nexus for someone to provide a funeral. But the epigraphical evidence shows us what was possible. Keith Bradley, who certainly does not glorify social conditions in antiquity, concludes that 'The circumstances of gladiators therefore may have been no worse than those of other elements of the lower-class population, but that can hardly have made their conditions more tolerable.'[60] If for no other reason, gladiators, whether slave or free, were well looked after because they represented a considerable investment to the trainer. If ancient writers made disparaging remarks about the food they got, these were intended as moral statements, not records of calories. Propertius describes the *sagina* on which gladiators were fattened up as 'unspeakable' to express his disapproval of freeborn youths selling themselves to trainers: 'qui dabit immundae venalia fata saginae'. He did not mean that its nutritional value was low. Juvenal's disparaging reference to the 'miscellanea ludi' has the same moral quality, as does Tacitus' comparison of the rations which Vitellius at the height of his power distributed to his soldiers to 'gladiatoriam saginam'. If gladiators were fattened up with barley porridge, as Pliny the Elder avers had once been customary, then this will not have been because their trainers were only prepared to give them food normally reserved for animals (though the phrase 'barley eaters', *hordearii*, may just hint at the idea that gladiators were sufficiently marginal to be thought of as eating the food of animals). A more likely reason will have been to build up the body fat in order to give them the maximum possible protection against sword-cuts, and maximum weight for combat, as suggested by the third-century AD Christian Cyprian: 'inpletur in sucum cibis fortioribus corpus, ut arvinae toris membrorum moles robusta pinguescat, ut saginatus in poenam carius pereat'. We are told that on the day before a contest, they would be given a special meal, presumably with a high meat content; similar meals are given to sportsmen today in order to maximise the energy available on the day when it is required.[61] There are other indications too of the care which trainers took over their gladiators. It was recognised that a favourable climate was required for gladiatorial schools, like that of Capua and Ravenna, where 'the place has been found to be so healthy that the government has ordered gladiators to be maintained and trained there'. While medical texts illustrate the excruciating wounds that gladiators might sustain in combat, they also show that trainers tried to ensure that they had the best medical attention that was available in antiquity: Galen himself spent some time looking after gladiators, and gained a great deal of his empirical knowledge of anatomy from examining their wounds. Scribonius Largus refers to cases involving the treatment of gladiators. Remedies developed as a result of the treatment of gladiators were applied in the wider society: the Elder Pliny lists some in his encyclopaedia.[62] And the presence of physicians employed by at least the larger imperial *ludi* is confirmed by inscriptions such as that of a physician (*medicus*) of the *ludus matutinus*. Those who fought against wild beasts were perhaps more likely to suffer wounds which were excruciating but not fatal; gladiators were taught to strike to kill without causing the opponent (with whom they had been training, perhaps for years) unnecessary pain. The θηρεύτορες ἀνδρὲς (*bestiarii*) of Corinth set up a bronze plaque honouring their physician. Apart from physicians, there are many inscriptions commemorating weapons' instructors (*doctores*, whose names are often typical of slaves, suggesting that they were themselves retired gladiators). The artificial group loyalty of different categories of gladiators was reinforced by the fact that different groups had their own specialised *doctores*: inscriptions record a 'doctor Thraec[orum]', a 'doctor murmillonum', a 'doctor secutorum', a 'doctor [h]oplomachor[um]', and a 'doctor velitum'. A 'doc[tor] ret[iariorum]' from Cordoba in Spain had the typical slave name 'Cursor'.[63] *Lanistae* also provided their gladiators with masseurs to keep them in trim; one such is mentioned in an inscription put up by thirty-two imperial gladiators under Commodus.[64]

The same inscription shows that gladiators, even if (like these members of the imperial *ludus*) of servile status, could like other slaves form friendly societies (*collegia*). In this case, the *collegium* dedicated itself to honour the god Silvanus. The members were organised hierarchically in groups of ten, *decuriae*, as was common with slaves. The first consisted of experienced fighters (*veterani*) whose skills lay in the use of a range of six different types of weaponry; the second was led by a *veteranus*, while the others consisted of men who had not yet fought in a formal contest, *tirones*. Other such colleges are mentioned in inscriptions. An inscription from Ankara refers in Greek to the κολλήγιον ἐν Ῥώμῃ τῶν σουμμαρούδων, i.e. of retired gladiators (*summa rudis*).[65] *Bestiarii* were similarly organised: a college is attested at Rome, and in Dea (Dié, South Gaul) there was a college of *venatores*.[66]

These formal sub-divisions within the body of gladiators served to create a corporate pride which was no less real for being as artificial as the emotional identification mobilised by an Oxford versus Cambridge boat race. Memorials show how gladiators liked to represent themselves as 'Summa rudis', 'Campani primarii', 'Thracians' or 'Retiarii'. As Georges Ville pointed out, the fact that some, or even most, gladiators provided their audience with a spectacle at all proves that they to some extent identified with their role, however unwillingly they had had it forced upon them. Seneca argues that a gladiator – even though the least honourable of people – nevertheless considers it an insult to have to fight a weaker opponent. He talks of how a gladiator would take a wound without uttering a cry. Each of the contests for which a gladiator trained might result in his recovering the right to life, or in a relatively swift death. Seneca also says that another of the skills gladiators were trained in was dying cleanly, without too much fuss.[67]

The purpose of the armour was to prevent stunning or minor wounds. If a fighter got through his opponent's defences, he was likely to reach the torso and inflict a fatal injury. In the case of criminals who were still alive after they had been mauled by wild beasts, the evidence suggests that they would be removed from the arena for the execution to be completed out of public view.[68] *A fortiori*, we may assume that gladiators were not just left to die in the open. There appears to be no evidence for the popular belief that they were dragged away by a hook, as crucified slaves were (p. 75 above). The Zliten mosaic shows two mobile beds with head rests available for disabled gladiators to be taken away for immediate medical treatment (figure 5; the height of the beds suggests that they were designed as operating tables as well as just stretchers). The armour was of course designed for other purposes as well as protecting those who wore it. Precious metals and intricate craftsmanship broadcast the liberality of the *editor* (p. 14 above). Helmets were perceived as a particularly important and fascinating part of the gladiator's equipment (figure 4). They served to identify the type of gladiator (thus the *murmillo*'s helmet marked him out as a 'fish' whom his opponent, the *retiarius*, would try to catch in his net). We may also suspect that one of the functions of the visored helmets which made gladiators look so sinister because their faces could not be seen, unlike much of the rest of their bodies, was to make it easier for an opponent to inflict pain and death upon a person with whom he had been living and training as part of the same troupe, perhaps for years: then as now, a fighter will have found it less nerve-racking to destroy an anonymous target than a fellow human-being and a friend. The gladiators' craft involved learning to kill, as well as dying. Not surprisingly, we find them being used as public executioners: the executioner whose hand trembled so much that he needed St Perpetua's help to cut off her head was a young trainee gladiator (*tirunculi gladiatoris*).

Both literary sources and visual representations concentrate on the spectacle of slaughter, and leave us with the impression that killing was a certainty rather than a possibility. Inscriptions are a corrective: it was worthy of note, and therefore unusual, for eleven gladiators to lose their lives out of eleven pairs.[69] Contests in which there was no possibility of reprieve for the loser (*munera sine missione*) were banned by Augustus, who took the opportunity to criticise the savagery of a powerful magnate, Nero's grandfather Gn. Domitius Ahenobarbus.[70] It was characteristic of bad emperors to ignore that convention. Particularly unacceptable was forcing a victorious gladiator to face another opponent immediately (a substitute, *suppositicius*). The widespread assumption that a gladiatorial show might involve a general mêlée in the arena, with several pairs of gladiators fighting at the same time (*gregatim*), is based on literary anecdotes about bad emperors,[71] and cannot be confirmed by pictorial evidence, since a sequence of events is often represented together. Thus the famous mural from Pompeii with a representation of the riot of AD 59 shows fighting outside the amphitheatre as well as in the arena: even if what is going on in the arena is gladiatorial rather than part of the riot, it still does not show that several pairs were fighting at the same time. From our point of view a gladiatorial combat is perceived as bringing death to (one of) the combatants; but it can equally be seen as giving a condemned man an opportunity to regain his physical and social life. We should be wary of assuming that few gladiators reached retirement before their deaths. The posters advertising games found at Pompeii suggest that those who had the fighting skills to survive their first four or five matches might well become popular enough with the public to avoid being killed altogether; the crowd would give the thumbs up sign if their opponent ever got the better of them. Pompeian advertisements refer to men who had survived twenty or thirty fights, but had only actually won about half of them. Furthermore, it was in the interests of the *editores*, the professional organisers who trained gladiators, to keep their expensively trained professionals in service for as long as possible. A gladiator's chances of survival should not be compared unfavourably with those of dying in a sporting accident in the modern world, but with the survival rates of antiquity. Although it is impossible to establish rates of life-expectancy for any part or social group in the Roman empire with absolute certainty, it was a world where three persons out of five would die before they reached their twenties.[72] Life as a gladiator might not be as hopeless as all that for, say, a skilled ex-soldier who had no wish or ability to become a farmer.

Inscriptions record a considerable number of men who had died – not necessarily in the arena – after a gladiatorial career lasting several years (we may assume a minimum of two contests a year, and the same individual may have been required to fight several times in one *munus*: ILS 5088 records a man who fought 9 times on 9 consecutive days in Trajan's games, and was then freed). There are references to 37 fights; 30 or 36 fights or victories; 27 fights; 25 fights; 20 fights; and 13 fights.[73] On the other hand there are also references to gladiators who were freed after only 3 or 7 combats.[74] Other inscriptions give us the age of gladiators at death. Those listed in Dessau reached the ages of 18, 20 years 8 months and 12 days, 22 years 5 months and 8 days, and 25 years. An inscription from Padua records a man who died after 5 fights at the age of 21, having spent four years in a training school.[75] A considerable number of inscriptions tell us how many combats gladiators had taken part in as well as their age at death. One man aged 22 had survived only 5 fights; another also aged 22, 13 fights. One aged 23 had survived 8 fights, and was killed in his ninth; two aged 25 had had 9 victories and 20 fights; two aged 27, 10 fights (dying in his eleventh) and 16 fights respectively; a Sicilian inscription ascribes 34 fights to a man who died at 30, including 21 victories, 9 'draws' and 4 defeats in which he had been allowed to survive.[76] Of course inscriptions are slanted towards commemorating those who were exceptionally successful, and those who left behind a family or friends with an interest in commemorating them; not to mention the other methodological problems involved in abstracting valid conclusions from such evidence, such as the tendency for Romans to estimate their age in *lustra*, multiples of five years.[77] Nevertheless some gladiators had a comparatively long life. One died aged 35 after 20 victories, another at 38 after 18 fights, another at the age of 45. An inscription from Rome mentions a man who died at the age of 48, with 19 victories behind him and (probably) 20 years' service in the *ludus Caesaris*. 'Flavius Sigerus, summa rudis', retired to Caesarea Mauretania and died at the age of 60. A *paegniarius* (see Glossary) did not fight to the kill. The *paegniarius* Secundus was able to claim on a Roman epitaph that he had lived 99 years 8 months and 18 days.[78]

Individual epitaphs cannot give a statistical picture of the 'average' gladiator's chances of survival. There is however a fragmentary inscription from Venusia which lists the ages of at least twenty-nine gladiators belonging to the troupe of one Gaius Salvius Capito and buried in the same tomb. They are classified by type. The names are accompanied by numbers, which the archaeologist Mau thought referred to the number of combats and victories each man had taken part in; Mommsen used a Greek parallel to show that the figures applied to victories won and the number of times the gladiator had been crowned. In either case the numbers represent the minimum number of times the gladiator in question had appeared in the arena. We may also note that not all these gladiators had died as a result of fighting; the inscription lists at least ten *tirones*, trainees, who were presumably as liable as similar groups such as soldiers to succumb to accidents or disease. Of the others, we can establish the minimum number of fights. Three died during, or after, their first fight, four after two, three after three, one after four, two after five, one after six, two after seven, and three after twelve. And some will no doubt have survived to win their freedom, lead an independent life, and be buried in a tomb of their own.[79]

If it seems perverse to talk about a gladiator's career prospects, funerary inscriptions nevertheless show that there were some gladiators who had wives and children and lived to a relatively ripe age. The references in the law codes to freedmen who had been gladiators do not simply illustrate society's need to maintain the distinctions between normal citizens and ex-gladiators, but also show that ex-gladiators might be integrated into civil society. While the laws insisted that those condemned *ad ludos* could never become Roman citizens, they also released slave gladiators who had won their freedom from the obligation to fight again as part of any *operae* that their ex-owners might require them to perform.[80] If slave gladiators did choose to fight again after having won their manumission, then this may have been because they had no other way of making a living, or because they knew that because they had already proved that they were good fighters, they would be highly regarded by the audience, and win substantial financial rewards.[81] There is literary, epigraphic and legal evidence that a gladiator who fought particularly bravely would be rewarded with a purse of coins.[82] The *Digest* refers to *lances* and *disci* given to *bestiarii*.[83] Juvenal mentions the financial rewards that might accrue to the successful gladiator, and Suetonius tells us that in Tiberius' reign, a retired gladiator was granted 100,000 sesterces, while Nero gave the *murmillo* Spiculus a palace and a triumphator's estate. Horace suggests it was conceivable for an ex-gladiator to retire to an estate in the country.[84] The very fact that manumitted gladiators left enough money for their families to set up a tombstone for them is some indication that they were in possession of a certain degree of wealth. An example is a funerary inscription from Vellitri in Etruria erected in accordance with the will of a freedman *lanista*:

C. Baebius CC L p[. . .
idem danista [*sic*] hoc commodum est [. . .
factum ex testamento ar[. . .
Pamphili.[85]

Only the tiniest minority of gladiators would have been able to amass prize-money on such a scale. Most would have needed a source of regular income; and they would have been helped in finding a job by the fact that their retirement from the arena proved their fighting skills. Nevertheless the legal impediments against those who had ever hired themselves out to fight as gladiators excluded them from the most obvious career in which their skills could have been put to use, that of a soldier. It was unprecedented for Caligula to give 'Thracian' gladiators (whom he supported) positions as officers of the emperor's Batavian bodyguard; these men were of course not citizens, but the personal dependants of the Caesars. One of these gladiators, Sabinus, later had to fight to the death again in the arena (presumably after being dismissed by Claudius); Messalina interceded for him, leading to accusations that he had been her lover.[86] It will have been much more usual for retired gladiators to be employed by powerful men as security guards: they might include provincial governors such as Junius Blaesus in Pannonia in AD 14, and of course emperors: when Nero went rioting through Rome at night, he was protected by a gang of gladiators.[87] Women might have such guards: an inscription from Cos mentions the φαμιλία μονο-μάχων καὶ ὑπόμνημα κυνηγέσιων of the wife of an Asiarch.[88] In late antiquity great landowners throughout the empire were frequently accompanied by gangs of armed retainers who were no longer classified as 'gladiators', but performed much the same functions, and made it difficult for the government to control them. A sixth-century AD inscription from Bonçuklar in Turkey states how the *Scribon* of the sacred palace in Constantinople was warned in a dream to ask the local bishop to suppress groups of retainers and exact an oath that each landowner keep a maximum of five bodyguards only.[89]

A rosy picture of a retired gladiator growing old in the service of a powerful employer, and dying in the company of his wife, children and pet dog (p. 96 above), corresponds too closely with our own need to come to terms with death in a world where up to 20 per cent of the population will soon be over retirement age. It was not a picture that would have helped most Romans come to terms with their anxieties about dying. Few survived into old age, and the absence of drugs and medical care meant that, even for those supported by their family, old age was harsh. Death could come at any time during the life cycle, and it was painful and often violent. Romans needed to watch how gladiators faced death in the arena, not in their beds.

NOTES

1 Plutarch, *Crassus* 8.1.
2 Appian, *Civilia* 1, 14.116; though, curiously, Appian says that he had previously fought in a Roman army.
3 *Tusculans* 2.41; *Pro Sestio* 134; Livy 28, 21.2.
4 Cicero, *Att.* 4, 4a.2; 8.2.
5 Florentinus, *Digest* 1, 5.2.
6 *Res gestae* 3.2.
7 *Panegyrici Latini* 6.12.3; 12.23.3.
8 Josephus BJ 6, 418; 7, 24.38.
9 Cassius Dio 60, 30.3.
10 E.g., *Testamentum Dasumii* lines 80 ff.: J. Gardner and T. Wiedemann, *The Roman Household* (Routledge, 1991), no. 158.
11 *Res gestae* 25.1.
12 Ὡς μηκέτ’ ὄντων, *Historia Ecclesiastica* 8.10 = PG 20.765.
13 *Digest* 48, 19.8.11; Pliny, *Letters* 10, 31.2 etc. Not 'ludi' meaning games.
14 11.7.4. Cf. Mommsen, *Strafrecht* 953 ff. Five years also appears as a standard measure of time in other aspects of Roman law, e.g. the *lustrum* for *postliminium*.
15 Pliny, *Letters* 10, 31: 'in opus damnati vel in ludum'.
16 Suetonius, *Vitellius* 12.
17 Gaius, *Institutes* 1, 13: qui ut ferro aut cum bestiis depugnarent traditi sint, inve ludum custodiamve coniecti fuerint.
18 *Historia Augusta*, Hadrian 18.7 f.
19 Gaius, *Institutes* 3, 146, an early text, perhaps from the second century AD.
20 Quintilian, *Declamationes* 9.21: in ludo fui – morabar inter sacrilegos, incendiarios et homicidas.
21 *Liber spectaculorum* 7, 7 ff.; pp. 77, 84 above.
22 ILS 5083/5083a. By contrast the thirty-two names on the list of members of an association of imperial gladiators dating to AD 177 all belong to men of servile birth: ILS 5084.
23 AE 1985.777: P. Folius Potitus Thraex.
24 Seneca, *Letters* 37, 1f.: eadem honestissimi huius et illius turpissimi auctoramenti verba sunt: uri, vinciri ferroque necari. Ab illis qui manus harenae locant et edunt ac bibunt quae per sanguinem reddant cavetur ut ista vel inviti patiantur.
25 *Satyricon* 117.5: in verba Eumolpi sacramentum iuravimus: uri

vinciri verberari ferroque necari, et quidquid aliud Eumolpus iussisset. Tanquam legitimi gladiatores domino corpora animosque religiosissime addicimus. Horace used almost the same words eighty years earlier: *Satires* 2, 7.58: quid refert, uri virgis, ferroque necari/ auctoratus eas . . .

26 11, 8: nec prohibente tribuno (for citizens to) scripturus leges et regia verba lanistae.

27 Seneca, *Controversiae* 10, 4.18.

28 Quintilian, *Declamationes* 302: auctoratus ob sepeliendum patrem; Lucian, *Toxaris* 58. Plutarch, *Moralia* 1099B also implies a gladiator with the freedom to marry and own slaves.

29 Tatian, *adversus Graecos* 23.

30 Fg. 14 f. Ribbeck; Cassius Dio 74, 2.5.

31 Cicero, *Pro Sestio* 9.

32 Cicero, *De oratore* 3, 86 = Lucilius fg. 1273 f. Marx.

33 Suetonius, *Julius* 26.3.

34 Manilius, *Astronomica* 4, 225 f.

35 *Ad martyres* 5.

36 ILS 6635 (Carsulae): pinn[irapus] iuvenum; AE 1935.27 (Paestum): summarudis iuvenum; CIL XII.533 (Aix-en-Provence): a youth who died aged 19 is said to have performed in the amphitheatre.

37 *Historia Augusta*, Macrinus 4, 3 and 5.

38 Cassius Dio 73, 20.

39 Suetonius, *Caligula* 54.1, Cassius Dio 59, 5.5.

40 Dio 66, 15.2; 67, 14.3.

41 *Historia Augusta*, Hadrian, 14.10; Marcus, 8.12.

42 *Historia Augusta*, Didius Julianus, 9.1; Cassius Dio 76, 7.1.

43 Dio 59, 10.2. For parallels, see D. Porch, *The French Foreign Legion* (London, 1991).

44 Cassius Dio 62/3, 2.1; Tacitus, *Annals* 15.32.

45 Suetonius, *Domitian* 4.1; *Liber spectaculorum* 6B.

46 Cassius Dio 76, 16.1.

47 Seneca, *Letters* 70.22; Symmachus, *Letters* 2, 46.

48 Plutarch, *Crassus* 8.1.

49 Suetonius, *Vitellius* 12: circumforano lanistae.

50 Suetonius, *Augustus* 42.3.

51 CIL IV.1182–4.

52 Paul, *Digest* 38, 1.37 pr.

53 Plutarch, *Moralia* 1099B.

54 ILS 5104, 5100, 5107, 5095, 5097 and 5101, 5102, 5098, 5112.

55 AE 1985.197.

56 ILS 5086, 5096.

57 AE 1982.137.

58 Plutarch, *Crassus* 8.3.

59 ILS 5128; cf. 5118, from Parma; ILS 5113.

60 Bradley, *Slavery and Rebellion* (London, 1989), 88.

61 Propertius 4, 8.25; Juvenal, *Satire* 11, 20; Tacitus, *Histories* 2, 88; Pliny NH 18, 72; Cyprian, *Ad Donatum* 7; cf. Galen, *Peri trophon Dynameos* 1, 19 = Kühn VI, 529.

62 Strabo 5, 1.7; Galen, *De comparanda medicina* 101, 203, 207, 208; Pliny, NH 26, 135.
63 *Ludus matutinus*: ILS 5152; Corinth: IG IV.365; *doctores*: ILS 5091, 5092; ILS 5103, CIL V.1907, VI.10174; ILS 5116; ILS 5099, 9241; ILS 9342; AE 1986.379.
64 ILS 5084, l.25.
65 IGR III.215.
66 ILS 7559, 'harenariorum'; 5148.
67 *De providentia* 3.4; *De constantia sapientis* 16.2; cf. Cicero, *Tusculans* 2, 41 and 46; Seneca, *Letters* 30.8.
68 Seneca, *Letters* 93, 12; *Historia Augusta*, Commodus 18, 3.5; *Passion of Perpetua and Felicity* 21.6.
69 ILS 5062.
70 Suetonius, *Augustus* 45.3.
71 Dio 67, 8.2.
72 On life expectancy in the Roman world, cf. R. Duncan-Jones, *Structure and Scale in the Roman Economy* (Cambridge, 1990), chapter 6. One of the best studies remains that of B. Frier, 'Roman Life Expectancy: Ulpian's Evidence', HSCPh 86 (1982), 213–51.
73 ILS 5096, 5094, 5117, 5101, 5093, 5111.
74 ILS 5102, 5086.
75 ILS 5109, 5089, 5125, 5087; Padua (*in ludo*): 5107.
76 ILS 5112; 5115; 5120, 5095; 5122, 5114; Sicily: *stans* 9, *missus* 4: 5113.
77 See R. Duncan-Jones, *Structure and Scale* (n. 72 above), chapters 5 and 6.
78 ILS 5098, 5090, 510; ILS 5106; ILS 5126.
79 Number of combats recorded on the Venusia tablets (ILS 5083): 1: Quartio, Amicus, Eleuther; 2: Secundus, Mycter, Anteros, Clodius; 3: Mandatus, Memmius, Strabo; 4: Atlans; 5: Fabius, Inclutus; 6: Dorus; 7: Masonius, Hilario; 12: Phileros, Donatus, Aquila.
80 On *operae*, cf. Callistratus, *Digest* 38, 1.38.
81 Petronius, *Satyricon* 45.4; Cassius Dio 60, 30.3.
82 AE 1986.726: Theveste, Algeria: 'Sadunti/ob merita/missos sacco'. Cf. the mosaic at Smirat depicting *bestiarii* who are 'saccis missos'. The distribution of money bags on the unpublished Maasbracht wall painting may be another example: p. 24 above.
83 *Digest* 12, 1.11 pr., 30, 51; 16, 3.26 §2; Marcus Aurelius limited the prize-money to 12,000 HS per event (p. 134 below).
84 Juvenal 6, 204; Suetonius, *Tiberius* 7.1; *Nero* 30.2; Horace, *Epistle* 1, 1.4 f.
85 AE 1984.161; first published in *Supplementa Italica* 2 (1983), p. 55, no. 24.
86 Sabinus: Josephus, *Antiquities* 19, 212; Suetonius, *Caligula* 55; Dio 60, 28.2.
87 Tacitus, *Annals* 1.22; *Annals* 13.25.
88 Mommsen, *Gesammelte Schriften* VIII, 517.6; cf. IG XII.8 no. 547 f. from Hekataea, on Thasos.

89 AE 1985.816: Boncuklar, Turkey: Cankiri Museum. Cf. *Novellae Justiniani* 30 (AD 536) and 149 (AD 569); R. Macmullen, *Corruption and the Decline of Rome* (Yale, 1988), p. 96 surprisingly argues that there was 'no sign' of such independent *possessores* in the classical period.

4

OPPOSITION AND ABOLITION

Roman gladiatorial games have evoked such revulsion on the part of western scholars since the nineteenth century that many of them have looked for evidence for opposition to them in antiquity itself. There are some interesting parallels here between the imperative to find evidence for ancient criticism of the games, and modern scholars' treatment of the wider subject of slavery. For example, a humanitarian programme to counter the cruelty involved in both institutions has been seen in what was in fact the ever-increasing tendency for emperors to try to control the lives of their subjects through legislation. Alternatively, Greek philosophy (especially the Stoic principle that 'man is sacred to man', *homo sacra res homini*) and/or Christianity have been claimed by some to have been responsible for the decline of one and the disappearance of the other in late antiquity.[1] Hostility to the Roman games was combined with the nineteenth-century preference for Greeks over Romans to produce the unsustainable idea that gladiatorial contests were rejected by the Greek half of the Roman empire. 'Le génie propre de la race grecque lui inspira pour les combats de gladiateurs une répugnance qu'elle ne surmonta jamais complètement'.[2] As late as 1940, when Louis Robert accumulated the wealth of archaeological and literary evidence for the popularity of gladiatorial games in the Greek world, he could not bring himself to accept the conclusion that by the second century AD, the Greek cities of the Roman empire were competing with one another to introduce gladiatorial contests as proof of their earnestness in adopting Roman culture. Scholars selectively interpreted what evidence there was in terms of their own predilections and presuppositions, and those presuppositions were often by no means as liberal as they appear. If Greeks appeared to be enjoying these contests, then these scholars assumed that they cannot have been true Greeks. Much of the eastern archaeological evidence originates from Asia Minor rather than from the old Greek territories (this is in fact only because these provinces had more wealth to spend on public institutions in the Roman period, and the literary sources make it clear that gladiators also appeared at Corinth, Athens or Rhodes).

When Friedländer and Lafaye wrote, it was possible to explain away the popularity of the games amongst this 'half-oriental racially mixed population' ('halborientalische Mischlingsbevölkerung') as the result of insufficient superior Greek blood, 'grâce aux instincts naturellement sanguinaires des populations orientales qui s'y trouvent en contact avec les Grecs'.[3]

On closer examination, ancient criticism of gladiatorial games, as of slavery, was given expression by specific groups or individuals in particular contexts which do not permit any conclusions to be drawn about widespread objections to the inhumanity of the games, even in late antiquity when they ceased to play a central role in Roman culture. Four respects may be considered in which scholars have sometimes been tempted to draw invalid conclusions from the evidence. First, the fact that any orator or philosopher in Greek or Roman antiquity did indeed have an entire armoury of arguments against the gladiatorial games available for him to use if required, and that these arguments can be found in surviving writings by philosophers, Roman as well as Greek, and Christian as well as pagan, do not prove that they thought that their audience or readership objected to the games as an institution, or even that the writer himself did. The writer and his readers may still have taken the games for granted, even if they could see that there were some negative things that might be said about them, at least in particular circumstances and on particular occasions. Those who express disapproval of certain aspects of behaviour by players or supporters at modern mass spectator sports do not necessarily want those sports abolished. Secondly, we should beware of assuming that the kinds of objections put are ones that we would find acceptable today, any more than Lafaye and Friedländer's explanation of the popularity of the games in racial terms. Nor is it clear that it was the objections of those who were implacably opposed to gladiatorial displays (as many Christian writers were, though as we shall see not necessarily for 'humanitarian' reasons) that led to imperial legislation against them. Governments have their own reasons for wanting to control public spectacles. When an emperor issued an edict banning gladiatorial games, as Honorius is reported as having done for Rome in AD 399, then that may have been for specific political reasons, even if contemporary Christians like Ambrose and Prudentius (p. 152 f.) supplied him with a collection of religious or moral arguments against them. Finally – and perhaps most crucially – there need have been little or no connection between the hostility against the games, whether by philosophers, Church fathers, or even emperors, and their decline: pagan and Greek intellectuals similarly expressed hostile opinions about chariot-races and theatrical displays, which continued for centuries. Instead of concentrating on the 'abolition' of the games – as though there were an analogy with the abolition of New World slavery – we would do well to look for cultural reasons for why people no longer felt that they needed this particular institution.

We may begin by noting that hostile comments about gladiators in no way need imply hostility to the games themselves. As we have seen, the gladiator was a marginal figure, regarded with fear and loathing as well as idolised. He was *infamis* under Roman law, and inscriptions assimilate him to those who commit suicide under disgraceful circumstances. For Seneca, the man who escapes the world to 'flee' to a *ludus gladiatorium* is like a man who has castrated himself. Christians shared this prejudice against professional gladiators: some of those sentenced *ad ludos* in the Diocletianic persecutions are said to have refused to train. Tatian, addressing a Greek audience in the second century AD, says that a man who has sold himself to the *lanista* had 'made a profession of idleness' and was a murderer and a bandit. But to describe gladiators as immoral is far from the same as condemning the contests in which they destroyed one another as immoral.[4]

It had always been imperative for an emperor who wanted to be seen as protecting good order to enact rules controlling gladiatorial spectacles. The Latin biographical tradition ascribes such enactment to 'good' emperors, while not maintaining the proper distinctions became a characteristic of accounts of the behaviour of 'bad' emperors.[5] When persons of honour such as senators or women were encouraged to take part, as under Nero or Domitian, then this symbolised the emperor's depravity. The ultimate threat to established morality was for an emperor to appear in the arena himself, as Caligula, Nero and Commodus did. Good emperors were expected to legislate against partici-pation by persons of high status: that was not legislation against the games themselves. The regulation restricting women (other than the six vestal virgins and members of the imperial family) to the uppermost tier of an amphitheatre, usually ascribed to Domitian but apparently already applying under the Julio-Claudians, or the attempts to make the audience wear formal clothing, illustrate basically moral concerns.[6] When Augustus required the audience to wear laurel wreaths, and male citizens to wear the toga as a sign of their status, at *ludi*, such regulations were appropriate to the public spectacles at which the Roman people assembled for ceremonial religious purposes. The trans-ference of such regulations to *munera* may be seen not so much as an illustration of the widening of the concept of public occa-sions as of the emperor's wish to regulate private occasions. Seating regulations had first been introduced for state *ludi* as early as 195 BC, when the introduction of permanent seating for the Circus Flaminius in the Campus Martius led the censors to insist on separate seats for senators. The enactments which might apply are listed by the *Lex Irnitana* – 'Quibus locis quaeque genera hominum ante hanc legem spectare solita sunt, isdem spectanto', in accordance with laws, decrees of the senate, edicts, and constitutions of Tiberius, Claudius, Galba, Vespasian, Titus and Domitian.[7]

In addition to these moral concerns, there were also practical reasons for such controls: the possibility of political demon-strations, danger to the audience as a result of the collapse of buildings, crushing, or the need to prevent burglaries while the population was engaged in watching the games (Augustus' overt reason for instituting an urban police force). The crushing of several thousand members of the audience at a *munus* given at Fidenae in AD 27 by a freedman called Atilius gives Tacitus a marvellous opportunity to describe a domestic incident with all the colour of a great military disaster (he claimed 50,000 dead). It was certainly serious enough for Tiberius to introduce restric-tions on *munera* outside Rome, including building regulations to ensure that in future amphitheatres would have sufficiently firm foundations.[8] His personal interest in this, as in his earlier restrictions on such games at Rome itself, may simply have been a dislike of such shows, or a wish to prevent other people from winning popularity in this way; but since the ban he introduced applied only to persons whose census was below that of an equestrian (400,000 HS), he is more likely to have been concerned that any games that were put on were properly funded. Similar government intervention originated from emperors who were very keen on *munera*. In AD 59, following the notorious riots between gangs of supporters from Nuceria and Pompeii, both cities were forbidden from putting on spectacles for ten years. The *editor* of these games, Livineius Regulus, had been expelled from the senate, presumably for immorality (Tacitus' account of this incident is lost); he was punished with exile.[9] Analogies may be drawn with the reasons for the abolition of public executions in nineteenth-century Europe. Anxieties about the problems posed by controlling a great crowd of spectators, and the disorder and crime that might ensue, began to outweigh the arguments for the spectacular visible execution of justice.

Apart from the wish to impede political rivals, fear of the potential danger which large concentrations of socially marginalised men trained to fight presented to public order will have played a role in the passing of regulations in the late republic, limiting the number of gladiators which *editores* were allowed to present. The Spartacus rebellion gave Romans good cause to fear the effects of training large numbers of gladiators together in one place. By 65 BC the Senate was introducing restrictions on the number of gladiators that Julius Caesar wished to provide. Although rumours that Catiline called on slaves to join his rebellion in 63 BC, promising them freedom from their masters as a reward, were unfounded and standard accusations against an enemy in civil war, the magistrates of Capua were sufficiently afraid of the possibility of unrest among trainee gladiators to expel Gaius Marcellus from their city under suspicion of soliciting their support. Further restrictions on the numbers of gladiators permitted at any one *munus* were introduced the following year.[10]

The ordinances about the presentation of public spectacles of all kinds introduced by Augustus in 22 BC clearly illustrate the way in which regulations whose primary purpose was political control were presented in terms of public morality. Ostensibly, Augustus was exercising censorial powers in association with the two censors who had been appointed in that year (Paullus Aemilius Lepidus and Lucius Munatius Plancus). Dio tells us that

> He abolished some public feasts completely, and placed restrictions on others. He put all religious festivals under the control of the praetors, ordering funds to be allocated them by the treasury, and forbidding any one of them to spend more from their own domestic resources than another, or from presenting a gladiatorial contest without the Senate's permission, or more than twice in the same year, or with more than one hundred and twenty men. He entrusted the task of putting out fires to the curule aediles, giving them a brigade of six hundred slaves to help them. And since both equestrians and women of status had appeared on the stage even at that time, he banned not just senators' sons (who had been forbidden from doing this hitherto) but also their grandsons if they were listed as equestrians from ever doing such a thing again.[11]

The passage illustrates several aspects of imperial control of public events: the creation of a police force (aliter a fire brigade); the inclusion of munera, formally 'private' affairs, within the scope of general regulations on what magistrates could or could not do; limits on the numbers of gladiators gathered together at one time; restrictions on overt competition by preventing any praetor from making more of a display than his colleagues; and – perhaps most crucially – the wish to reinforce visibly the moral division between those of high status in the audience, and those who were infames appearing on the stage.[12]

Augustus' successors continued to intervene to control different kinds of public spectacle; on different occasions they will have been motivated by different concerns. Tiberius was notoriously hostile to public shows. One of his first acts on coming to power in AD 14 was to take away from the popular assemblies any real part in the process of election of praetors; the effect was that junior magistrates (aediles) no longer felt it necessary to invest in putting on grand displays with a view to winning the people's support for the next round of elections. He also imposed maximum rates on the prize-money allowed to actors and gladiators, and repeated controls on maximum numbers.[13] Nero's motives for banning provincial governors and imperial procurators from giving gladiatorial *munera*, *venationes*, or theatrical shows of any kind in the provinces in AD 57 were more complicated; Tacitus suggests that the ostensible reason was to protect provincials from having to pay the costs of such shows, a substantial source of unpopularity, but it may also have been his desire that such spectacles should be concentrated at Rome, where the ensuing popularity would accrue to him. In the same year he had had a wooden amphitheatre constructed on the Campus Martius.[14] Imperial control over the provision of *munera* by the political elite at Rome was completed by Domitian, who reportedly banned all games not put on by magistrates on the emperor's own behalf.

Tacitus' comments show that control over *munera* was not just a matter of public order or a political move to protect the interests of emperors or, in the republic, rival politicians who feared the popularity that a particularly spectacular show would bring the man who put it on. As the obligation to provide shows became more and more of a burden on provincial magnates, they were correspondingly more grateful for imperial restrictions on the amount that it was permitted to spend. The most famous evidence for this is an inscription on a bronze tablet found at Italica (near Seville) and now in Madrid, minuting a debate apparently held at Lyon, the centre of the imperial cult for the three Gallic provinces, in AD 177, profusely thanking the emperor Marcus Aurelius for a senatorial decree the previous year which introduced detailed restrictions on the permitted expenditure for the annual gladiatorial shows which provincial *flamines* had to provide in honour of the imperial household.[15]

The decree appears to have divided gladiatorial games into five separate categories, depending on the outlay: under 30,000 sesterces; 30 to 60,000; 60 to 100,000; 100 to 150,000; and 150 to 200,000 sesterces, the upper limit (and still half the equestrian census rating). Gladiators too were categorised by different price-bands: the lowest were *gregarii*, 'ordinary' ones, costing between 1,000 and 2,000 sesterces; more expensive ones were assigned to three (possibly five) categories, the maximum being 15,000 sesterces. For each of the five categories of games, regulations were set limiting the proportions and numbers of gladiators of different bands. If the *munus* were in one of the higher classes, then on each day at least half the gladiators had to be *gregarii*. In accordance with the best traditions of Roman legislative procedure, the drafting committee had made provisions for possible objections. If the *lanistae* claimed that they could not provide enough *gregarii* to make up the required proportion, then better class fighters could be used, but they had to be paid for at the rate of a *gregarius*. These rules were to apply to major cities; in smaller places, notional prices had to be estimated, based on the average prices of gladiators put on show there during the preceding ten years. The enactment went on to specify further complicated provisions: 25 per cent of the prize money was to be reserved for *auctorati*, 20 per cent for slaves; those who fought voluntarily (i.e., gladiators of free birth) were to receive 2,000 HS; freed slaves (*liberati*) who were prepared to fight again could be given up to 12,000 HS in prize-money.

One of Marcus' motives for this very detailed piece of legislation was to protect the wealth of provincial notables from being exploited by the demands of central government officials (as with Nero's restrictions in AD 57), or of their own competitiveness. But fiscal considerations may also have played a part. The combination of the plague which followed the war against Persia in the AD 160s and the serious incursions into the empire on the Danube frontier in the AD 170s resulted in a fiscal shortfall so serious that Marcus had publicly to advertise it with an auction of effects belonging to the imperial household, and a proposal to conscript slaves for military service, something which in the classical world signalled a military threat of extreme proportions. Attempts to prevent wealth from being spent on conspicuous consumption, particularly where such consumption was unpopular with taxpayers, fit into this picture of economic difficulty. There were precedents for cutting back on expenditure on spectacles to demonstrate the need for fiscal retrenchment: after Domitian's overthrow in AD 96, Nerva had not only 'sold many ceremonial garments and gold and silver accoutrements and furniture belonging both to his private household and the imperial one', but also 'abolished many sacrifices (i.e., *ludi*), horseraces and other spectacles, to cut down the expense as far as he could'.[16] We can reject Dindorf's view that Nerva intended to abolish gladiatorial games altogether. His motives were fiscal, not humanitarian, and he did not single out *munera* as opposed to other spectacles.

In the case of Marcus Aurelius too, we may be hesitant to ascribe control of the expenditure of games to any humanitarian considerations. Admittedly, Cassius Dio gives us a whole chapter about Marcus' unwillingness to see human blood spilt, as part of his explanation for why he exercised such restraint in punishing those involved in Avidius Cassius' rebellion (AD 175): he watched gladiators only when they fought with blunted weapons, and refused spectators' demands that a man who had trained a lion to eat human flesh should be manumitted. But the fact that not even Marcus felt able to refuse the populace's demand that the lion should be displayed in the arena illustrates the limits of an emperor's power.[17] In the case of the Italica inscription, the repeated references the speaker makes to the ignoble nature of gladiatorial games (lines 6 ff.) serve as explanations for why Marcus had abolished taxes on them. Disparaging comments about the vile nature of *lanistae* mirror traditional Roman prejudices – and of course the high cost of *munera* could be blamed on their rapacity (line 37). The speaker also says that such spectacles do not in any way accord with Marcus' *secta*, i.e., Stoicism. But as we shall see, philosophical objections to these games were not based on what we would identify as humanitarian grounds, but on the belief that they were not appropriate to the rational elite; in that respect, *munera* were not to be distinguished from any other spectacle that appealed to the emotions.

The motives of provincial notables in drawing this issue to the emperor's attention may have been equally complicated. They may have been afraid that one of their own number would wish to increase his prestige by exceeding the permitted total. But perhaps they were more afraid of what would happen when Marcus was emperor no longer and had been succeeded by his son. Marcus' only surviving male child, Commodus, was born on 31 August AD 161; in 177 he was holding his first consulship, and had been granted the titles *Augustus* and *Pater Patriae* by the Senate. Two years before he had been co-opted into all the major priesthoods, he joined his father on the Danube frontier and was declared to have come of age on 7 July AD 175. It was clear that he would be Marcus' successor; and it will also have been clear to those who had to provide *munera* that he had a very special interest in gladiators. There were good reasons to fear that once Commodus ascended the throne, he would expect them to provide games of hitherto unparalleled expense – and that he might be ready to listen to accusations from rival magnates against those who were not so happy to spend their wealth in this way. Under these circumstances, public documentation of formal limits on the expenses required would be very much to the provincials' advantage. There is some other epigraphical evidence for pressure on provincial cities during these years to win Commodus' favour by means of new or better spectacles, and consequent concern about the expenditure this might commit provincials to: for instance, the text of a speech to the Senate by Marcus Aurelius in October/December AD 177, replying to a request that Miletus had made through Commodus to improve the games at Didyma, explicitly excuses other cities from feeling that they had to compete.[18]

Members of the elite also had ambivalent feelings about being required to spend large sums of money on an institution that might bring immediate glory, but glory which could soon be dissipated (hence the wish to preserve the memory of particular *munera* in the form of pictorial representations). In a public speech, Cicero was willing to emphasise his role in participating in giving games; but he gave his relatives different advice in private. In the *De Officiis*, the moral treatise Cicero wrote for the benefit of his son, the pleasure the games give to the public at large is contrasted with the meagre returns accruing to the *editor*. 'This sort of amusement gives pleasure to children, silly women, slaves and free persons with the characters of slaves; but an intelligent man who weighs such matters with sound judgement cannot possibly approve of them.' If a rich man wanted to parade his liberality, Cicero advised him to give the voters a banquet, or to ransom fellow-citizens who had been captured by brigands or pirates.[19] Complaints about the expense of *munera* given by others are to be found in Cicero's letters to his brother Quintus. Again, he advises providing citizens with feasts or ransoming them from captivity as more constructive ways of winning the people's favour.[20] The concern felt by the wealthy at the ever-increasing demands on them to provide games is given expression by anecdotes about the prices of gladiators. These were often associated with bad emperors: at an enforced auction of imperial property, Caligula was said to notice that the ex-praetor Aponius Saturninus had fallen asleep, and drew the auctioneer's attention to his constant nodding. The senator was said to have woken up to find that he had just bid for thirteen gladiators at the cost of nine million sesterces. Suetonius tells the story to illustrate the rapacity characteristic of a tyrant; but the story also expresses the elite's reservations about the increasing demands *munera* were making on them.[21]

As gladiatorial contests spread throughout the Greek world, we find similar objections being made by Greek writers. Plutarch notes that politicians have to borrow money to lay on shows, either from moneylenders or from friends, causing annoyance.

> We must not let ourselves feel overawed or impressed by the immediate popularity with the masses which comes from spectacles (θεάτρων), public feasts or mass events (πολυανδρίων), since it is of short duration, and ends at the very same moment as the gladiatorial combat or the show ends; it has nothing honourable or dignified.

Plutarch argues that a poor man can have as much political influence as a rich man, unconvincingly emphasising the importance of rhetorical ability over wealth. Dio Chrysostom, in an essay on 'Public Reputation', notes that 'the masses are insatiable and people spend limitless sums of money in trying to please them' to support the argument that it is degrading for a political leader to try constantly to win the approval of the people through feasts of food and wine and spectacles. The *topos* of expense is mentioned in passing by Christian writers, too.[22]

The moral concerns that lay behind imperial legislation were not those that inform modern objections. Did any ancient commentator share our humanitarian concern at the 'cruelty' of the games? Attitudes to the shedding of blood are complex. The wish to protect the innocent (or fellow-citizens, or those of high rank) does not necessarily apply to criminals or dangerous beasts. While Tacitus illustrates the ugly character of Tiberius' son Drusus by referring to his unhealthy keenness to watch blood being spilt in the arena, he also notes that it was worthless blood.[23] There is only minimal evidence for concern about cruelty against criminals. Cicero mentions that 'the gladiatorial spectacle seems to some people to be cruel and inhumane', but goes on to explain that this was because it involved not just criminals, but free men who have sold themselves to fight.[24] The evidence rather suggests that it was meant to be part of the Roman character to be able to watch the bloodshed of the arena. An inability to look at executions was childish: Caracalla as a child cried and turned his eyes away when he was present at punishments in the arena.[25] In an adult, not to be able to see the blood of a criminal being shed was a moral weakness, which an orator could turn against (for example) a husband who had failed to execute his wife's lover caught *in flagrante*: 'there are some adults who cannot even look at blood, and many who turn away from the wounds suffered by gladiators' – suggesting that those who suffered from this common weakness did not therefore desist from attending the games.[26] Marcus Aurelius' unwillingness to watch combats except when the gladiators had blunted weapons was a peculiarity comparable to his failure to hunt out and punish those who had conspired against him in Avidius Cassius' rebellion.[27]

The lack of sympathy for criminals is nowhere more starkly illustrated than in Symmachus' remarks about the Saxon prisoners who committed suicide rather than appear in his praetorian games: he says that they were more worthless than Spartacus and his companions – and compares the way he patiently accepted the loss this constituted for his games to Socrates' patience in accepting his death. It is hard to see that the ancient evidence warrants the weight which modern scholars have put on occasional philosophical arguments about the sacredness of man. When Seneca criticises the interest in seeing men and beasts killed in the arena, it is as part of a general onslaught on the modern world: it was in the Golden Age that men did not kill each other, or even animals.[28]

The entire context of the events which went on in the arena militated against the expression of anxieties about the suffering of criminals. The process of taking the life of another human being itself elicited feelings of anxiety, and as we have seen (Chapter 2 above) different modes of execution sought to minimise those anxieties; but that was not the same as having any reservations about the need to destroy hostile animals, prisoners-of-war or convicted criminals. The protests uttered by the crowd when elephants were slaughtered in Pompey's games have been taken as evidence of humane feelings: 'the result of the slaughter was a certain compassion (*misericordia*) and some kind of feeling that there was fellowship (*societas*) between this huge beast and humanity.' But Cicero's reason for reporting this sympathy has to be taken into account: the letter to Marius is intended to console him for having had to miss Pompey's games because of illness, and Cicero marshalls every possible argument to suggest that the games were a failure.[29] While there was little sympathy for condemned criminals, there are a number of references which imply an awareness of the possibility that persons might be forced to participate in *munera* unjustly, and sympathy for those who suffered in consequence. The unjust condemnation of the innocent was a required theme of rhetorical invective; one of the most famous, and most fantastic, invectives was Cicero's attack on Piso, the consul of 58 BC. One of the crimes he is accused of is having sent provincials to Rome to fight in the wild beast shows put on by Cicero's arch-rival Publius Clodius.[30] More historically reliable is a story Cicero reports in a letter of 43 BC about L. Cornelius Balbus, Caesar's quartermaster, who was said to have tried to force a Pompeian officer called Fadius to fight twice as a gladiator in Balbus' home town of Gades and, when he refused, to have had him burnt alive in a gladiatorial school. Cicero mentions other stories about illegal executions of Roman citizens by being thrown to the beasts – one of them for no other apparent reason than that he was physically malformed. Given the autocratic powers of a Roman provincial governor (see Chapter 2, p. 68 above), it is hardly surprising that such concerns about magistrates ignoring citizens' rights are frequently expressed.[31]

What applied to the wicked provincial governor applied *a fortiori* to the tyrannous emperor. Cassius Dio condemns Caligula for forcing citizens to fight as gladiators. Suetonius mentions a specific example. Caligula wanted to have the leading centurion (*primuspilus*) Aesius Proculus executed; the anecdote fails to ascribe a plausible motive, but we may assume that there was more to it than just that Proculus was outstandingly handsome. Caligula had him dragged from his place in the amphitheatre and ordered to fight two gladiators sent against him in succession; when Proculus defeated them both, he was beheaded. The cruelty did not lie in the form of punishment, but in the abuse of judicial procedures.[32]

There were other vices associated with gladiatorial games, but again they are not evidence of opposition to them on humanitarian grounds. It was not good to be too interested in bloodletting. As we have seen, Tacitus illustrates the ugly character of Tiberius' son Drusus by referring to his unhealthy keenness to watch blood being spilt in the arena; but he also notes that it was worthless blood. Claudius was criticised for being so interested in watching the killings of beasts and the midday executions that he arrived early in the morning and stayed during the lunchbreak. Suetonius says that he took so much pleasure in *venationes* that he condemned men to too high a penalty; once he ordered the immediate execution of the stage-hands when the set failed. This is represented as the cruelty characteristic of a tyrant. But we may note these stage hands had not only humiliated Claudius as the giver of the games; they were also his slaves, and as their master he was legally entitled to decide on their punishment.[33]

The criticism of Claudius' interest in those elements of the show that Seneca described as *mera homicidia* was an elitist one that could be applied to any spectacle: they were only suitable for people of simple tastes. Educated people ought to avoid such pastimes, and attend to better (intellectual) pursuits. Seneca's objection is not that they were cruel, but that they were boring and demonstrated no skill, 'sine arte', and he goes on to complain that they degrade the audience. In the letter consoling Marius for having been too ill to come to Rome to see Pompey's victory games, Cicero writes: 'What pleasure can an educated man possibly take in seeing either some puny human being mangled by a powerful beast, or . . .' But these arguments do not prevent Cicero from hoping that, if his consolation has not had the effect of diminishing Marius' regret at having missed the games, then 'I am still consoled by the fact that you will come to the *ludi* at some future occasion and pay me a visit, and not leave your hopes to be entertained to depend solely on my letters'. Pliny the Younger calls circus races boring, and says that the spectators act like children, 'pueriliter'. Marcus Aurelius says the same: 'the shows in the amphitheatre and similar places grate upon you as an everlasting impression of the same sight, and the constant repetition makes the spectacle uninteresting'. His rhetoric teacher, Marcus Cornelius Fronto, says the same about the theatre: 'idem theatrum, idem odium'. In the fourth century AD Libanius in his autobiography claims that as a boy he lost interest in the characteristic pleasures of (incompletely rational) children: 'pigeons, chariot races, the stage and gladiatorial combats' (pigeons represent toys in general). It is worth noticing that this criticism is not confined to the gladiatorial shows, and that it implies no feelings of 'humanity'.[34]

Of the criticisms in ancient literary sources levelled specifically at gladiatorial games, that which occurs most frequently is that they mobilised the emotions of the onlookers in such a way as to cloud their reason; they made them less rational, less properly human. This too was essentially an elitist argument. In the Greek city-states, the ruling groups justified their hold on social and political power, both to themselves and to those they ruled, on the grounds that it was to everyone's advantage for those who possessed reason (Gk. *logos*) to lead, instruct, and in the final analysis suppress those whose actions were guided by emotion rather than reason; those persons, in fact, whose lifestyle had more in common with animals than with rational human beings. This emphasis on *logos* had been used, from the fourth century BC on, to distinguish Greeks from non-Greek speaking barbarians, the free population from slaves, adults from children, and men from women. The increasing gulf between rich and poor during the Hellenistic and Roman periods predictably led to the argument being used to emphasize distinctions between ordinary citizens, most of them craftsmen or peasant farmers, and the wealthy; their wealth gave them time for leisure, including the leisure to study philosophy, and that made them more rational, in turn legitimating their exercise of power.

Warnings about the violent emotions that can be stirred up by mass spectacles go back at least as far as Plato, who at one point says that he would banish all poetry that excites the emotions from his ideal city, even Homer. He would allow his citizens to watch, and be influenced by, only those theatrical displays that represent men acting virtuously, and performances of hymns in praise of the gods.[35] Later both Stoics, with their emphasis that life should be lived in accordance with reason, and Epicureans, who emphasised that violent emotions had to be avoided, found Plato's view congenial. Roman writers who wished to adapt such ideas to an Italian audience found public *ludi* ideal material. Being part of a crowd, as ancient philosophers correctly noted, makes it more difficult for people to think clearly, and easier for emotions to be whipped up and lead to actions which may later be regretted.

> Nothing is so damaging to good character than the habit of wasting time at the Games; for then it is that vice steals secretly upon you through the avenue of pleasure . . . I come home more greedy, more ambitious, more

voluptuous, even more cruel and more inhumane, because I have been among human-beings.[36]

Criticism of public spectacles along these lines was a standard element of Stoicism, and is found in Plutarch, Aulus Gellius, and Philostratus. The second-century Stoic Favorinus of Arles is even said to have written a monograph on gladiators (ὑπὲϱ τῶν μονομάχων), though we have no idea what it said. There is no need to evoke 'humanity' in the modern sense to explain the allusion in the Italica inscription to the aversion to gladiatorial spectacles of Marcus Aurelius' *secta*. For Epicurean philosophers too, the emotions evoked by over-identification with gladiators were examples of what the educated and self-controlled man ought to avoid: it is stupid to get emotional about whether Castor or Docilis is the better gladiator, says Horace. Gladiators exemplified the sort of trivia that a philosopher ought to avoid talking about. Another of Horace's poems suggests in all serious-ness that these trivial topics were precisely the sort of thing that polite conversation might consist of: the patron (Maecenas) honours the client (Horace) by asking him the time, telling him about the weather, or discussing whether the Thracian Gallina could put up a fight against Syrus.

Did these philosophical objections lead to changes in actual behaviour? One possible consequence of the Platonic view that the good ruler was someone whose superior reason enabled him to lead his fellow-citizens by argument was that he had a respon-sibility not to degrade them by providing them with occasions for emotion. Philosophers, Romans as well as Greeks, pointed out that gladiatorial and wild-beast games, like strip-tease shows, tended to engage the emotions of the onlookers to an extent that made them incapable of rational thought. Plutarch, in his essay of advice on 'How to be a Politician' objects strongly to winning popular support through 'banquets or gifts of money or *pyrrichae* or gladiatorial games'. The pleasure involved in such things was more appropriate to animals than to reasonable human beings:

A people or a community should be led chiefly by the ears, and not – as is done by some who are no good at public speaking and try to control the people by uncul-tured and unskilled means such as appealing to their bellies – by providing feasts or distributions of money or putting on Pyrric dances or gladiatorial shows so as to lead the masses, or rather win popularity. But leading a people means leading those who can be persuaded by reason (*logos*); enticing the masses by the methods I have mentioned is just like hunting and rounding up wild boars.

In practice, those who had had personal experience of the political process like Plutarch admitted that one should grant the people 'either what is good or what is necessary, or at least something that is pleasant and enjoyable without being harmful or disgraceful'.[37]

But the practical effects would have been rare. Only the most radical pagan legislator, the emperor Julian, drew the consequences: he banned his newly established pagan priesthood from attending either *venationes* or theatrical shows (gladiators are not specified); even at the sacred *ludi*, they may only attend if no women are present.[38]

What objections there were to gladiatorial spectacles on the part of Greek (or Roman) philosophers can hardly, then, be classified as 'humanitarian' in our sense; rather, they expressed the elitist prejudice against the emotions thought to govern less rational members of society, and applied to many other kinds of shows apart from *munera*. Nevertheless, there are some traces of an undercurrent of resistance specifically to the introduction of gladiatorial combats in the eastern part of the Roman empire. A particularly interesting text occurs in Lucian's essay *Demonax*.[39] He notes that the only reason why the Athenians introduced these games was out of rivalry with the Corinthians (for the gladiatorial displays which the Corinthians held in order to emphasise their privileges as Roman colonists, see p. 43 above). Before doing so, argues Demonax, the Athenians should have removed the altar of the goddess *Eleos*, 'Pity'. This is a curious argument, since gladiators who fought bravely (unlike criminals due to be executed) could precisely expect to elicit sympathy from the audience. Only Athens and Epidauros are known to have honoured such a deity, suggesting that Lucian's point was that a specifically Athenian ritual should not have been replaced by a widespread Roman one. Like other rhetorical commonplaces used by some Greek writers to criticise gladiatorial shows, we may suspect that Lucian is looking for plausible arguments to give support to his underlying objection, not made explicit: a fear that such shows represent a threat to Greek culture as he understood it. In the 'second Sophistic' that was a literary culture, the social success of litterateurs such as Lucian (who came from a non-Greek speaking background from Samosata in Syria) depended upon their ability to attract an audience to their public lectures. The literary spectacles provided by Sophists were just as much public displays as *monomachiai* were, though they claimed that their performances in the Odeion were as much superior to those in the theatre as the ear was superior to the eye.[40] Terence had already noted how hard it had been for his comedy Hecyra to compete with a gladiatorial contest in 164 BC;[41] it is not surprising that those who won fame and public esteem as orators should feel that gladiators represented a direct threat to Hellenic culture.

Lucian's unease about the threat which these games presented to Greek culture is shared by a slightly earlier orator, the Bithynian Dio Chrysostom. In a speech attacking the Rhodians' practice of re-using old statues to honour new benefactors, he addresses the stock rhetorical procedure (which his opponents might appeal to) of comparing the Rhodians' customs with those of other great cities, in particular the Athenians; he argues that not all Athenian customs are good. The example he gives to support his argument is that of gladiatorial games. But his objection is not humanitarian in the sense that we would understand it: it is that killing is an unclean act, and that therefore it is inappropriate to hold gladiatorial games in the theatre of Dionysus, as the Athenians do. Executions should take place outside the city, in a dingy and insalubrious place such as that properly used by the Corinthians for their games.[42]

There is little to support the view that any Greeks objected to gladiatorial contests on what we would describe as humanitarian grounds, even if for rhetorical purposes some mileage could be got out of the proposition that they were un-Greek, or specifically un-Athenian. The argument can even be found that gladiatorial games are superior when the participants are Greek: Plutarch suggests that Greeks who take up fighting are not beasts like other gladiators.[43] The concern of those who owed their status to the literary culture associated with the manipulation of Attic Greek was cultural, not moral.

For the Jews, culture was indissolubly bound up with piety and morality. The popularity of such spectacles within the territory of Jewish client-kings therefore constituted a threat not just to local Jewish culture, but to ancestral morality. References to gladiators in Hebrew texts are virtually non-existent. For Josephus, the quinquennial games in honour of the emperor which Herod Agrippa instituted at Jerusalem, including gladiatorial shows held in a newly built amphitheatre in the plain below the city, were in direct competition with the pious practices enjoined by tradition. 'Herod went even further in departing from ancestral custom; through foreign practices he gradually corrupted the traditional way of life, which had so far been inviolable'; 'When the practice began of making wild animals fight one another, or setting condemned criminals to fight them, non-Jews were astonished at the expense, and at the same time found the excitement and danger entertaining; but for Jews it meant an open challenge to the customs they held in honour.' Although gladiators are not specifically mentioned, Josephus criticises both Hellenic forms of competition such as wrestling and chariot-racing, and the Roman *venationes* and execution of prisoners *ad bestias*. It was 'sheer impiety (ἀσέβες) to throw men to the wild beasts to afford delight to spectators'. Josephus' criticism uses both the rhetorical argument about the expense of such shows, and that of cruelty: but it is the effect on Jewish tradition that ultimately concerns him.[44] Gladiators are explicitly mentioned in Josephus' account of Herod Agrippa's generosity to the people of the Roman colony of Berytus; apart from a theatre, baths and porticoes, he built them an amphitheatre, and demonstrated his munificence by displaying a great number of gladiators; Josephus mentions one show in which seven hundred pairs were made to fight, including any condemned criminals Agrippa had available. While Josephus refrains from criticism in this particular account, the context shows that there was a substantial feeling amongst those versed in Jewish law (Simon, §4) who thought that Agrippa's behaviour was improper.[45]

Like Josephus, the early Christian writers could draw on the armoury of pagan philosophical objections to public shows in defence of their religious reservations about gladiatorial spectacles. For some Greeks, gladiatorial games represented a threat to their literary culture; for Jews, culture – that is to say, ethnic tradition – and morality were closely associated; but for (gentile) Christians, their religion represented a rejection of their inherited (pagan) culture, and criticisms of particular features of secular culture could be made on moral grounds alone. Surviving patristic writings, both Latin and Greek, confront their readers (generally Christians rather than pagans, but invariably members of the literate elite) with a range of arguments against the moral acceptability of *munera*. Some of these are specifically Christian, but many are culled from the common classical stock of philosophical reservations about passionate shows. We do not have to assume that these were the grounds that ultimately concerned Christians; in fact we have to go further, and assume that many or all contemporary Christians may not have been fully conscious of what it was about gladiatorial games specifically (as opposed to other elements of secular culture) that gave them such concern, apart from their 'impiety' in general.

In his handbook on the Christian's moral development, the *Paedagogus*, Clement of Alexandria (died ca. AD 215) warns the young tutee that the arena is a frivolous and confusing place where the onlooker may find himself caught up in a riot. Like other public spectacles, the games are also morally dangerous because they are attended by men and women together.[46] Latin Christians were no less hostile than Greek ones. Clement's contemporary Tertullian divides spectacles into three separate categories in order to attack them, in accordance with the prescriptions of rhetorical theory. He speaks of chariot-racing as 'mad', gladiatorial contests as 'savage', and theatrical shows as 'titillating': circus furens, cavea saeviens, scaena lasciviens.[47] But the 'savagery' Tertullian deprecates is not the savagery inflicted on each other by the gladiators, but the emotion experienced by the onlooker. The three non-rational characteristics listed by Tertullian have to be seen as parallel: in each case it is their effect on the audience, not on the actors, that worries him. In the early fifth century – perhaps after gladiatorial combats, though not wild beast hunts, had ceased – both St Jerome and St Augustine still use the same three terms: 'harena saevit, circus insanit, theatra luxuriant' and 'turpitudines variae theatrorum, insania circi, crudelitas amphitheatri'.[48] A slightly different term had been applied to gladiatorial contests in the mid-third century by Minucius Felix in a dialogue aimed at educated pagans. He divides spectacles into the same three categories, but talks of madness, manslaughter, and immorality.[49] Here it is the activity itself rather than its effect on the audience to which the negative characteristic is being ascribed. It was the effect on the onlooker that was the primary concern of Christian moralists, just like their Stoic predecessors, as is made clear in a diatribe by the Latin rhetor Lactantius.[50] He discusses the effect which various kinds of spectacles have in destroying the capacity of their audience to act rationally, and concludes by wondering whether it is not in fact the theatre with its sexually titillating displays that does the most damage to morals (§27). Many other warnings against the harmful effects of *munera* on the onlooker by the early Greek Fathers could be cited.[51]

Of all the Church fathers, it was perhaps Augustine whose concern about the psychological damage that external experience might inflict on the Christian soul was expressed with the greatest immediacy. Anything that diverts the mind from the serious concerns of life is reprehensible: he found it disgraceful that the wealthy Roman refugees who arrived in North Africa after the sack of Rome and devastation of their Italian estates by Alaric's army in AD 410 should spend their time applauding their favourite actors in the theatre. Both amphitheatre and theatre are described as 'concilium vanitatis', the meeting-place of irrelevance. He talks about gladiatorial games as 'trifles', *nugacia munerum*, in a sermon apparently delivered to his congregation on a day when the rest of the population were attending such a show. While the pagan watches the games, the Christian should be listening to the word of God.[52]

If the *nugacia* of spectacles distracted both pagans and Christians from matters of merely secular importance, then their effect on morals was even more dangerous. One of the finest accounts of how attending such a show perverted the moral sense of one of Augustine's own fellow students at Carthage in the AD 360s occurs in the *Confessions*.

> When he saw the blood, it was as though he had drunk a deep draught of savage passion. Instead of turning away, he fixed his eyes upon the scene and drank in all its frenzy, unaware of what he was doing. He revelled in the wickedness of the fighting and was drunk with the fascination of bloodshed . . . He watched and cheered and grew hot with excitement, and when he left the arena, he carried away with him a diseased mind which would leave him no peace

until he came back again, no longer simply together with the friends who had first dragged him there, but at their head, leading new sheep to the slaughter.[53]

Another moral objection to gladiatorial games which the Church fathers shared with pagan thinkers concerned the status of the gladiator. Augustine exploits the association in Roman thought between the prostitute, the pimp, and the gladiator: all ought to be denied baptism.[54] The gladiator suffered from *infamia*: did it not follow that he was someone to whom no one should pay any attention – 'Sed infamis est ille qui spectatur; qui spectat, honestus est?'[55] Christian references to cruelty should be seen in the context of the same discourse about gladiators, rather than as attacks on the cruelty of the games as an institution. In the *City of God*, Augustine criticises those who watch the games on the grounds that it is the gladiator himself who is evil and cruel. Where Christian writers apparently attack the games as cruel, the argument they are using is that such cruelty defiles the (Christian) onlooker. Tertullian, in a defence of Christianity which may have been intended for a wider readership, argues that it is terrible for the death of an evil-doer condemned to perform as a *bestiarius* to be a source of entertainment: but it is the fact that the performer is an evil-doer, a *malus homo*, that concerns Tertullian, not the cruelty of the mode of execution (still less the cruelty directed against the animals).[56]

Christian attitudes to the cruelty associated with the exercise of magisterial power were varied and complex; what surviving literary sources have in common is that they see the moral problem of cruelty from the point of view of the Christian who may have to witness or even inflict it, not that of the convict or gladiator who suffers it. Even for the perfectionist Pelagians in the early fifth century AD, the exercise of secular power was a moral problem for the Christian magistrate, not something that called for a humanitarian abolitionist movement:

> In your sight the bodies of men, human beings like yourselves, are beaten with leaden whips, broken with sticks, torn by the torturers' hooks, and burnt in the flames. Christian compassion can witness this, Christian eyes can bear to look at it – and not just to look at it, but to give the order for the torture to begin, out of the pride that comes from exercising power . . . You entertain your dinner-

guests by giving them an account of the event, telling them just how each man died and what tortures he underwent, and how you had the body flung on the ground in the presence of the crowd. But you do not want to give your guests indigestion; so you say that you were just carrying out the law.[57]

The attack on gladiatorial games as 'despicable and defiled' by one of the earliest Greek apologists, Tatian, in the mid-second century, has to be seen as part of a wider attack on pagan rituals.[58] Instances of objections to gladiatorial combat on the grounds found in Josephus, that it is shocking that men should suffer at Rome to give pleasure to others, are few in the extreme; the argument occurs in Prudentius' armoury of objections in his attack on the Vestal Virgins, but notwithstanding those who have wished to argue that Christians had a distinctively humanitarian approach to pain, it cannot there be taken seriously: Prudentius goes on to say that criminals should be sentenced to be killed by wild beasts instead. Any objections there may have been to the cruelty inflicted in the amphitheatre did not prevent Tertullian from seeing the Second Coming in terms of a spectacle: the mass execution of traitors, i.e. pagans, in a cosmic arena under the presidency of Christ. This was not a compassionate Christ, just as no compassion had been shown to those convicted of the crime of Christianity. Earlier Christian visions of the Last Judgement had been in terms of the destruction of an earthly city in warfare.[59] For Roman Christians, the arena was an essential feature of the culture they shared with pagans, and the imagery of the arena, with its wild beasts, torture, burning, and weapons, provided Christians with some of the imagery for the picture of hell that was to persist through the centuries. The imagery of the arena was taken for granted by Christians, and some of them, as Romans, shared the belief that the arena was the place where a brave fighter achieves resurrection in the midst of death. The martyrs' bravery had overcome physical suffering in 'the contest of God, the battle of Christ'. Cyprian, bishop of Carthage in the AD 250s, exhorted those in danger of execution to remain steadfast in the faith.

The tortured showed more bravery than the torturers . . .
The blood which flowed might have sufficed to put out the fire of persecution, even to put out the flames of Gehenna

with its glorious gore . . . What a spectacle this was for the Lord – how sublime, how magnificent, how acceptable to God's eyes is the allegiance and devotion of his soldiers.[60]

The metaphor of military bravery is strikingly applied to women martyrs in the *Passion of Perpetua and Felicity*. Their execution is represented as a battle against the devil in the Carthaginian arena; the president's box is occupied not by the proconsul, but by the Lord. Since Perpetua was a *honestior*, her execution was in fact a swift one, by the sword: 'When the swordsman's hand shook (for he was only a trainee), Perpetua herself placed it in position on her neck.' The story of Perpetua's dream before her execution represents it as a gladiatorial contest, in which the martyr slays her opponent, a great black devil; for a Christian lady, playing the ambivalent figure of a gladiator might be as subconsciously attractive as for the pagan woman of high status satirised by Juvenal. The martyrs in ecstasy feel no physical pain:

> Perpetua . . . was so much in the ecstasy of the Spirit that she was like someone waking up from sleep; she started by looking round her, and then, to the surprise of everyone who was there, asked 'When are we to be thrown to the bull?' When she heard that this had already happened, she would not believe them, until she saw how her body and her clothing had been torn.

For the Roman hagiographer, the suffering of the saints does not matter because they are above ordinary mortality; a proposition which assumes that the sufferings of criminals, as witnessed year after year in the same amphitheatres, are to be taken for granted because they are below humanity.

The fact that Christian moralists had to point out the idolatrous associations of the arena again and again to their Christian readers over the centuries suggests that many or most Christians did not see them as sufficiently strong reasons for rejecting *munera* in theory, or staying away in practice. In the tract *On Spectacles*, Tertullian has to make the most of any pagan religious association that he can think of: this is one of the few ancient texts which explicitly explains the origins of *munera* as offerings to the *manes*, the souls of the deceased. Amphitheatres are pagan temples, dedicated to particular gods, and contain images of those gods. Victims are sacrificed to the underworld god Dis or Pluto. Two centuries later, Prudentius produced a particularly sustained critique of gladiatorial spectacles at the conclusion of his two long hexameter poems *Against Symmachus*. These literary essays were inspired by the publication at the end of the fourth century of the attack on the cult of the goddess Victory by St Ambrose, bishop of Milan from AD 374 to 397. Ambrose's letters were themselves a reply to an appeal in AD 384 to the emperor Valentinian by the orator Symmachus in his capacity as Urban Prefect, to allow the altar of Victory to be set up again in the Roman senate house, whence it had earlier been removed by Gratian. Symmachus' appeal had been rejected at the time, thanks largely to Ambrose's efforts.

Prudentius' first book is a general attack on paganism as a dying religion, while the second answers some of the specific arguments that had been made by Symmachus. One of these had been a plea for the restoration of the privileges of the Vestal Virgins.[61] Prudentius selects this as a hook on which to append the attack on gladiatorial contests with which his poem ends. He begins with an attack on the supposed chastity of the Vestals, on the grounds that, since they were appointed between the ages of six and ten, they could not be said to have in any real sense chosen virginity, as shown by the fact that many of them married when they had finished their thirty years' service to Vesta. The reference to the marriage ceremony leads Prudentius to discuss the procession in which the Vestals were taken to watch the games in the arena. His description of a spectator's behaviour denigrates the Vestals' claim to chastity by emphasising the sexuality associated with gladiators:

> What a sweet and gentle spirit she has! She leaps up at each stroke, and every time that the victorious gladiator plunges his sword into his opponent's neck, she calls him her sweetheart, and turning her thumb downwards this modest maiden orders the breast of the prone gladiator to be torn open so that no part of his soul should be hidden, while the *secutor* looms above him, panting as he presses in with his weapon.[62]

Prudentius asks whether the Vestals deserve their privileges because they perform animal sacrifices 'to redeem the life of the people and the salvation of their leaders', or whether it is because 'Sitting in the better part of the amphitheatre they look closely at the bronze-covered face, smashed by repeated casts of the trident, and at the part of the arena which a bleeding gladiator stains with his gaping wounds as he tries to flee, and at how many steps he can manage, marked by his blood.'[63] He concludes by appealing to Honorius to remove this wretched rite, 'tam triste sacrum', from golden Rome, using the rhetorical commonplace that his Christian father, Theodosius, had only refrained from doing so himself in order to leave his son an opportunity for such a virtuous action. 'He forbad the city from being stained by the blood of (sacrificed) bulls, you must prohibit propitiation by putting wretched men to death.' Prudentius clearly wants to see an end to gladiators as such, and not just the pagan religious associations of the arena. But it is not violent behaviour as such that he objects to, but the shedding of human blood: 'Let no one fall dead in the City, whose punishment gives pleasure to others. Nor should girls' eyes take pleasure in killing. Let the ignoble arena be content with beasts alone; and let there be no man-killing games involving bloody weapons.'[64]

The unease of Christians about *munera* is striking, and requires explanation. Certainly gladiatorial games had not become entirely 'secular', any more than other Roman spectacles. But Christian Rome and Byzantium found no difficulties in suppressing any pagan associations of chariot races and wild-beast shows and integrating these activities into a Christian polity. Prudentius did not perceive cruelty to criminals by using the *infamis arena*, the amphitheatre popular with the lower orders, for executions as a moral problem of any kind: on the contrary, he says that a city in which that happened would be devoted to God (*sit devota deo*, 2, 1130). The legislative enactments of Christian emperors from Constantine on show no inhibitions about extending the range of crimes calling for torture and execution by fire or wild beasts, as well as introducing more novel refinements such as the mutilation of various parts of the body used in committing particular crimes, and pouring molten lead down the throat of someone involved in the abduction of a virgin.[65] There may be doubts about the extent to which late Roman criminal legislation was really more savage than that of the classical period, or merely reduced everyone apart from the elite to the level of judicial violence that had always been held for slaves and *dediticii* (rightless provincials); and it may also be the case that the penalties preserved in the law-codes were intended to reassure the public that, no matter how ineffective, the government at least intended to maintain law and order. At times emperors may have made the punishments they publicly proclaimed rather more savage than anything they actually intended to impose in order to give themselves scope to exercise the imperial virtue of *clementia*.[66]

But despite these caveats, it remains the case that Christians would have had no difficulty in coming to terms with the cruelty of gladiatorial games if they had not had other grounds for disliking them. Cruelty towards wild beasts was as little a problem for Christians as cruelty towards prisoners: both mosaics and literary descriptions show that *venationes* continued to be a feature of Roman life in North Africa until the Arab conquest, and in Christian Iberia and areas of southern France they continue to the present day in the form of the bull-fight.[66a] The ivory diptych advertising the consular games of Aerobindus in AD 506 shows, on one of its leaves, the crowd in the Circus at Constantinople watching acrobats baiting bears, and on the other four *bestiarii* despatching lions with their spears in much the same poses as on representations four centuries earlier (figure 8). A letter composed by Cassiodorus for the Ostrogothic King Theoderic encourages the consul of AD 523 to provide *venationes*, while also expressing the elite's disdain for such popular spectacles (another letter makes the same criticisms about chariot races). Several of the Latin poems contained in the sixth-century North African anthology (in the *Codex Salmasianus*) honour either charioteers or *bestiarii*. There are a number of explicitly Christian tombstones to charioteers, and the importance of chariot races in the Byzantine world is well documented.[67] Both chariot-races and the destruction of wild beasts could even be given a new significance by Christians, as symbols of the struggle of virtue against vice. The wild beasts slaughtered by the *bestiarius* were the vices the Christian needed to control in himself. For Christians as for pagans, the lion was the dangerous beast *par excellence*; in the Golden Age, domestic animals would no longer have cause to fear them, in Vergil's messianic eclogue as in Isaiah. A very early apocryphal text, the *Acts of Paul and Thecla* (perhaps composed ca. AD 185/95) tells the story of how St Paul was attacked by a lion; the beast was converted by the saint, and baptised.[68] Several late antique

Christian sarcophagi represent the scene of the saint over-coming the lion. On one in the Museo Torlonia in the Vatican, the lion holds a gazelle between its paws, but does it no harm: an inversion, rather than a development, of earlier mosaics such as one found at Verulamium which represent the lion as having destroyed a gentler animal. In the archiepiscopal chapel at Ravenna, built in the time of Peter II (AD 494–519), there is a mosaic of Christ as the true life, destroying a lion and a serpent (perhaps a reference to Psalm 90:13): beasts continued to represent the dangerous natural world which man had to overcome to attain salvation.[69]

This leads one to suspect that it was not the element of death or suffering in a gladiatorial performance that Christians found impossible to come to terms with, but the possibility of resurrection. We may recall the association between gladiators and funeral games: it was exactly this association that Tertullian was reduced to appealing to in his claim that the games were inextricably linked to pagan ritual, with little conviction. Apart from their alleged origins in the cult of the *manes*, he noted the appearance of umpires and assistants in the guise of Charon, the Etruscan Mercury; a very tenuous proof that the worship of pagan gods was an essential part of a *munus*. Whether Christians were conscious of it or not, the link with death and renewal might have been more worrying than the honour granted to any pagan god. We have seen that the Roman games were closely associated with the winter solstice, with five days before and five after the Saturnalia: the last day of gladiatorial *munera* corresponded to Christmas eve. The Christian celebration of the winter solstice as the time when the saviour-god was born developed in the course of the later fourth century, precisely at the time when the performance of gladiatorial games during the preceding fortnight fell into abeyance, in spite of the efforts of pagans like Symmachus. Unlike the *venatio* and the execution of criminals, the games were an expression of the belief, which had been fundamental to Roman society for centuries, that a person who was *infamis*, had no claim to respect from society, might nevertheless prove his *virtus* by fighting well in the arena. That was not the way in which Christians saw resurrection. Unlike the chariot-racing and *venationes*, gladiatorial games could not be tolerated by Christians, not because of any residual pagan religious rituals (which could easily have been excluded from such spectacles), but because they usurped the symbolism of Christian religious sacraments in providing salvation. They also assigned the source of that salvation, not to a divine being or his representative, the Christian church, but to a secular human entity: the Roman people. Rufinus of Aquileia, in the late fourth century, was adamant that the final judge was God, not the *vulgus*, and advised the Christian to provide only those *munera* over which God would preside: 'munificus esse in huiuscemodi largitionibus, in quibus iudex residet Dominus'.

What effect, then, did the acceptance of Christianity as the organising principle of public life in late antiquity have on gladiatorial contests? Some nineteenth-century scholars posited a simple connection in terms of formal abolition by Christian legislators, analogous to the process by means of which New World slavery had been abolished by law in their own experience. They pointed in particular to a rescript issued by Constantine at Berytus on 1 October AD 325, addressed to the Praetorian Prefect Maximus, Vicar of the Oriens (roughly, the Asiatic provinces with Egypt):

> In an age of public peace and domestic tranquillity, spec-
> tacles involving the shedding of blood displease us. We
> therefore utterly forbid the existence of gladiators; ensure
> that those persons who, because of their crimes, used to be
> sentenced to become gladiators, should now be sentenced
> to the mines, so that they can pay the penalty for their
> criminal behaviour without having to shed their blood.

The rescript is apparently unambiguous, but – as has been pointed out most succinctly recently by Ramsey Macmullen – gladiatorial contests continued to exist, both in real life and in literature. Three years after the Berytus ruling, a gladiatorial contest took place in Antioch, a city which had a reputation of being exceptionally 'Christian'. Mommsen, with his unshakable belief that imperial commands could not have been disobeyed, explained away the inconsistency by assuming that Constantine forbad only the judicial *damnatio ad ludos*, not voluntary enlistment as a gladiator. But the argument used by Constantine in the Berytus rescript was patently not the purpose of the decree: that was to provide a new source of labour for the mines, presumably to replace the Christians who had been condemned

to hard labour by Licinius, from whom Constantine had conquered the eastern part of the empire in the previous year. The
argument against 'cruenta spectacula' served as a rhetorical
justification for Constantine's ordinance, as it had earlier done
in the case of Marcus Aurelius.[70]
   One respect in which Constantine may have contributed significantly to the decline of the symbolic importance of gladiators
was by founding his new residence at Constantinople as an
overtly Christian city; and there is no evidence that gladiators
ever appeared there. This explains why Christian polemic ema-
nating from Constantinople does not need to attack gladiators,
unlike *venationes* (e.g. in the writings of John Chrysostom). But
elsewhere there was no question of systematic suppression. In a
rescript dating to the AD 330s addressed to the Umbrian city of
Hispellum, Constantine himself guaranteed the city's right to
maintain its gladiatorial fiesta in order not to have to attend the
one put on by the rival city of Volsinii across the mountains.[71] A
generation later, Valentinian addressed a rescript on the subject
dated 5 January AD 365 to the Urban Prefect Symmachus. It
threatens with a heavy fine any judge who sentences a Christian
'to the arena'.[72] 'Harenarius' normally refers to gladiators; the
rescript implies both that at this point (perhaps specifically in the
course of the praetorian games held in the previous December)
some of those forced to fight in this way had been Christians,
and that non-Christians would continue to be liable to condemnation *ad ludum*. In other words, gladiatorial games were not
being 'abolished', but Christians were being granted the privilege of suffering other penalties. Nevertheless, if this enactment
was taken seriously, then it would represent an additional, if
minor, reason for the gradual decline of gladiators: as the
number of non-Christian criminals declined, so did the number
of those who could be sentenced to become gladiators.
   As late as AD 384, Symmachus, as Urban Prefect, reports
senatorial regulations limiting expenses on both theatrical and
gladiatorial spectacles,[73] and of course he was concerned to
ensure that the quaestorian games he provided in the name of
his son were as spectacular as anything in Roman tradition.
Prudentius' attack makes it clear that Theodosius' legislation
against public pagan ceremonies in AD 388, and again after his
victory over the last pagan pretender for the imperial office,
Eugenius, at the battle of the river Frigidus in September 394,

had suppressed such games at Rome only temporarily, if at all. Epigraphic evidence has invalidly been taken to indicate that gladiatorial schools were abolished (presumably as the result of the discontinuing of imperial funding) in AD 399. One of the last references to gladiators, as opposed to wild beast shows, is the story of the monk Telemachus, who was torn apart by an irate crowd when he tried to intervene to stop a *munus* at Rome.[74] In consequence, Honorius is said to have banned games. But that ban cannot have applied throughout the empire; it was a temporary punishment of one particular community, like that of Pompeii in the reign of Nero. As late as the AD 430s or 440s, contorniates (medallions commemorating the holders of consulships) depict gladiators in combat; one from 410 or later is inscribed 'May the restoration of the *munus* have a happy outcome'.[75]

After that, references to gladiators cease. The argument from silence is of course a weak one, but it is significant that (for instance) the sustained attack by Salvian on public spectacles in the AD 440s mentions *venationes*, theatrical shows, and chariot-races in many parts of the western empire, but not gladiators (who would have given him much scope for his rhetoric). Western Church councils in the fifth century do not repeat the threats of excommunication against gladiators which are found in Augustine. When the emperors Anthemius and Armasius decree that Sundays must be kept free from litigation and obscene spectacles in AD 469, the spectacles they specify are 'scaena theatralis aut circense certamen aut ferarum lacrimosa spectacula'. When Justinian laid down regulations for the consular games in AD 536, he specified two days for chariot races and two days for *venationes*; there were no gladiators.[76] The poems of the *Codex Salmasianus*, consular diptychs, and reliefs all show pride in *venationes* and, increasingly, chariot-racing, but gladiators no longer appear.

The disappearance of references to gladiators in imperial legislation and in historical narratives does not coincide with the political victory of a Christian dynasty of emperors. Nor does the disappearance of gladiators as literary symbols. In some contexts, it could be argued that such references are simply part of the tradition of moralising: like his predecessors, Gregory of Nazianzen in the AD 360s refers to 'fools who take a great interest in unnatural dances, men killing one another, and the slaughter of wild beasts'; this does not prove that gladiatorial contests were still being held in the Greek part of the empire, any more than the failure of Gregory's friend Basil to include gladiators in a list of 'pancratists, and men fighting wild beasts' whom a wealthy man will provide for the sake of secular honour proves that gladiatorial contests were no longer popular.[77] There are other passages in fourth-century texts which suggest something more than just rhetorical topoi, but rather that the writer assumed that his audience knew what gladiators were and what they signified. In one of his first works, a hagiography of the Palestinian hermit Hilarion, Jerome told the story of two devils who came to plague the anchorite: they were a charioteer, and a gladiator who asked that Hilarion give him a Christian burial. But here too there are problems. Leaving aside the question of whether the gladiator was 'real' or 'symbolic' and whether the story was Jerome's own or had appeared in his source, a panegyric by Bishop Epiphanius of Salamis, the dramatic date of the episode is early in the saint's career – perhaps in the first quarter of the fourth century. At that time gladiatorial contests were clearly still acceptable to many, even in 'Christian' cities such as Antioch, in the eastern and central Mediterranean. When the Sicilian senator Firmicius Maternus wrote his astrological handbook during the last years of Constantine's reign (ca. AD 334–7), he analysed several horoscopes of gladiators, including gruesome details of the way they lost their lives.[78]

In the north-western provinces, the marginalisation of gladiatorial contests may have begun earlier, and that in its turn may have had an effect on the personal taste of Constantine: he came from the west, where firm evidence for gladiatorial games, as opposed to wild beast shows, disappears after the third century. The western provinces were the least Christianised part of the empire, yet the area where references to gladiators first become sparse. But it does not quite follow that 'The role of Christianity in the abandoning of most western gladiatorial combat was nil' (Macmullen). Constantine may have shared the tastes of the north-west, where he had grown up. This did not make him any more humane. In AD 313, when Constantine was making his preference for the Christian God publicly clear following the 'Christian' victory at the battle of the Milvian Bridge, the author of a panegyric in praise of the

emperor had no qualms about referring in glowing terms to his
slaughter of captured Germanic prisoners of war by wild beasts,
presumably in the amphitheatre at Trier, as a spectacle, *ludibrio*.
The panegyricist does not explicitly say that these prisoners
were forced to fight as gladiators.[79]
   In Italy, things were different. Two years later, Constantine
was condemning kidnappers to fight as gladiators:

> Kidnappers who inflict on parents the lamentable bereave-
> ment of their living children were formerly sentenced to
> the mines or other similar punishments. In future, if any
> person is charged with such a crime and his guilt is mani-
> fest, then if he is a slave or freedman he shall be thrown to
> the wild beasts at the next public spectacle; but if he is
> freeborn, he shall be handed to a gladiatorial school under
> the proviso that before he does anything to escape punish-
> ment, he shall be destroyed by the sword.[80]

   The role of Christianity in the suppression of gladiatorial
contests is a complex one. Neither the cruelty inflicted on the
participants, nor the pagan rituals associated with them, need
have been insuperable reasons for their suppression. Nor was
their disappearance due to direct intervention by Christian
emperors, let alone bishops or theologians. But the Christian
society of late antiquity no longer needed them as a symbol of
the dividing line between who belonged and who did not: as
the means by which the outsider can enter, or re-enter, respectable society. That route for entry, or even – for sinners –
re-entry into the only society that mattered was by way of the
sacraments of baptism and penance. There were other factors,
too: Roman Christians could no longer hold that only those
who shared Mediterranean urban culture 'belonged'. In north-
west Europe, the decline in gladiatorial displays seems to
coincide with the assimilation of barbarians into the Roman
army. If outsiders could join the Roman army as fighting men,
it was difficult to define the margins of the civilised world in
such a way as to exclude them, even if you were a pagan –
though those who valued the classical literary heritage, like
Ammianus Marcellinus, continued to write as though the old
categories persisted. Gladiators had a symbolic role only for
those who saw Rome as the ultimate classical city.

OPPOSITION AND ABOLITION

NOTES

1 For a recent critique of this attitude, cf. R. Macmullen, 'Late Roman Slavery', *Changes in the Roman Empire* (Princeton, 1990), chapter 23; also 'What Difference Did Christianity Make?', chapter 13.
2 G. Lafaye, 'Gladiateurs', D-S II (1896), 1565.
3 D-S II, 1566.
4 Cf. Chapter 1; Seneca, *Quaestiones Naturales* 7.31, Tacitus, *Annals* 15.32 etc.; Eusebius, *De martyribus Palaestinae* 8.1; Tatian, *Adversus Graecos* 23.
5 The *Historia Augusta*'s account of good emperors: Antoninus Pius 12, 3; Marcus 11, 4.27.6.
6 Suetonius, *Augustus* 44.2; Calpurnius Siculus, *Eclogue* 7, 26 ff; 80 ff.; Martial 5, 8.1.
7 Suetonius, *Augustus* 58.1 (Augustus acts in his capacity of *pater patriae*). By Cassius Dio's time, laurel wreaths were worn by senators at *venationes*, and presumably also other *munera*: Dio 72, 21.2; Livy 34, 44.4 and 54. 4–8; AE 1986.333 §81.
8 Tacitus, *Annals* 4, 63.
9 Tacitus, *Annals* 14, 17.
10 Legislation on numbers 65 BC: Plutarch, *Caesar* 10.2, Pliny NH 33, 53. Cicero, *In Vatinium* 37.
11 Cassius Dio 54, 2.4 17.4; cf. B. Levick, 'The *Senatus Consultum* from Larinum', JRS 73 (1983), 108.
12 On the status of actors, see C.H. Edwards (p. 26 and n. 77 above).
13 Suetonius, *Tiberius* 34.1; cf. 47.
14 Tacitus, *Annals* 13, 31.
15 ILS 5163 = CIL II.6278; there are other excerpts of the decree on an inscription found at Sardis. For text and translation, see J.H. Oliver and R.E.A. Palmer, *Hesperia* 24 (1955), 320 ff. (arguing that Marcus' enactment was a response to the martyrdom of Blandina and her companions at Lyon); Th. Mommsen, 'Observationes epigraphicae xli: Senatus consultum de sumptibus ludorum gladiatorum minuendis factum a. p. C. 176/7' = *Gesammelte Schriften* VIII (Berlin, 1913), 499–531.
16 Dio 68, 2.3; Zonaras 9, 20; *Chronicon Paschale* I, p. 469, 12.
17 Cassius Dio 72, 29.3–4.
18 AE 1977.801.
19 *Pro Murena* 40; *De Officiis* 2, 16 and 60; the views on liberality perhaps taken from Aristotle. See p. 141 for further disparaging remarks about the pleasure to be found in watching spectacles.
20 *Ad Quintum fratrem* 3, 8.6.
21 Suetonius, *Caligula* 38.4.
22 Plutarch, *De republica gerenda* 29–31 = *Moralia* 823E; Dio Chrysostom, *Or.* 66 (cf. *Or.* 32.45); Clement of Alexandria, *Paedagogus* 3, 11.77.
23 *Quamquam vili sanguine nimis gaudens*, *Annals* 1, 76.
24 *Tusculans* 2, 17.41: *crudele gladiatorium spectaculum et inhumanum nonnullis videri solet.*

25 *Historia Augusta*, Caracalla 1,5.
26 Pseudo-Quintilian, *Declamationes* 279, p. 137.20 Ritter: esse quos-
   dam maiores qui ne conspicere quidem cruorem sufficerent: multi
   se a gladiatorum vulneribus avertunt.
27 Cassius Dio 72, 29.3 f.
28 Symmachus, *Letters* 2, 46; Seneca, *Letters* 90.45 and 95.33; 7.2 ff.
29 Cicero, *Ad Fam.* 7.1.
30 Cicero, *In Pisonem* 89.
31 Cicero, *Ad Fam.* 10. 32.3.
32 Cassius Dio 59, 10.4; Suetonius, *Caligula* 35.2.
33 Cf. n. 23 above; Suetonius, *Claudius* 14, 34.2.
34 Cicero, *Ad Fam.* 7, 1; Pliny, *Letters* 9, 6; Marcus, *Meditations* 6.46;
   Fronto, *Letters* 2.6; Libanius, *Oration* 1.5; for other examples of
   disparaging references to shows, cf. Cicero, *Ad Fam.* 12, 18.2;
   Horace, *Epistles* 2, 1.200 ff.; and Seneca, *Letters* 7, below.
35 Plato, *Republic* 3, 397; 10, 605. On the philosophical tradition of
   opposing the senses and the intellect, cf. B. Gibbs, 'Higher and
   Lower Pleasures', *Philosophy* 61 (1986), 31–59.
36 Seneca, *Letters* 7.3: Nihil vero tam damnosum bonis moribus quam
   in aliquo spectaculo desidere: tunc enim per voluptatem facilius
   vitia subrepunt. Quid me existimas dicere avarior redeo, ambitio-
   sior, luxoriosior immo vero crudelior et inhumanior, quia inter
   homines fui. Seneca introduced the vice of 'inhumanity' in order to
   make a word-play on 'homines'. Plutarch: *Moralia* 802D; 821F–
   823F; Aulus Gellius, *Attic Nights* 17, 12; Philostratus, *Sophists* 1, 25.9;
   Horace, *Epistles* 1, 18.19; Epictetus, *Enchiridion* 33.2; Horace, *Satires*
   2, 6.44.
37 Plutarch, *De Republica Gerenda* = *Moralia* 822.
38 Julian, *Letters* 304B-D.
39 Lucian, *Demonax* 57.
40 The comparison of eyes and ears to the advantage of the latter was
   a rhetorical commonplace. Cf. Isocrates, *Panathenaicus* 150; *Panegyricus* 30.
41 Terence, *Hecyra*, prologue 31.
42 Dio Chrysostom 31, 121.
43 Plutarch, *Moralia* 1099B; cf. p. 115 above.
44 Josephus, *Antiquities* 15, 8.1.
45 Josephus, *Antiquities* 19, 7.5.
46 *Paedagogus* 3, 11.77.
47 *Adv. Marcianum* 1, 27.5. Cf. *De pudicitia* 7.15; *Ad Martyres*.
48 *Letters* 43.3; *Sermones* 199.3.
49 Insania, homicidium, turpitudo: 37.11.
50 *Divinae Institutiones* 6, 20.9–14.
51 Athenagoras, *Legat.* 35 = PG 6.96 A, who includes *venationes*;
   Theophilus, *Ad Autolycum* 3.15 = PG 6.1141 A; Irenaeus, *Contra
   Haereseos* 1, 6.3 = PG 7.508; Novatian, *De spectaculis* 4 = PL 4.814;
   Cyril of Jerusalem, *Constitution Apostolica* = PG 33, 1069–72. Cf. G.
   Ville, 'Les Jeux de gladiateurs dans l'Empire Chrétien', *Mélanges de
   l'école Français à Rome* 72 (1960), 272–335.

52 *City of God* 1, 32 ff.; *Enarratio in psalm.* 25.9; *Sermones* 19, 51; *City of God* 2, 11–13.

53 *Confessions* 6.8; tr. Pine-Coffin.

54 *De Fide et Operibus* 18.33 = PL 40.220.

55 S. *Augustini sermones post Maurinos reperti.* ed. Dom G. Morin (Vatican, 1930), 68.13.

56 Augustine, *City of God* 3,14; Tertullian, *Apologeticum* 9.6; Cf. Petronius 45 for 'bestiarius' as man condemned to the beasts.

57 Ps.-Pelagius, *De Divitiis* 6 = PL suppl.I, 1385 f. Cf. G. Clark, 'Let Every Soul Be Subject', in L. Alexander (ed.), *Images of Empire* (Sheffield, 1991), 251–75.

58 Tatian, *Oratio ad Graecos* 23: πονεϱῶν καὶ μιαϱῶν ἔϱγων.

59 B.E. Daley, *The Hope of the Early Church* (Cambridge, 1991).

60 Cyprian, *Letter* 7/10.

61 Symmachus, *Relatio* 3, 11.

62 2, 1095–101.:

> O tenerum mitemque animum! consurgit ad ictus
> Et quotiens victor ferrum iugulo inserit, illa
> Delicias ait esse suas pectusque iacentis
> Virgo modesta iubet converso pollice rumpi
> ne lateat pars ulla animae vitalibus imis,
> Altius impresso dum palpitat ense secutor.

63 2, 1109–112:

> An quoniam podii meliore in parte sedentes
> Spectant aeratam faciem, quam crebra tridenti
> Impacto quatiant hastilia, saucius et quam
> Vulneribus patulis partem perfundat arenae
> cum fugit et quanto vestigia sanguine signet?

64 2, 1126–9:

> Nullus in urbe cadat, cuius sit poena voluptas,
> Nec sua virginitas oblectet caedibus ora.
> Iam solis contenta feris infamis arena
> Nulla cruentatis homicidia ludat in armis.

65 CTh. 9, 24.1.1.

66 Cf. p. 104 above; R. MacMullen, 'Judicial Savagery in the Roman Empire', *Changes in the Roman Empire* (Princeton, 1990), chapter 20.

66a We may add the survival of camel-wrestling at Ephesus: London *Times* Magazine, June 19 1993, p. 34.

67 Cassiodorus, *Variae* 5, 42 and 3, 51 = MGHAA 12, 168 ff.; 106 f. AE 1982.384 (near Aquileia); ILCV IV.10549, ILS 5303 (Rome); A. Cameron, *Circus Factions* (Oxford, 1976).

68 *Eclogue* 4, 22: nec magnos metuent armenta leones; Isaiah 11.6; *Paul and Thecla*: E. Hennecke, *Neutestamentliche Apokryphen* (3rd edn, Tübingen, 1964), 2, 221–68.

69 Hönle p. 66 argues that the Christian scene parallels the representation of a bearded man controlling a lion on the Nennig mosaic;

EMPERORS AND GLADIATORS

but on that – heavily restored – scene, the gazelle's head between the lion's paws clearly belongs to a dead gazelle. On another of the Nennig scenes, another tame animal is being destroyed by a tiger. The Ravenna mosaic is in F.W. Deichmann, *Frühchristliche Bauten und Mosaiken in Ravenna* (Baden-Baden, 1958), plates 216 f. Even executions *ad bestias* continued under Christian emperors: the latest known to me is recorded for AD 568 in the *Chronicle of John of Biclaro* §4: K.B. Wolf, *Conquerors and Chroniclers of Early Medieval Spain* (Liverpool, 1990).

70 CTh. 15, 12.1 = CJ 11.44.1; Wallon, *Histoire de l'esclavage* III, 387 ff. 'What Difference did Christianity make?' = *Changes in the Roman Empire*, pp. 147 ff. Cf. also *Christianising the Roman Empire* (New Haven, 1984).

71 ILS 705.= CIL XI.5265.

72 CTh. 9, 40.8.

73 *Relatio* 8.3.

74 Dated to AD 404: Theodoret, *Historia Ecclesiastica* 5, 26 = PG 82.1256. The view that the state discontinued *ludi* (schools) in ca. AD 399 depends on a highly speculative interpretation of CIL XIV.300.

75 Reparatio muneris feliciter: A.Alföldi, *Die Kontorniaten* (1943), no.176; cf. no.204.

76 *De gubernatione Dei* 6, 10; *Code of Justinian* 3, 12.9; *Novellae* 105, §2.

77 Gregory of Nazianzen, *Poemata* 2.4 lines 150–7 = PG 37.1515 f.; Basil, *Homilia in Luc.* 3 = PG 31.268D f.

78 Jerome, *Vita Hilarionis* 7 = PL 23, 32; Firmicius Maternus, *Mathesis* 3, 4.23; 7, 8.7.26.2; 8, 7.5.10.4; 23.4; 24.7.

79 *Panegyrici Latini* 12 (9), 23.3: Tantam captivorum multitudinem bestiis obicit, ut ingrati et perfidi non minus doloris ex ludibrio sui quam ex ipsa morte patiantur.

80 CTh. 9, 18.1.

5

CONCLUSION: IMPERIAL SOVEREIGNTY AND POPULAR SOVEREIGNTY

A gladiator was a man who might lack any positive quality except the skill to fight to the death. But that *virtus* was so important in defining who was a Roman that its public display might lead to the gladiator's being accepted back into the community of Romans. Although Rome had effectively ceased to be a city-state generations before the first three pairs of gladiators fought at Junius Brutus Pera's funeral in 264 BC, the city-state principle that sovereignty ultimately resided with the body of adult male citizens was adhered to even under the emperors. Consequently it was not the *editor* of the games, even if that *editor* was the emperor himself, but the assembled people that decided whether a defeated gladiator had shown enough courage to be granted his life, and whether a successful gladiator deserved to be restored to the privileges of citizenship. Reports of what the crowd demanded in the amphitheatre primarily refer to favours for particular fighters; this applies to the literary evidence, and to the occasional archaeological item such as the Tunisian mosaic commemorating the *venatio* of Magerius (p. 16 f.). The literary evidence is anecdotal, and emphasises demands made in the presence of an emperor. Anecdotes are recorded because of the light they shed on the emperor's character, particularly when those demands expressed friction between people and emperor, even on apparently non-political matters: the *Historia Augusta* notes the refusal of Hadrian and Gallienus to grant popular fighters what the people demanded, and Suetonius records the hostility of both Caligula and Domitian towards those who supported gladiators of a different type from their own favourites. The *Book of Spectacles* refers to the audience's demand that a particular gladiator be allowed to leave the arena alive, *missio*.[1]

The power to represent the legitimate sovereign, the true Roman people, might be claimed by crowds assembling in many different contexts, of which the amphitheatre was only one. During the republic, the people assembled to give their opinion not just in electoral and legislative assemblies of various kinds, but also in *contiones*, assemblies summoned by magistrates (or tribunes) for the purpose of making political announcements or suggesting possible courses of action, and gauging the reaction of the electorate. There was thus no clear dividing line between contexts where the assembled crowd formally represented the Roman people, and those where the people present spoke (or shouted) only for themselves; during the political upheavals of the late republic, it became quite clear that the answer to the question whether a particular crowd was simply a crowd or legitimately constituted the sovereign people expressing its will in electing a magistrate or passing a law largely depended on whether one approved of the faction the crowd supported. In the late republic, those politicians who classified themselves as *populares* in the tradition of the Gracchi had used mass support to challenge other sources of political authority; but this did not discredit the theory that the people were sovereign even after the republican constitution had been 'restored' by Augustus. Politicians like Cicero did not challenge that theory (at least, not in practical contexts); they merely argued that any crowd of a few thousand men collected by a *popularis* politician could not possibly be truly representative of Roman citizens, of whom there were nearly a million in the mid-first century BC. Indeed, Cicero argues that the audiences assembled at the *ludi* in the Circus or the theatre are much better representatives of the real opinions of the sovereign people, since they consist of respectable citizens and persons associated with the elite through networks of patronage.

In the amphitheatre, just as in the Circus and in the theatre, the people might give expression to their political opinions. In a letter to Atticus, Cicero reports popular acclaim as he appeared at a gladiatorial contest; in 59 BC, he claims that Caesar's opponents were cheered at a gladiatorial contest, while his supporters were booed and hissed or received in silence; at a performance in the theatre, the actor Diphilus was forced to repeat a line which could be interpreted as an attack on

Pompey.[2] Popular private individuals who were not magistrates might occasionally be so acclaimed, such as Vergil, according to one account.[3] The people might make concrete demands rather than just formal statements of approval or disapproval. During Caligula's reign a section of the crowd at a Circus *ludus* demanded a tax reduction.[4] The right of the people to bestow life was most evident on the occasions when they appealed for a condemned criminal to be reprieved, as in the romantic tale of Androclus. But it was not the lion who had the power of reprieve: Androclus might have been fed to some other beast, as happened to the martyr Germanicus (p. 80 above). It was the people who were convinced that Androclus deserved to live.[5] Again in Caligula's reign, the crowd demanded that a bandit called Tetrinius should be brought forward and given his freedom: Caligula accused them of being Tetrinius' accomplices.[6] The most famous example is a provincial one. The sovereign power of the Roman people extended throughtout the empire: as early as the reign of Tiberius, at the Jewish passover feast, the Roman prefect of Judaea could use the right of life and death that he had received, via the emperor, from the sovereign people to allow the crowd to request the release of a condemned criminal.

As the Gospel narratives show, the crowd had the right to bestow life, and also to condemn to death. The legal situation was bypassed. They might demand the execution of an unpopular person, even when no formal charges had been lodged against them: for example, Nero's praetorian prefect Tigellinus during the reign of Galba, and Titus' alleged opponents. Suetonius tells us that during Vespasian's reign his son, as Praetorian Prefect, arranged for partisans of his to be distributed amongst the theatre audience to demand the execution of individuals whom Titus suspected of opposing him. The fall of Commodus' favourite Cleander was engineered by a demonstration in the Circus, sparked off by a woman and a crowd of children uttering slogans.[7] The best attested category of unpopular persons attacked at public spectacles are of course Christians.

The crowd's demands were not restricted by legal niceties. They might ask for the manumission of a slave belonging to someone who was not the *editor*: Tiberius only acceded to such a demand when he had obtained the permission of the slave's owner. It was said that the wish to avoid being under pressures of this kind was a major reason why Tiberius gave up attending spectacles. Hadrian also refused to permit the manumission of slaves in response to the demands of the audience without the permission of the slave's owner. The law codes confirm that these were not just literary anecdotes: Marcus Aurelius had to forbid the enforced freeing by the presiding magistrate of a condemned slave whose freedom was demanded by the populace against the wishes of his owner.[8]

But the crowd might also make more explicitly political demands at such public celebrations, though our sources do not specifically assign examples of such demands at *munera*. Anti-war demonstrations were particularly frequent in the Circus: instances are recorded in 40 BC, and AD 196 (there were of course a number of occasions under the republic when war-weary citizens opposed the wishes of particular magistrates to lead them into a war, but in that period they could give expression to their views at *contiones* formally summoned by the tribunes). There was a demonstration by the people against rises in the price of grain in AD 32, and objections were made to Tiberius' removal to his palace of a favourite antique statue by the famous Greek sculptor Lysippus: Tiberius was forced to have the statue put back in its place.[9]

Any formal popular gathering therefore raised the question of how political power was distributed at Rome, and drew attention to the complex relationship between the formal sovereignty of the people, the *imperium* which had been awarded to presiding magistrates or military commanders who were celebrating a triumph, and the extra-constitutional but not unconstitutional wealth, influence and authority of powerful individuals and families. Even under the republic, spectacular displays such as Metellus Pius' celebrations and Pompey's games were expressions not just of the competition between political leaders, but also of the balance of power between the leadership collectively and the rest of the community. The concentration of political leadership in the hands of one person by Augustus made the question of that relationship much more obvious (and also had the effect of giving the rest of the political class a highly ambiguous position as both servants of the imperial system, and part of the 'people': accounts of the curious behaviour of senators during demonstrations illustrate their difficulty in deciding which way to face). This constant struggle between emperor and people as to how power was to be distributed, and (more formally) where sovereignty lay, was particularly liable to surface in the amphitheatre, since the three categories of activities that went on there were particularly symbolic of the exercise of power: power over the natural world, the enforcement of law, and the power to decide whether a particular gladiator was or was not to be classified as a virtuous Roman.

Notwithstanding its popularity, it is hard to accept the idea that *ludi* and *munera* were a means to divert the people away from politics. The theory is not a modern invention. An anecdote was told about Augustus' complaining about the popularity of pantomime actors; the leading such actor, Pylades, was said to have told the emperor that he ought to be pleased that the people spent their free time supporting actors instead of political opponents.[10] A first-century AD rhetorical exercise purporting to be a letter of advice to Julius Caesar written by the historian Sallust advises that the people be kept occupied to prevent their interfering in politics.[11] Fronto reported that Trajan had discussed the advantages of winning popular support by giving games rather than distributions of largesse or of grain (not the position that Cicero and Plutarch would have taken: cf. p. 137 f.), on the grounds that it kept the people out of trouble by giving them something to do with their time.[12]

But attendance at *munera* subjected emperors to pressure from the people, rather than diverting potential expressions of political will in other directions. Tiberius preferred to keep away altogether to avoid such pressure; but the unpopularity which this brought upon him shows that it was a mistake which later emperors knew they could not afford to repeat. The emperor could not of course appear at every *munus* anywhere in Italy or in the provinces. But not to appear at all would have been a challenge to the people by denying that the power exercised at these events was shared, even if only symbolically, between emperor and people. From the time when Augustus monopolised power, emperors consequently had an obligation to share that power with the people by providing them with games. In the emperor's absence from Rome, he had to make arrangements for *ludi* and *munera* to carry on, as Marcus Aurelius did during his absences on the northern frontier (thus allowing the boy Commodus to become more interested in the arena than he would otherwise have been), and in late antiquity emperors repeatedly legislated to ensure that games would be regularly provided by the Roman senatorial families.[13]

Apart from providing finance for the shows themselves and building the amphitheatres in which they were performed, the most significant contribution the emperors had to make were the permanent training schools, *ludi*, for gladiators and wild beast fighters. There had been both imperial and 'private' training schools in Rome before Augustus, though we cannot be certain when such schools were first set up in the capital; the gladiators referred to in Cicero's speeches, whose large numbers caused both resentment and fear when put on display by Caesar, need not have been trained in the capital. Horace mentions an 'Aemilium ludum'; there is no need to associate it with the construction of Statilius Taurus' amphitheatre in 29 BC.[14] We have seen that there were imperial slaves in charge of gladiatorial equipment at least from the time of Tiberius (p. 22 above). Caligula appears to have had his gladiators trained at Rome, and once (according to Suetonius) had a superintendant, *curator munerum ac venationum*, whipped to death.[15] Later inscriptions show that the careers of these procurators were part of the regular establishment of the imperial household. Some of them had previously served as military tribunes of legions, others as financial officials. Nor was this procuratorship a dead-end job; one was subsequently promoted to the administration of the 5 per cent inheritance tax. The procurator was assisted by a deputy.[16] In addition to maintaining the *ludi* at Rome, the emperors also instituted gladiatorial training schools in other cities in Italy and the provinces. The fact that Tacitus refers to imperial interference in a gladiatorial *ludus* at Praeneste (Palestrina) does not in itself prove that it was funded by the emperor. The evidence that there were gladiators at Capua called *Iuliani* and *Neroniani* comes from the notoriously unreliable *Historia Augusta*, but is confirmed by inscriptions. There is also epigraphic evidence relating to the two one-time Hellenistic royal residences in the East, Alexandria and Pergamum. An inscription from Rome mentions a 'procur[ator] famil[iae] glad[iatoriae] Caes[arianae] Alexandreae ad Aegyptum' as early as Augustus.[17] Furthermore, the emperors had to maintain a network of associated administrators of gangs of gladiators (*familiae*) which covered the whole of the empire. Some of these procurators had authority over wide geographical areas covering several provinces. One was responsible for Northern Italy and the Illyrian provinces, another covered the later prefecture of the Gauls (Gaul, Britain, Spain, the Germanies and Rhaetia), and an inscription from Prusias in Bithynia refers to a 'procurator Augustorum ad familias gladiatorias per Asiam et cohaerentes provincias'. These procurators were presumably not themselves responsible for training, like the *curatores* of the *ludi*, but for acquiring potential gladiators (from among convicts or captured prisoners of war rather than volunteers) and seeing that they reached Rome.[18]

With the exception of Alexandria and Pergamum, the Caesars seem in principle to have provided gladiatorial games only for Rome itself. When emperors happened to be in a major city other than Rome for pleasure or, as happened with increasing frequency from the end of the second century AD onwards, on campaign, they sometimes provided games for the population of these other residences; the improvements to the amphitheatre at Pozzuoli in AD 65 may be associated with Nero's visits to the town, which he raised to the status of a colony; an early example from outside Italy is that of the games held in honour of Vespasian by his son Titus in Berytus in AD 69/70. Hadrian's visit to Greece resulted in a new cycle of 'imperial Nemeans' at Argos (p. 47 above); and major improvements were made to the theatre at Corinth for *munera* which Caracalla was expected to put on during a prospective visit in AD 217 (but he was killed before he arrived).[19]

When an emperor was at Rome, then his personal presence at *munera* was expected. An emperor who was unpopular might be criticised either for being too interested in these games, or not interested enough: the tightrope which each emperor had to walk was a necessary consequence of the ambiguous position of the emperor as both autocrat and servant of the Roman people. The description of how an emperor behaved is often coloured by perceptions of whether he was good or bad: thus support for a particular chariot team or type of gladiator could be a good thing[20] or a bad.[21] 'Good' emperors were those later deified: Augustus, Claudius, Vespasian, Titus, then Nerva and his successors up to Marcus Aurelius. In order to avoid the criticisms that had been levelled at Julius Caesar for dealing with his correspondence during shows, Augustus paid full attention to what was going on. In this as in other respects, the behaviour of Augustus became a standard against which later emperors were judged.[22] Marcus Aurelius was criticised for reading or dealing with petitioners during games. The imperative for emperors to be accessible to the people, at least visually, meant that 'bad' emperors were attacked for watching from a special box – Nero watched from such a box at the beginning of his reign; Domitian's box was removed by Trajan when he rebuilt the Circus Maximus.[23]

Easy communication was another requirement. Instead of making announcements formally to the assembled people through heralds, emperors were praised for having placards paraded with information about what was going on. Sometimes an emperor might hope that communication by tablet would deflect the people's displeasure when he had not acceded to their demands, as when Hadrian refused to manumit a charioteer who was someone else's slave. Conversely, the use of a herald was a sign that an emperor was angry with the behaviour of the people, for instance when the people expressed incomprehension at Gallienus' decision to honour a bad bullfighter.[24]

Occasionally an emperor later classifed as 'tyrannical' was clearly popular with the people; this needed to be explained, for instance through the claim that he had bought the favour of the less rational elements of people, typically women and youngsters. Josephus makes no distinction in this respect between Caligula's distributions of meat, theatrical shows and gladiatorial games; only the third of these categories could be interpreted by Josephus in terms of his picture of Caligula as a bloodthirsty tyrant.[25] Rational and educated members of the elite ought not take base pleasure in the shedding of blood, and bloodthirstiness was a stock accusation: Tiberius' son Drusus was said to have developed a specially sharp gladiatorial sword. We have already noted criticism of Claudius' interest in *venationes* and midday executions. Nero was another tyrant-figure; Tacitus says that those ordinary Romans who had enjoyed the Circus and theatre games he had presented regretted his overthrow, and intellectuals explained away his posthumous popularity as due to his expenditure on theatrical displays. The popularity with the lower orders of Septimius Severus, an emperor who had a strong negative reputation for stinginess towards the elite, could be explained in terms of the money he devoted to games.[26]

It did not follow that an emperor who pursued the opposite course, and refused to bribe the less rational elements of the populace in this way, won the approbation of posterity. Unlike his predecessor Augustus (or his own son Drusus), Tiberius showed little interest in public spectacles of any kind, though we are told that at the beginning of his reign he attended shows. One of his first acts on coming to power in AD 14 was to take away from the popular assemblies any real part in the process of election of praetors; the effect was that junior magistrates (*aediles*) no longer felt it necessary to win the people's favour with a view to winning their votes in the next round of elections. He also imposed maximum rates on the bonuses allowed to actors and gladiators. The resulting unpopularity turned any attempt by other public figures to put on a special display into a challenge to the emperor: Tiberius' Praetorian Prefect Sejanus put on shows during his consulship, just before his fall.[27]

Caligula was the first Julio-Claudian to lose the support of the elite. Consequently a series of anecdotes is reported illustrating his wickedness in the context of gladiators such as that of Apronius Saturninus, forced to pay nine million sesterces for thirteen gladiators at an imperial auction because he nodded off to sleep – an expression of the concern of the wealthy at the expense of such shows under an emperor who enjoyed them. As we have seen, it was a rhetorical commonplace for a wicked magistrate to be accused of condemning people falsely. It is not surprising that Caligula is reported to have forced freeborn citizens to fight in the arena. One anecdote concerns the *primuspilus* Aesius Proculus, whom Caligula first forced to fight two gladiators in succession, and then had beheaded. Characteristically, the tyrant is accused of having had no more serious motive for the murder than jealousy of the victim's physical beauty. In Domitian's case, too, occasions when members of the elite were persuaded to fight were turned into hostile anecdotes: for instance, Acilius Glabrio, who is said to have fought in the arena before – perhaps at a *juventus*-display – and was therefore induced by Domitian to fight and kill a lion in Domitian's private arena in the Alban Hills at Domitian's own *Juvenalia*.[28]

The case of Claudius is a particularly interesting example of how difficult it was for emperors to demonstrate just the right degree of interest. Tiberius had been immensely unpopular for absenting himself from public events. Claudius demonstratively took his public role seriously. He communicated with the people informally, through placards, joining in jokes, counting out the participants' prize-money on his fingers along with the audience, and – significantly – addressing the crowd by the respectable title 'lords', *domini*. Yet he was criticised for taking so much pleasure in *venationes* that he condemned men to that penalty when their crimes did not deserve it, such as the stage-hands responsible when the set failed at a public spectacle.[29] It is ironic that Claudius won this reputation for cruelty and injustice, since it arose as a hostile interpretation of his concern to be seen to be maintaining law and order. Only with the principate was there a political force at Rome powerful enough to give its backing to the development of a coherent legal system; under the republic, different jurists had expressed authoritative opinions on legal issues, but their interpretations had not been powerful enough to be recognised as superior to other factors, such as the force of rhetorical persuasion exploited by Cicero. It was only when Augustus and his successors gave the backing of their personal authority to a limited number of legal experts that their opinions could count for more than social prestige or rhetorical ability; not because they were experts in the law, but because their responses were *ex auctoritate principis*, backed by the social power of the emperor. The primacy of the law at Rome was not possible without the backing of the emperor. Later, emperors could safely leave the courts under the supervision of their Praetorian Prefects; but in the Julio-Claudian period, the direct participation of the emperor in the law courts was as important an aspect of his duties as attendance at *munera*. Tiberius had absented himself from both, thus jeopardising his authority as emperor. Claudius was adamant that he would not repeat Tiberius' mistake in failing to devote sufficient time to solving legal disputes: in a surviving decision about the citizen status of a north Italian community called the Anauni, he explicitly attacks Tiberius' consistent truancy, 'apsentia pertinaci patrui mei'.[30] It is as part of this concern that the emperor should be seen to carry out legal judgements that his attendance at the midday executions should be interpreted: a good emperor devotes time to the law courts, but also devotes time to, literally, seeing that malefactors are punished.

As the focus of conflict between the power of the emperor and that of the people, the arena was as much a place where the people were on show as the ruler. Emperors might disapprove of the crowd's demands, although, as the anecdote about Caligula's response to the crowd's support for a rival type of gladiator shows, a 'bad' emperor might find that any humorous comments he made would be turned against him: he had wished that the Roman people had only a single neck (sc. for the opposing gladiator to plunge his sword into: see p. 96 and figure 9d). Augustus was displeased when the people rose to acclaim his grandsons, Gaius and Lucius Caesar, who were not yet adults. Tacitus complains that the Circus and Theatre were places for unbridled licence, 'seditiosis vocibus'. It was there that individuals collectively found the courage to shout disapproval of an emperor's shortcomings. They might also attack other powerful men with *maledicta*, whether on political or other grounds. In the time of Augustus, an ex-slave called Sarmentus attained the dignity of an equestrian, and watched a ceremony from the places reserved for equestrians; the crowd's chants of disapproval are preserved in a scholion on Juvenal. As late as AD 509, Cassiodorus can refer to the Circus as the place where the people exercise their right to free speech; and the connection between the Circus at Constantinople and political and religious disputes has been studied in detail.[31] The organised ritual chanting of the crowd is well-attested for the Byzantine world, and it is clear that such chanting in the Greek world went well back into the Hellenistic period. At Rome, it had certainly become customary by Nero's reign.[32]

Uncertainty about the distribution of power between emperor and people meant that no one could predict how the people would greet an emperor in times of crisis. The events in the amphitheatre or at the Circus were consequently given the force of omens. The chants of the people were ominous: under Commodus, a race-horse called Pertinax won a race, and the crowd expressed the hope that 'Pertinax (the later emperor) might win'; there are many such near-contemporary references in Cassius Dio. Before his assassination, Caligula had been spattered with blood at a performance of the Laureolus mime, and Commodus had changed his dress to the black cloak worn at *munera* just before his death. Even things that happened to the building itself might be ominous. In AD 217 the Colosseum was hit by lightning and badly damaged on the day of the Volcanalia, the feast of the fire-god, portending the political disasters that followed Caracalla's demise.[33]

What happened at public spectacles thus signified the power not just of the emperor, but also of the people. Just as emperors had to behave well, so did the spectators. There is a well-known anecdote about Augustus humiliating an equestrian whom he saw having a drink. There are many stories of emperors rebuking the populace for their behaviour through edicts or by the voice of a herald. The maintenance of discipline at public spectacles became the responsibility of the Urban Prefect; given the large number of people from all over Italy who came to watch such games, even in the republic, public order was naturally a problem. At Julius Caesar's triumphal games, two senators were crushed to death. From Augustus' time on, one of the duties of the *vigiles* was to patrol the streets to prevent burglaries and looting during Circus games.[34]

But imperial interventions were not just a matter of policing, or asserting the emperor's dominance; they were also a matter of maintaining the honour of the Roman people. Since the republic, there had been regulations about dress and seating arrangements relating to the *ludi*; these were revised by both Julius Caesar and Augustus, and later emperors. In the Forum and the Circus, the toga had to be worn as an external mark of Roman citizenship (p. 131). There were rules about appearing with or without shoes in the summer, and hats. Cloaks were permitted in bad weather, though many people were said to have died of colds after Domitian refused to allow cloaks to be put on during a downpour. He also forbad coloured clothing and allowed umbrellas.[35] Some of these regulations clearly applied only to *ludi*; *munera* had not originally been public festivals but funerals, and the dress expected to be worn there was not the toga but the dark cloak (*pullum*) associated with mourning.

As we have seen, it was considered an important part of the emperor's duties to maintain the status distinctions between different levels of citizens, and to prevent those of high status from becoming *infamis* by appearing in the arena, thereby subverting the reinforcement of social order which any public games represented. The crowd in the amphitheatre represented the Roman people, the dominant people whose capital was the centre of the world. The arena was the place where their sovereignty might visibly be usurped by the emperor. In his

celebration of the inauguration of the Colosseum, the poet of the
Book of Spectacles says that all peoples hailed Titus as *pater patriae*:

> What people is so cut off, what people so barbarous,
> Caesar, that it has not sent someone to your city as a
> spectator? A Rhodopian peasant has come, from Mt.
> Haemus, associated with Orpheus; a Sarmatian has come,
> who gets his nourishment from mare's milk; one who
> drinks from the sources of the Nile; one who is pounded by
> the waves of the distant Atlantic. The Arab has hastened to
> Rome, and the Yemenites, and the Cilicians have enjoyed
> the perfume which their own country produces. The
> Sygambrans have come, their hair twisted into a knot, and
> the Aethiopians, their hair twisted in a different way. The
> language spoken by these peoples differs, but it becomes
> one when you are justly addressed as *Pater Patriae*.[36]

It was an essential feature of the Augustan 'constitution' that
there was no formal agreement between the emperor and other
elements in the Roman political system as to where the limits of
imperial power lay. In terms of the relationship between
emperor and people, the amphitheatre was as important as the
Circus in giving emperors (and, to a lesser extent, the people)
opportunities to test the limits of their power. Hence the paradox that some emperors imposed regulations banning others
from appearing as actors or gladiators, and then appeared as
such themselves. Such anecdotes are regularly told of emperors
who failed in their attempt to identify just how far they could go
without turning into tyrants (Caligula, Nero, Domitian). The
most spectacular instance is that of Commodus. His gladiatorial
interests developed while he was a teenager, during his father
Marcus Aurelius' absences on campaign. It is possible that the
anxieties of provincial magnates about the costs of games in the
AD 170s were not just the result of economic difficulties, but
expressed concern about the role that *munera* were likely to play
once Commodus succeeded his father (see p. 136 f.). Before he
became emperor, he was said to have fought in 365 contests, and
1,000 altogether in his life. His passion for gladiators was such
that he was rumoured to be a gladiator's child, the product of an
affair on the part of Marcus' wife Faustina.[37]

Commodus took a similar interest in *venationes*. He is said
to have appeared in the arena in person to kill wild beasts,

decapitating ostriches by shooting sickle-headed arrows at them. It is in the context of his appearances as a *bestiarius* and a gladiator that Commodus had himself represented as Hercules, as in the famous bust in the Conservatori Museum at Rome. Sir Mortimer Wheeler described it as grotesque – 'No doubt it delighted, as it revealed, the sadistic pervert whom it so faithfully immortalized.' But the association between a political leader who fights as a gladiator and Hercules goes back to Mark Antony. Coin issues reveal a whole line of emperors, by no means all of them sadistic perverts, who identified themselves with Hercules. They include Trajan, Antoninus Pius, and of course some of the Tetrarchs in the late third century.[38]

The Roman Hercules was closely associated with gladiators; a shrine to Hercules was found in the London amphitheatre on the Guildhall site in 1988. When they were allowed to retire, gladiators dedicated their weaponry to Hercules.[39] For Romans, the Hercules they worshipped at the Ara Maxima in the Forum was the creator of order and destroyer of barbarism, akin to the Herakles who was hero of the Greek colonies of the west.[40] As the founder of the city of Rome, Romulus was seen as playing the role of creating an ordered society which Hercules fulfilled elsewhere (and the founding hero Theseus did at Athens). Hence Romulus was represented as Hercules, in stories and on coins.[41]

The order that Romulus had first created in founding Rome, and for which he was, like Hercules, rewarded with a place in heaven, was reconstituted by Augustus and maintained by his successors. An emperor might quite reasonably hope that, if he continued to protect that order, his people would see him too as a Hercules-like figure, and like Hercules he might ultimately be rewarded with divinity. If such an emperor wished to demonstrate his likeness to Hercules publicly by appearing in the arena, then that was a symbolic realisation of his ambition both to win divinity himself and to preserve Roman civilisation. It was a dangerous assumption: if he lost the favour of the people (or, more precisely, of those members of the elite whose histories survive), he was likely to be represented as mad rather than divine. The madness of bad emperors was expressed in their association with the 'mad' Hercules.[42] For Christians, the qualities attributed to Hercules made him a rival of Christ as a man who had won immortality by bringing civilisation and salvation to the world. Christian martyrs are explicitly compared to Hercules: Augustine says that, when the thirteen-year-old St Agnes overcame the devil, she was conquering a more dangerous enemy than Cacus and Cerberus had ever been. Not surprisingly, Julian the Apostate encouraged the cult of Hercules as Christ's rival, claiming that the story of Hercules and the cup of the sun actually referred to his walking on water, thus proving his divinity, like Christ.[43]

Cacus and Cerberus between them represent several aspects of Hercules' civilising mission: the destruction of beasts and monsters, the punishment of criminals, and the conquest of Hades. In Seneca's tragedy *Hercules Oetaeus*, Hercules uses the words of the gladiator at the moment of his death and apotheosis: 'habet'.[44] The arena was where Roman society dealt not just with the chaos represented by wild beasts and of crime, but also the chaos of death. It was a symbol of the ordered world, the cosmos; it was the place where the civilised world confronted lawless nature. To kill wild beasts was to share in the divine mission of Hercules, and indeed of all the other great heroes:

If Carpophorus had been born in the Olden Times, Caesar, then barbarian lands would have had no cause to fear the wild boar of Parthaon, nor Marathon the bull, nor leafy Nemea the lion, nor Arcadia the wild boar of Maenalus. If Carpophorus had taken up his weapon, there would have been a single death for the hydra; all three elements of the Chimaera would have died at one blow from him; without Medea's help, he could have yoked the fire-breathing bulls, and he could have destroyed either of Pasiphae's two monsters. If the myth of the sea-monster were to happen again, he on his own could set free both Hesione and Andromeda. Let the glories that make Hercules famous be counted up: it is a greater achievement to have killed twenty beasts on one occasion.[45]

The Roman emperor was not supposed to be a tyrant like Caligula, but rather a guarantor of law and order like Hercules. The Colosseum was not just a monument to the successful suppression of the Jewish revolt, but also to the restoration of traditional Roman 'freedom' by Vespasian following the civil wars of 68–9 and the overthrow of Nero:

Here where the heavenly colossus is nearer to the stars it looks upon, and the tall scaffolding rises up in the middle of the highway, the hated palace of a wild tyrant used to stretch out, and a single house used to cover the entire city. Nero's fishponds used to be here, where the amazing mass of the amphitheatre is being raised up, visible from far away . . . Rome has been restored to herself, and under your presidency, Caesar, what was once enjoyed by a tyrant is now enjoyed by the people.[46]

The Colosseum was built on the site of Nero's highly unpopular Golden House, on land he had sequestered from its owners after the fire of AD 64; when Vespasian had an amphitheatre built on the site, he was symbolising his own legitimacy as emperor by claiming that he had restored to the Roman people its right to decide on life and death. It was appropriate that at its inauguration, the new birth of Roman liberty should be celebrated not just by the traditional slaughter of animals – the destruction of natural evil – but also by the spectacle of a pregnant sow being killed in such a way as to give birth to its young in the arena, in the full view of the Roman people.[47] On each occasion when they fought, gladiators enacted a spectacle of death and rebirth; and they did that in the presence of the Roman people, enabling individuals to come to terms with their mortality by reflecting on the unprecedented power and continuity of Rome's universal rule.

NOTES

1 Suetonius, *Caligula* 30.2; *Liber spectaculorum* 29.3.
2 Cicero, *Ad Att.* 1, 16.11; 2, 19.3; cf. 13, 44.1; 14, 2.1; *pro Sestio* 115 ff.
3 Tacitus, *Dialogus* 13.3; cf. Seneca *Letters* 29.12.
4 Josephus, *Antiquities* 19, 25.
5 Aulus Gellius 5, 14.29 f.; cf. Fronto, *Letters to Marcus* 1, 8 = p. 21 Naber.
6 Suetonius, *Caligula* 30.2.
7 Plutarch, *Galba* 17; Tacitus, *Histories* 1, 72; Suetonius, *Titus* 6.1; Dio 72, 13.3 f.; Herodian 1, 12.5.
8 Cassius Dio 57, 11.6; Suetonius, *Tiberius* 47; Paul, *Digest* 40, 9.17 pr.
9 Dio 48, 31.5; Suetonius, *Augustus* 16.2; Dio 75, 4.5 f.; Tacitus, *Annals* 6, 13; Pliny NH 34, 62.
10 Macrobius, *Saturnalia* 2, 7.19: ἀχαριστεῖς, βασιλεῦ, ἔασον αὐτοὺς περὶ ἡμᾶς ἀσχολεῖσθαι; cf. Cassius Dio 54, 17.5.
11 *Ad Caesarem*, 1, 17.
12 Fronto, *Princip. hist.* p. 210 ed. Naber.

CONCLUSION

13 *Historia Augusta*, Marcus 17, 7.23, 4; CTh. 6, 4.
14 Horace, *Ars Poetica* 32.
15 Suetonius, *Caligula* 27, 4; Josephus, *Antiquities* 19, 253; Pliny NH 11, 144/245.
16 ILS 1428; 1397; 1420; 1437; 1338; 9002; CIL VIII. 8328 (cf. p. 968); ILS 1406.
17 Juliani: *Historia Augusta*, Didius Julianus 8.3. A relief in the Museo Nazionale at Rome, representing a Samnite and dated to the first century BC, labels him as IVL VCV, i.e., a member of the *ludus Julianus* who had fought five times and had been crowned for five victories. Procurators: ILS 1397; cf. papyrus Lips. 57 (AD 261) and U. Wilcken, *Archiv f. Papyruskunde* III (1906), p. 566; CIL X. 1685; III.14192, no.12.
18 ILS 9014; 1396; CIL III. 6994.
19 H.S. Robinson, 'Chiron at Corinth', AJA 73 (1969), 193–7.
20 Suetonius, *Titus* 8.2.
21 Vitellius; Suetonius, *Domitian* 10, 1; 13.1; Pliny, *Panegyric* 33.3. f.
22 Suetonius, *Augustus* 45; Tacitus, *Annals* 1, 54.
23 Suetonius, *Nero* 12.2; Pliny, *Panegyric* 51.5.
24 Claudius: Cassius Dio 60, 13.1.5. Cf. Aulus Gellius' account of the Androclus' story: NA 5, 14.29; Dio 69, 16.3; Dio 69, 6.1, Hadrian again; *Historia Augusta*, Gallieni Duo 12.3 f. On the importance of communication (as well as other issues) see A. Cameron, *Bread and Circuses: the Roman Emperor and his People* (inaugural lecture, King's College London, 1973; Oxford, 1974).
25 *Antiquities* 19. 130.
26 *Antiquities* 19, 130; Dio 60, 13.1.5; Tacitus, *Histories* 1, 4; Dio Chrysostom, *Oratio* 71.9 f. = II, 28 Arnim; Herodian 3, 8.9 f.
27 Dio 57, 11.5; Suetonius, *Tiberius* 47, 34.1.
28 Suetonius, *Caligula* 38.4; Cassius Dio 59, 10.4; Suetonius, *Caligula* 35.2; Dio 67, 14.3 (see p. 110 above).
29 Suetonius, *Claudius* 21.5; 14; 34.2.
30 ILS 206. On the development of Roman law, see p. 40 above.
31 Suetonius, *Caligula* 30.2; *Augustus*, 56.2; Tacitus, *Histories* 1, 72; Tertullian, *De spectaculis* 16; *Ad nationes* 1, 17; Schol. Juv. 5, 3; Cassiodorus, *Variae* 1, 27.5; Cameron, *Circus Factions*.
32 Tacitus, *Annals* 16, 4; certis modis plausuque composito. Cf. Dio 73, 2.3. Otho was acclaimed as Nero: Plutarch, *Otho* 3. For an example, see p. 17.
33 Dio 73, 4.2; Dio 72, 9.3; Dio 78, 26.1.
34 Quintilian 6, 3.63; *Digest* 1, 12, 1.13; Suetonius, *Caesar* 39, 4; *Augustus* 43, 1.
35 Dio 59, 7.7 f.; Suetonius, *Claudius* 6.1; Dio 67, 8.3; Martial praises Domitian for his regulations: 5, 23; 4, 2; 5, 8; cf. 14, 131 and 137; 14, 28.
36 *Liber spectaculorum* 3:

> Quae tam seposita est, quae gens tam barbara, Caesar,
> ex qua spectator non sit in urbe tua?

181

venit ab Orpheo cultor Rhodopeius Haemo,
venit et epoto Sarmata pastus equo
et qui prima bibit deprensi flumina Nili,
et quem supremae Tethyos unda ferit;
festinavit Arabs, festinavere Sabaei,
et Cilices nimbis hic maduere suis.
crinibus in nodum torti venere Sicambri,
atque saliter tortis crinibus Aethiopes.
vox diversa sonat popularum, tum tamen una est,
cum verus patriae diceris esse pater.

37 References to Commodus' gladiatorial interests are legion. Important examples: Cassius Dio 72, 17 ff.; 72, 20; 73, 22.2; Herodian 1, 15.8; *Historia Augusta*, Marcus 19.4 f., Commodus 8.5; 11.10 ff.; 12, 10 f.; 18.12; Clodius Albinus 6.7.

38 Cicero, *Philippic* 2, 63; Plutarch, *Antony* 4.1; Appian, *Civilia* 3.16; Trajan as Hercules: Pliny, *Pan.* 83; Ph. Strack, *Untersuchungen zur Reichsprägung des 2. Jhdts* I (1931), 95 ff. with coins of AD 100 representing Hercules Gaditanus. Marcus Aurelius: Dio Cassius 72, 29, 3–4. Commodus as Hercules: M.P. Speidel, 'Commodus the God: Emperor and the Army', JRS 83 (1993), 109–14.

39 Horace, *Epistles* 1, 1.5: 'Herculis ad postem . . .'.

40 G. Karl Galinsky, *The Herakles Theme* (Blackwell, Oxford, 1972); Jean Bayet, *Les Origines de l'Hercule romaine* (Paris, 1925); Diodorus 4, 21.3–4.

41 Livy 1.7.15; BMC Republic 2.124–5, nos. 28–33; Sydenham, *Coinage of the Roman Republic*, 2 no. 6.

42 Caligula: Dio 59.26; Nero: Suetonius, *Nero* 21 and 53; cf. Suetonius, *Vespasian* 12.2; Domitian is described in Herculean terms by Martial, *Epigrams* 9, 101 and 64; 9, 65: as 'maior Alcides'.

43 M. Simon, *Hercule et le Christianisme* (Paris, 1955), 125–66; Augustine, *Sermones* = 273.6 = PL 38.1250; Julian, *Oratio* 7, 219C–220 ; cf. *Caesares* 319D, 325A, 335D; *Letter to Themistius* 253C and 264A.

44 *Hercules* 1472; another comparison between Hercules and a gladiator at 1457. Cf. *De constantia sapientis* 16.2; *De tranquillitate animae* 11.5; *De providentia* 2, 115.

45 *Liber spectaculorum* 27:

Saecula Carpophorum, Caesar, si prisca tulissent,
    non Parthaoniam barbara terra feram,
Non Marathon taurum, Nemee frondosa leonem,
    Arcas Maenalium non timuisset aprum.
Hoc armante manus hydrae mors una fuisset,
    huic percussa foret tota Chimaera semel.
igniferos possit sine Colchide iungere tauros,
    possit utramque feram vincere Pasiphaes.
si sit, ut aequorei revocetur fabula monstri,
    Hesionem solvet solus et Andromedam.
Herculeae laudis numeretur gloria: plus est
    Bis denas pariter perdomuisse feras.

(Poem 6B expresses the same theme.)

46 *Liber spectaculorum* 2:

> Hic ubi sidereus propius videt astra colossus
> et crescunt media pegmata celsa via,
> invidiosa feri radiabant atria regis
> unaque iam tota stabat in urbe domus.
> Hic ubi conspicui venerabilis Amphitheatri
> erigitur moles, stagna Neronis erant. . . .

(11) reddita Roma sibi est et sunt te praeside, Caesar,
> deliciae populi, quae fuerant domini.

47 *Liber spectaculorum* 12–14.

GLOSSARY

auctoratus: a man who has hired himself out: therefore, someone who has taken the gladiator's oath. The discharged gladiator is *exauctoratus.*

bestiarius: professional wild-beast fighter.

ad bestias: form of judicial execution by throwing to wild animals.

campus: site for military training, normally outside the city-walls; e.g. the Campus Martius at Rome.

confector: executioner.

crematio: execution *ad flammas.*

crupellarii: term used by Tacitus (*Annals* 3, 43) for heavily armed slaves made to fight each other as a punishment in Gaul. There seems to be no connection with so-called 'Gallic' gladiators.

doctor: weapons instructor, often an ex-gladiator.

editor: the person who provided and paid for a *munus.*

equites: 'horsemen': gladiators, initially fighting from horseback, who opened the fighting. They are not to be confused with the equestrian order (also *equites*).

essedarius: rare term for gladiator fighting from a chariot.

familia: group of slaves in the ownership of the same master; consequently group of gladiators training together.

flamen: priest, including the priests of the imperial cult elected by provincial councils.

184

ad flammas: form of judicial execution by burning, sometimes in a tunic impregnated with pitch (*tunica molesta*).

Gallus: (normally pre-Augustan) term for *murmillo*.

harenarius: legal term for criminal sentenced to the arena (either as a gladiator or as a *bestiarius*).

honestiores: legally privileged classes in late antiquity, as opposed to the *humiliores*.

hoplomachus: rare term for a gladiator armed with a long oblong shield, pitted against a *Thraex*.

juventus: organisations which introduced young Romans to weapons-training.

lanista: the owner of a gang of gladiators, responsible for their training and for the practicalities of a *munus*.

ludi: (a) festivals in honour of particular divinities, often including chariot-racing (*ludi circenses*) or plays (*ludi scaenici*). Major festivals included the *ludi Romani* (from 366 BC), *ludi Plebeii* (from 216) and *ludi Apollinares* (from 212);
  (b) training schools for gladiators or *bestiarii* (*ludus matutinus*); the emperors extended their control over the *ludi* at Rome (the *ludus Magnus*, *Gallicus*, and *Dacicus*). Hence:
  ad ludos, judicial penalty of period of three years as gladiator, followed by deprivation of liberty for two more years.

missio: discharge from service; for gladiators, either final retirement, or release from execution in a particular contest (*sine missione* meant a fight to the death). *Missus*, 'let go', applied to a gladiator who had lost his fight but demonstrated enough bravery to be reprieved from death.

monomachia: Greek for gladiatorial combat.

munus, pl. *munera:* obligatory service or gift, e.g. contribution by a rich citizen to his community; funerals, as something 'owed' to the deceased, were called *munera*, and so, consequently, were the gladiatorial shows associated with them.

murmillo or *mirmillo:* post-Augustan word for a 'Gallic' gladiator; heavily armed with a rectangular shield, he was normally pitted against the *retiarus*; his visored helmet had a symbolic fish on it.

naumachiae: in Caesar's time, demonstrations of seamanship in mock-battles, later effectively mass-executions.

paegniarius: gladiator who competed using wooden weapons or whips, possibly during the midday interlude.

pompa: the ritual procession at a funeral or *munus.*

pyrrichae: displays by performing animals (which might feature actors, or criminals).

Quinquatrus: spring festival in honour of Minerva, 19–23 March.

retiarius: lightly clad gladiator who fought with a net and trident, pitted against either *murmillo* or *secutor.*

Samnis, pl. *Samnites:* (normally pre-Augustan) term for *secutor.*

Saturnalia: the Roman mid-winter festival, starting on 17 December.

secutor: post-Augustan word for a 'Samnite' gladiator; carried a rectangular shield, visored helmet, greaves, and a protected sword-arm; normally pitted against a *retiarius.*

stans: 'standing', term used when a contest ended without either gladiator having won a clear victory.

summa rudis: wooden sword or stick used for weapons training and symbolically given to a gladiator on discharge. *Rudiarii* frequently continued as trainers.

Thraex or *Threx:* technical term for gladiator using a round shield and curved short sword (perhaps originally 'Thracian' weapons, but note the difference in spelling).

tiro: trainee.

venationes: hunting; consequently the word used for the killing of beasts in the arena; *venator,* hunter = *bestiarius.*

SELECT BIBLIOGRAPHY

This bibliography only includes modern works cited more than once. For information about the ancient authors and texts cited, see, e.g., the *Oxford Classical Dictionary* (2nd edn, 1970).

L. Alexander (ed.), *Images of Empire* (Sheffield, 1991).

J.K. Anderson, *Hunting in the Ancient World* (1985).

R. Auguet, *Cruauté et civilisation: Les jeux romaines* (Paris, 1970; Engl. trans.).

A. Balil, *La ley gladiatoria de Italica* (Madrid, 1961).

E. Baltrusch, 'Die Verstaatlichung der Gladiatorenspiele', *Hermes* 116 (1988), 324 ff.

A. Barbet, 'La Representation des Gladiateurs dans la Peinture Murale Romaine', *Les Gladiateurs* (Lattes/Toulouse exhibition catalogue, 1987), 69–74.

H. W. Benario, 'Amphitheatres of the Roman World', *Classical Journal* (1980), 255–8.

L. Berger and M. Joos, *Das Augster Gladiatorenmosaik* (Augst, BL, 1971).

K. Bradley, *Slavery and Rebellion in the Roman Empire* (London, 1989).

A. Cameron, *Bread and Circuses: The Roman Emperor and his People* (Oxford, 1974).

—— *Circus Factions* (Oxford, 1976).

K.M. Coleman, 'Fatal Charades: Roman Executions staged as Mythological Enactments', JRS 80 (1990), 44–73.

A.-M. Colini and L. Cozza, *Ludus Magnus* (Rome, 1962).

R.I. Curtis, 'A Slur on Lucius Asicius, the Pompeian Gladiator', TAPhA 110 (1981), 51–61.

R. Duncan-Jones, *Structure and Scale in the Roman Economy* (Cambridge, 1990).

K.M.D. Dunbabin, *The Mosaics of Roman North Africa* (Oxford, 1978).

F. Dupont, *L'Acteur Roi* (Paris, 1985).

R. Etienne, 'La naissance de l'amphithéâtre, le mot et la chose', REL 43 (1966), 213–20.

D. French, 'Two Gladiatorial Texts from Claudiopolis in Bithynia', *Epigraphica Anatolica* 13 (1989), 91–7.

L. Friedländer/G. Wissowa, *Darstellungen aus der Sittengeschichte Roms*, (9th edn, Leipzig, 1920), II, 51 ff.

G.K. Galinsky, *The Herakles Theme* (Oxford, 1972).

A. Garcia y Bellido, 'Lapidas funerarias de gladiadores de Hispania', *Archivio espanol de arquaeologia* 33 (1960).

J.-C. Golvin, *L'Amphithéâtre Romain* (2 vols, Paris, 1988).

J.-C. Golvin and C. Landes, *Amphithéâtres et Gladiateurs* (CNRS, 1990).

R. Graefe, *Vela erunt: Die Zeltdächer der römischen Theater und ähnlicher Anlagen* (Mainz, 1979).

M. Grant, *The Gladiators* (Harmondsworth, 1970).

A.H.J. Greenidge, *Infamia* (Oxford, 1894; repr. Aalen, 1977).

F. Habel, 'Ludi publici', Pauly-Wissowa Suppl. 5 (1931), col. 608–30.

A. Hönle and A. Henze, *Römische Amphitheater und Stadien* (Lucerne, 1981).

K. Hopkins, *Conquerors and Slaves* (Cambridge, 1978).

—— *Death and Renewal* (Cambridge, 1983).

J.H. Humphrey, *Roman Circuses* (London, 1984).

G. Jennison, *Animals for Show and Pleasure in Ancient Rome* (Manchester, 1937).

M. Kokolakis, 'Gladiatorial games and Animal-baiting in Lucian', ΠΛΑΤΩΝ 10 (Athens, 1958).

J.-C. Lachaux, *Théâtres et amphithéâtres d'Afrique Proconsulaire* (Aix-en-Provence, 1979).

G. Lafaye, 'Gladiator', Daremberg-Saglio, *Dictionnaire des Antiquites*, vol. II, 2, p. 1563–99.

R. Lane Fox, *Pagans and Christians* (London, 1986).

K. Latte, *Römische Religionsgeschichte* (Munich, 1960).

J. Mackenzie, *The Empire of Nature* (Manchester, 1988).

R. MacMullen, *Corruption and the Decline of Rome* (Yale, 1988).

—— *Changes in the Roman Empire* (Princeton, 1990).

A. Mau, *Pompeii* (1899; reprint Washington, 1973).

V. Maxfield, *Military Decorations of the Roman Army* (London, 1981).

C. Nicolet, *The World of the Citizen in Republican Rome* (London, 1980).

K. Parlasca, *Römische Mosaiken in Deutschland. Römisch-Germanische Forschungen* 23 (1959).

E. Rawson, *Roman Culture and Society* (Oxford, 1990).

L. Robert, *Les gladiateurs dans l'Orient grec* (Paris, 1940).

P. Sabbatini-Tumolesi, *Gladiatorum Paria, Annunci di spettacoli gladiatorii a Pompeii* (Rome, 1980).

P. Sabbatini-Tumolesi, *Epigrafia amfiteatrale dell'occidente romano, I: Roma* (Rome, 1988).

K. Schneider, 'Gladiatores', *Realencyclopaedie*, Supplementband III (1918), col. 760–84.

H. Stern, *Receuil general des mosaïques de la Gaule* (Paris).

J. Toynbee, *Animals in Roman Life and Art* (London, 1973).

J. Väterlein, *Roma Ludens* (Amsterdam, 1976).

H. Versnel, *Triumphus* (Leiden, 1970).

P. Veyne, *Le Pain et le Cirque* (Paris, 1976) = *Bread and Circuses* (tr. B. Pearce, Harmondsworth, 1990).

G. Ville, 'Les coupes de Trimalcion figurantes gladiateurs et une serie de verres sigilles gaulois', *Hommages à Jean Bayet* (1964), 722–33.

—— 'Les jeux de gladiateurs dans l'Empire chrétien', *Mélanges d'archéologie et d'histoire publiés par l'école française de Rome* LXXII (1960), 273–335.

—— 'La guerre et le Munus', J.-P. Brisson (ed.), *Problémes de la guerre à Rome* (Paris, 1969), 185–95.

—— 'Religion et politique: Comment ont pris fin les combats de Gladiateurs', *Annales E.S.C.* (1979), 651.

—— *La Gladiature en Occident des Origines à la Mort de Domitien* (Ecole Française de Rome, 1981).

J. Vogt, *Sklaverei und Humanität, Ergänzungsheft* (Wiesbaden, 1983).

C.W. Weber, *Panem et Circenses, Massenunterhaltung als Politik im antiken Rom* (Düsseldorf/Wien, 1983).

W. Weismann, 'Gladiator', *RAC* XI (1981), 23–45.

P.J. Wilkins, 'Amphitheatres and Private Munificence in Roman Africa', *ZPE* 75 (1988), 216 ff.

INDEX